BROKEN

CAPITALISM

THIS IS HOW WE FIX IT

FERRIS EANFAR

All book proceeds support the
nonprofit, nonpartisan AngelPay Foundation.

ANGELPAY

**Returning Wealth & Power to the
Creators of Value.**

The AngelPay Foundation
1710 First Ave., #178, New York, NY 10128

First edition published in 2017 by The AngelPay Foundation,
a nonprofit, 501(c)(3) corporation.
The AngelPay Foundation
1710 First Ave. #178
New York, New York, 10128.
Website address: AngelPayHQ.org

THE LIBRARY OF CONGRESS HAS CATALOGUED
THIS TITLE AS FOLLOWS:

Names: Eanfar, Ferris.
Title: Broken capitalism : this is how we fix it / Ferris Eanfar.
Description: New York, NY: The AngelPay Foundation, 2017. | Summary:
Provides unique and refreshing insight into the murky waters of Earth's economic
and political systems, banking systems, globalism, artificial intelligence, corporate
governance, and the geopolitical affairs that have shaped and distorted our global
economy.
Identifiers: LCCN 2017909289 | ISBN 9780999112113 (hardcover) |
9780999112106 (paperback) | 9780999112120 (ebook)
Subjects: Economic history—1990- | Capitalism. | Globalization—Economic
aspects. | Globalization—Political aspects. | International economic relations. |
Equality. | Income distribution. | International finance. | Economic policy. |
Corporate governance.
Classification: LCC HC59.15 .E26 2017 | DDC 330.9—dc23

Dedication

This book is dedicated to all the humans on Earth who are suffering from Broken Capitalism today.

You deserve a functional and prosperous economy.

Let's build a better future together.

Contents

Acknowledgments

I appreciate all the thoughtful and accomplished people in my life who have given me encouragement over the years, but a few human angels were exceptionally encouraging during the development of this book. Words are not enough to capture my appreciation for them, but I must start somewhere; so, these words are a down payment toward the debt of gratitude I owe them all. I thank . . .

Jeff Knowles, for his unassuming intelligence, attention to detail, serenity under pressure, and appreciation for the philosophical aspects of our lives and professional projects. I also appreciate him for sharing with me his decades of technical knowledge and experience in the payment processing industry. Nobody knows this industry and how to build financial services technologies better than him. It's difficult to imagine a human with more complementary professional strengths to balance my weaknesses, which is one of the reasons we work so well together. I am blessed to have Jeff as one of my dearest friends and professional partners.

Jen Bawden, for her unyielding encouragement and enthusiasm for life and everything we do together. She is truly a force of nature. Within seconds, anybody who meets her can see that she is likely not from Earth. I have known her for years and I still wonder if she might be an angel sent from the heavens, temporarily inhabiting a gorgeous human shell, precision-engineered to attract the most thoughtful and intelligent souls on Earth into her orbit, so that she can complete her mission to elevate humanity to her angelic level of consciousness. Imagine a creature with the DNA of Mother Teresa, Joan of Arc, Rita Hayworth, Jesus Christ, Reese Witherspoon, Catherine Deneuve, a tenacious pit bull, a glittering unicorn, and a bright rainbow hugging the horizon—that's Jen, the Universe's gift to humanity.

David Townes, for his irrepressible curiosity, philosophical spirit, deep knowledge of the many wonders of our planet, and decades of experience exploring dimensions of Earth most people don't even know exist. His unparalleled experience in the worlds of investment banking and business served as a meaningful foil during many late-night philosophical adventures into the deepest and darkest depths of human civilization.

Preface

Welcome to Earth

Escaping the Womb. When humans are launched from the womb at birth, every aspect of our world seems mysterious and chaotic. Then as we grow older and fill our heads with something resembling knowledge, planet Earth starts to make a little more sense . . . until we start listening to politicians and commentators in the media who sound like they're from Mars. Then many earthlings just want to crawl right back into the womb.

Demystifying the World of International Political Economy. Economic and political systems can seem mysterious, alien, and confusing, but this book will help many people achieve a level of deep awareness that few people ever experience. This may seem like a grandiose claim at this early stage of our journey together, but after you've read this book, I think you will agree that everything a citizen needs to know about what's wrong with the global economy today, and how to substantially fix it, is explained in this book.

Focused on Solutions. This is a book about solutions. Some of the solutions are organizational tools, knowledge, and systems that can be implemented immediately. Other solutions in this book are clearly defined, nonpartisan economic policies, which we should all demand from our elected government officials.

I Respect Your Time. This book is intended to be thought-provoking, engaging, and sometimes entertaining, but the primary purpose of this book is to inspire action. Learning about problems and solutions without learning how to effectively implement the solutions is a waste of time. This book respects your time by delivering practical knowledge, timeless wisdom, and specific tools that can make an immediate impact in your organization, in your country, and in your life.

Navigational Guides

Our Purpose. This book explores many interconnected economic, political, and social challenges facing humans around the world today. Given the complexity of some of the topics in this book, we often need to dive deep into the heart of various issues. Our purpose here together is to wrap our minds around the core principles and underlying social, political and economic phenomena that are causing the problems described in each chapter so that we can understand and embrace the corresponding solutions.

Our Mission: Fix Broken Capitalism. Exploring the deepest recesses of the human condition, wrestling with timeless existential questions, and uncovering the hidden machinations of a nation's political and economic systems can sometimes be disorienting. This creates the need for a clear structure and guideposts along the path to help us periodically reorient ourselves with the landscape and to stay focused on our primary mission: Fix Broken Capitalism.

Easy Navigation. Compasses and guideposts help explorers navigate treacherous environments. At times, it will feel like we are explorers on a nail-biting journey into uncharted psychological, philosophical, economic, and nonpartisan political territory. To maintain our bearing and to stay focused and mentally organized throughout this journey, each chapter ends with a section called "Key Points." This section summarizes the top-three principles in each chapter to maximize your retention of the most important concepts.

Unique Structure. The structure of this book is substantially different than most other books because it's intended to be an educational *and* practical handbook for busy people when they're discussing the nonpartisan principles herein with their friends, family and colleagues. To make it easy to navigate, I've added many page and paragraph headings throughout every chapter. This enables people to scan any page and quickly absorb the most important principles in seconds. This is especially useful for people who need to refresh their memory about a particular concept just before an important meeting or event.

Authentic Delivery. The tone of the human voice conveys approximately 30-40% of the total payload of meaning in verbal communications. This means reading a book without orienting the reader to the sound of the author's real voice can sometimes lead to misunderstood phrases, misinterpreted intentions, and less authentic human engagement with the material. For this reason, I've provided many audio clips from the Broken Capitalism audiobook for free on the official AngelPay Channel on YouTube (YouTube.com/AngelPay). Listening to those audio clips only takes a few minutes, but I think it will add a deeper human dimension as you read the rest of this book.

Geographical Scope

Global Perspective. I'm an American citizen and I frequently write nonpartisan articles about economic and geopolitical issues related to American domestic and foreign policies. I've traveled to dozens of countries throughout this ever-shrinking world—including in Europe, Asia, the Middle East, Africa, North and South America—and I have studied other governments, economies, cultures, and languages as much as possible over the years. I've learned enough about this planet to confirm that broken capitalism is not limited to the United States. In fact, the same problems are unfolding in virtually every nation on Earth today.

Universally Applicable to Every Democratic Nation. The solutions that I describe in this book are just as applicable to other democratic countries as they are to the United States. In fact, it might even be easier to implement these solutions in other countries because the political systems and economies in most other OECD (Organization for Economic Cooperation and Development) nations are not as systemically corrupt and controlled by special interest groups as the political system and economy of the United States.

Nonpartisan, Non-Biased Perspective. Anybody who has read my articles knows that I write from a *nonpartisan and non-biased* perspective.[1] The first two books I wrote were about systemic government corruption, special interest influences in the U.S. Federal Government, and how to fix those problems. Those books are important, but I decided not to publish

---

[1] See my article online, "Building a Non-Biased Political System," if you're not sure about the difference between "unbiased" and "non-biased." You can also get a taste of the topics in my other books if you read any of my other articles at Eanfar.org.

them until I have the time to properly nurture them in the wild. Books like that are lightning rods for controversy and I need to focus on a few other important goals first before I dedicate several years of my life to promoting and defending those books.

This Book is My "Vacation". In contrast to tackling the toxic swamp of systemic government and special interest corruption, writing this book and helping people understand the causes and solutions for broken capitalism is like a vacation. Obviously, no public policy reform is easy when powerful special interest groups have a vested interest in defending the status quo, but who could possibly be against economic policies that would create more jobs and more widespread economic prosperity, right?[2]

We Can't Please Everybody All the Time. Even if a divine angel glided down a gleaming shaft of light from the heavens and delivered this book directly, I'm sure several special interest groups would still find reasons to attack this book and me personally. Nevertheless, I suspect most people will appreciate it based on the feedback I've received so far. And if the billions of people worldwide who are suffering from broken capitalism today are lucky, maybe our elected government officials will take the time to understand why this is the only book they ever need to read to understand what is truly causing broken capitalism and how to fix it.

Thank you for taking the time to read this book. Now I think we're ready to embark on our adventure. I've enjoyed writing this book for you. I hope you enjoy the journey.

My best,

Ferris Eanfar

New York, NY

---

[2] It turns out, there are some people who don't want these outcomes, as we shall see in later chapters.

Part 1

The Price of Broken Capitalism

- Chapter 1 -
Introduction

"Civilization is a race between
education and catastrophe." — H.G. Wells

The American Dream

There are nearly 800 million Americans; 500 million adults are unemployed.
Average life expectancy for rich Americans is 150 years; for the poor, it's 65
years. The top-1% richest Americans own 99% of all national wealth. The
middle class is extinct. The poor have no economic or political power.
Democracy is a quaint memory.

Many cities are in ruins due to neglect, economic insolvency, and
shifting climate patterns. FEMA is broke and can't help because nobody
will lend money to a nation with a $130-trillion debt. Over 400 million
Americans live in crude medical triage camps. Medicaid and Medicare are
broke. Government assistance is handed to over 600 million Americans by
military soldiers at sprawling, chaotic, putrid food and water distribution
centers.

The U.S. economy represents less than 10% of global GDP. The
vast majority of economic activity is in Asia. International trade and
diplomacy are dominated by Asian nations. The Federal Reserve can't print
money because the U.S. Dollar lost its global reserve currency status.
Interest rates are prohibitively high for all but a tiny number of super-
wealthy individuals and corporations. Raising capital for new technology,
energy, and biotech companies is impossible because relatively lower-risk,
high-yield U.S. Treasury Junk Bonds have squeezed out the private capital
market. With no competition from new startups, the economy is centrally
planned by the Dow 30: the last remaining corporate goliaths that control
the U.S. economy. Capitalism in America collapsed years ago.

Humans can communicate using direct-brain connections over the Internet; the NSA is listening to your thoughts right now. Swarms of micro-drones fly silently through the air; they're watching you now. The IRS is monitoring your banking activity to find millions of terrorists; the same connection automatically withdrawals your taxes and other life-long debt payments, regardless of whether you have enough money left for food. No political or economic system is perfect, but at least you're still breathing.

Understanding the Trends

The Reality Distortion Machine. Based on current economic, technological, demographic, and political trends, the description above is one of the *best-case* future scenarios for the United States, which millions of Americans *living today* may see in their lifetimes. In fact, *these trends* are already easy to see today. Throughout Part 1 of this book, we will explore the major political and economic dynamics that are transforming the American Dream into an American Nightmare. This nightmare is *currently* unimaginable for many Americans because the unholy alliance between the federal government and corporate America has created the ultimate Reality Distortion Machine. This machine is fueled by a relentless pipeline of propaganda, distributed throughout a sprawling ecosystem of captured media, special interest groups, and organizations that seek to tranquilize and monetize as many humans as possible.

I've provided many charts and graphs throughout this book to illustrate the problems plaguing the U.S. and global economies today. The following chart is probably the most useful because it captures all the most significant factors in a single picture.

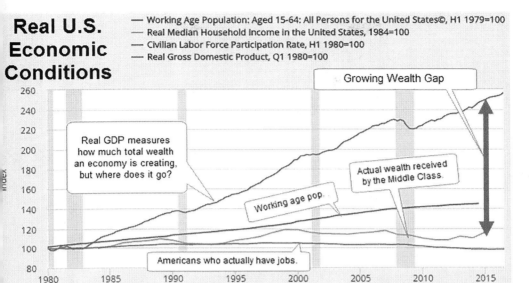

Real U.S. Economic Conditions

— Working Age Population: Aged 15-64: All Persons for the United States©, H1 1979=100
— Real Median Household Income in the United States, 1984=100
— Civilian Labor Force Participation Rate, H1 1980=100
— Real Gross Domestic Product, Q1 1980=100

Growing Wealth Gap

Real GDP measures how much total wealth an economy is creating, but where does it go?

Actual wealth received by the Middle Class.

Working age pop.

Americans who actually have jobs.

Raw data source: U.S. Census Bureau, the U.S. Bureau of Labor Statistics, and the St. Louis Federal Reserve; Chart produced by Ferris Eanfar.

Context is Everything. The analysis and solutions presented in this book are specific to the context of a planet in which *billions of humans will soon have no economic purpose*. In that rapidly approaching world, it's not enough to cling to ideologically-spawned notions of pure economic liberty and *laissez-faire* economic policies. If we want to avoid a Soviet-style revolution on a global scale, we should not fall prey to normalcy bias. Within the next 25-50 years, the quasi-free-market economic policies that exist in capitalistic economies today will produce subsistence income for only 25-50% of the global human population. What should we do about the other 50-75% of humanity?

How Do We Avoid the Malthusian Nightmare? Unless societies in each country want their governments to implement forced sterilization programs or some other Malthusian "thin the herd" policy that obliterates virtually all human rights, we must assume those 2 to 4 billion *economically useless* people are going to fight. They're not going to starve to death quietly. They're not going to gleefully accept a life of abject poverty. They're not going to voluntarily corral themselves into hundreds of massive economic refugee camps, each the size of New York City's population. They are going to rise up, take control of all forms of wealth (including yours), and redistribute it according to what *feels right*, which probably will

3

not result in the optimal outcome for capitalists, workers, your family, or human civilization.

No Conspiracy Theories Needed. This is not a book about conspiracy theories. We don't need conspiracy theories when the truth is already shocking enough; and the truth is sufficient to explain everything that is wrong with Capitalism today. In fact, I provide nearly 200 independent, *nonpartisan* references throughout this book to allow you to independently verify and explore everything you learn here. On this journey, you will learn why global economies and political systems behave the way they do today and how all the trends and their consequences are culminating into another high-probability scenario, which is even less optimistic than the scenario in this chapter's opening paragraph.

What is "Broken Capitalism"? Part 1 of this book is focused on diagnosing *the problem* and describing how it impacts our world. This will ensure that we are mentally prepared to understand why the solutions in Part 2 are practical, viable, and truly necessary. But what do we call *the problem*? Since Capitalism feels *broken* to at least 80% of Americans and billions of people on Earth today, I frequently call it "Broken Capitalism" throughout this book.[3] And I generally avoid more inflammatory labels like Crony Capitalism, Plutocracy, Kleptocracy, etc., because those labels are often associated with partisan innuendo and they can mean different things to different people. In contrast, "Broken Capitalism" is simple for anybody to understand, it doesn't imply that one political party or another is to blame, and it captures the essence of what we are talking about: the *broken* socioeconomic system that is *unnecessarily* preventing billions of people from achieving a higher quality of life.

Achieving Positive Results Requires Focus and Discipline. There are hundreds of economic and social policies that are distorted by Broken Capitalism, but only two policy areas drive approximately 95% of all the problems in our global economy today: The size of corporations and the impact of what I call "Globalism 1.0." Accurately diagnosing and curing the diseases in these two policy areas is all that really matters to fixing Broken Capitalism worldwide. It may not seem obvious now, but after you've finished reading this book, I think you will agree that all the other problems and distortions in our global economy today are byproducts of

---

[3] See the "Toxic Cloud" section later in this chapter for the data and references to substantiate this.

the size of corporations and Globalism 1.0. That means virtually all the other socioeconomic problems in our world today will naturally heal, or they will be much easier to resolve, if we can cure the diseases in these two policy areas.

Any Demons Lurking Below? No matter where you live along the ideological spectrum between complete Laissez Faire Capitalism and centrally-planned Communism, this book should give you rational reasons to reconsider some of your assumptions about how a modern economy should work. I don't expect you to believe me now, but if you read to the end of this book, I'm confident you will see that I don't approach any topic with a partisan lens and I'm not a slave to ideology. I think most people can see that our society is being ripped to shreds by irrational partisan tribalism. So as you read this book, please try not to allow my words to be distorted by any partisan or ideological demons that may be lurking just below your conscious mind.

The Rise of Donald Trump

Predicting Brexit and the Trump Wave. I was one of the few humans on Earth to publicly write about and predict the outcomes of two of the most influential geopolitical events in recent history: The June 2016 "Brexit" referendum in Britain and the rise of Donald Trump. I predicted those events because they were both triggered by the same underlying socioeconomic dynamics that I have been studying and analyzing for over a decade. And it was clear to me that nobody in the mainstream media and academia could see, let alone predict, why these events were happening.

Dinner with the Trump Family. Approximately half the American voting population voted for Donald Trump in the 2016 U.S. Presidential Election, but very few people actually believed he could win; and even fewer were willing to make any meaningful public statements about his chances of winning. In June of 2015, around the time that Trump announced that he was running for president (nearly 18 months before he surprised the world by winning the election), my girlfriend and I had dinner with several members of the Trump family at their home in upstate New York. We had a relaxed and candid conversation about Trump's chances of winning.

At that point, I had already finished my first book about how to fix the broken U.S. political system and I was working on my second book, which is a deeper dive into the systemically corruptive influence of special interest groups. All the research and analysis I did for those books made it abundantly clear to me that the 2016 election was going to be a different kind of election than any election in modern political history.

Trump Rides the Wave of Populism. In my other books, I described in detail how the populism of America was reaching a political boiling point far hotter than the 2011 Occupy Wall Street protests. I also described in exhaustive detail how the dysfunctional American political class is catering so much to the wealthiest and most powerful special interest groups that they can't even see the same America that most Americans see today. For these reasons, I knew the political class and mainstream media would severely underestimate the intensity of the disgust that most Americans living between New York and California feel toward the economic, media, and cultural *elite* in the United States.

During our dinner with the Trumps, I said:

> *I think the intelligentsia and media will underestimate Donald's chances of winning. And the reason they will underestimate him is because he sounds and looks different than them and he seems unpolished, which they will mistake for incompetence and assume he can't possibly win. But Donald's simple message will resonate very strongly with the majority of Americans, his financial independence from special interest groups will be very appealing to most Americans, and the fact that he is not a career politician is probably his greatest asset. You'll see, I guarantee he will win the primary election and he will probably win the general election.[4] . . .*

Those were my words about 18 months before the election. And I wrote publicly about Trump several times thereafter before the 2016 November election, adding more detail about why I believed he would likely win. This was not the result of any particular ideological or personal affinity for Trump; it was simply the logical conclusion of all the data and evidence I had analyzed up to that point.

We Can Respect and Appreciate People Even if We Don't Agree with Everything They Say. To be clear, I don't endorse all of Trump's personal lifestyle choices; and I don't agree with all his domestic or

---

[4] This is a condensed summary. The full conversation was much longer.

foreign policies, but I appreciate what he represented during the 2016 election: An alternative to the toxic political establishment. This is not about partisan ideology. Regardless of whether a candidate runs as a Democrat, Republican, Libertarian, Independent, or Socialist, any candidate who is not beholden to special interest groups and is not a career politician is more tolerable to most Americans today than the uninspiring electoral diet that Americans have been spoon-fed for decades.

Why Is This Book Different?

Unusual Childhood Experiences. I was born in Beverly Hills and most of my family was very wealthy. They all lived along the "Gold Coast" in Washington State where Bill Gates, Jeff Bezos, Paul Allen, and other billionaires call home. However, I was not born with a silver spoon in my mouth. Or more precisely: The silver spoon I might have had was ripped out of my mouth before I was six months old. In fact, I suffered from wretched poverty and a broken home throughout my childhood. I only met my father once in my life. Due to tension between my mother and the rest of our family, after I was six months old, I was raised by my mother and step-father in a very poor area of San Diego, California.

Understanding the Rich and the Poor. As a child without any other options, my neighbors and many of my friends were drug addicts and gang-bangers. We listened to Rap music by Eazy-E, Dr. Dre, Ice Cube, and Snoop Dog, with lyrics about sex, drugs, and gang-banging. While my *Gold Coast family* was pondering new apartment complexes to acquire for their real estate portfolio, I watched one of my primary school teachers get stabbed to death in front of our ghetto apartment.

Fighting to Survive. While my *Gold Coast family* was sun-tanning in the French Riviera, I carried my fishing poles, bait, and tackle to the lagoon to catch sand sharks and Spotfin Croakers for dinner. Fishing was not a hobby; it was an existential necessity because my mother's government assistance was not enough to pay for food and all the things I needed for school. Neighborhood fights, armed robberies, and gang shootings were frequent existential threats.

Overcoming Adversity. I could feel and taste sumptuous wealth when I was summoned up to the Gold Coast for chilly family reunions, but I never received a single penny from the wealthy side of my family. I was invisible to them. As a Caucasian in a very poor neighborhood, I was an ethnic minority all throughout my childhood years. I was teased mercilessly in school for being White and small because I started school at a younger age than the other kids. Virtually all my childhood friends were Samoan, Hispanic, and African-American. Eventually I earned their respect as an accomplished athlete and a trustworthy confidante to the popular kids. In return, they made me their Homecoming Prince in my junior year and Prom King in my senior year—a white boy in a multicolor sea of humanity.

An Exceptionally Diverse Background. Since leaving home when I was 16 years old, I've tasted the euphoria of business success and I've suffered heart-breaking business failure at various times in my life. I've traveled to many countries around the world for business and to observe which cultures and economic policies succeed or fail. I've been on humanitarian missions to build houses and provide food to desperate people in poor countries. I've lived in the lap of luxury in La Jolla and Beverly Hills, CA; The Hamptons and Manhattan, NY; Palm Beach, FL; London, United Kingdom; and Zurich, Switzerland. I've worked inside the U.S. Federal Government, the U.S. Intelligence Community, the U.S. Air Force as a Cryptological Linguist, and in the private sector in the commodities trading and financial services industries. I have many technical and financial industry certifications and a formal university education in International Political Economy. And I've written many nonpartisan articles and several books about political and economic systems.

Real-World Experience on Both Sides of the Poverty Wall. In short, I've had some pretty diverse life experiences, which have given me a level of sensitivity, insight, and awareness about Earth's geopolitical and socioeconomic systems that few people have the opportunity to develop. Along the way, I've learned that pain and adversity are the crucibles of character, but poverty is the great existential wall that divides humanity into two mental countries: Utopia and Dystopia. In Utopia, the wealthy elite see a world full of opportunity and pleasure with occasional episodes of pain when death and taxes strike. In contrast, the impoverished humans in Dystopia see a world full of deprivation and pain with occasional episodes of pleasure when they escape into self-stimulatory binges of liquor, drugs, video games, and sex.

Dual Citizen of Utopia and Dystopia. Neither Utopia nor Dystopia alone can reveal the complete picture of Broken Capitalism today, but together, they represent the full spectrum of human experience in today's dysfunctional capitalistic societies. The deepest insights about

Capitalism can only be truly understood and experienced as a dual citizen of Utopia *and* Dystopia. The life experience of a dual citizen combines the bitter taste of Dystopia's constant deprivation, existential uncertainty, and the 24/7 anxiety of wretched poverty, psychologically contrasted against Utopia's sweet taste of life in places like the Gold Coast, The Hamptons, and 24/7 concierge pampering in Manhattan skyscrapers overlooking 5th Avenue and Central Park. I don't think it's possible to write a credible book about Broken Capitalism and how to fix it without being a dual citizen of Utopia and Dystopia.

Transcending the Crude Labels of Social Class and Partisan Politics. Some people mistake me for an "elite" because of some of my life experiences and the people I know in Utopia, but I'm pretty sure my life experience transcends the crude, stereotypical class and ideological labels that some people use to pigeonhole others. Everything I write is from a nonpartisan and egalitarian perspective and I'm not blinded by ideology. Ideology prevents people from seeing problems clearly, diagnosing them accurately, and developing practical and viable solutions. Nobody can solve problems that they don't truly understand, or that they can't even see.

Broad Scope and Depth. I've spent many years researching, working, living, and writing about business and International Political Economy. So I know it can take years to develop a broad and deep enough understanding to appreciate why the solutions in this book would be more effective than other ideas discussed in many policymaking circles today. To accelerate the learning process for my readers, this book succinctly summarizes a wide range of topics, including the most interesting and significant historical, cultural, technological, philosophical, and geopolitical facts and events that are necessary to understand why and how Capitalism is broken today.

Concise Structure & Delivery. I don't have years to bring my readers up to speed on these topics. So the structure of this book is designed to communicate the most important concepts in very potent, concise, informal language, without unnecessary fluff or fillers. My style is unorthodox, but I think this is the best way to achieve maximum readability, comprehension, and retention, with an occasional dash of humor and irony to keep things interesting.[5]

---

[5] The "Navigation Tools / Structure" section in the Prologue provides additional details about the unique structure of this book.

Call to Action. A book is just a whisper in time unless it achieves some kind of meaningful impact. The purpose of this book is to empower and inspire meaningful action. Please forgive the repetition, but there is a call to action at the end of several chapters. This is because each person is different: You might understand the importance of this book and the nonprofit AngelPay Foundation after one chapter, or you might not truly understand it until the last chapter. Regardless, the moment you understand why it's so important to help us fix Broken Capitalism, please visit us online at AngelPayHQ.org to learn more about The AngelPay Foundation.

I see black storm clouds building on the horizon. Wait . . . no . . . those aren't storm clouds—it's a *massive Toxic Cloud* choking the life out of everything in its path. . . .

The Toxic Cloud

The American Dream is Dying. What do *you* think is wrong with the United States today? Are you satisfied with the federal government? If you're an American citizen, do you feel powerful right now? Based on many major public opinion polls and personal conversations with Americans across the socioeconomic and ideological spectra, it's clear that the sentiment of most Americans today can be summarized as follows: Democracy and Capitalism in America are broken. Ordinary Americans are being squeezed out of the American Dream. American citizens feel powerless to do anything about it.

The Toxic Cloud. To provide contextual awareness, Part 1 of this book summarizes many elements of the swirling, interconnected cloud of political and economic problems, which collectively, I call the "Toxic Cloud." The Toxic Cloud is the byproduct of Broken Capitalism, a structurally broken American political electoral system, and a toxic political culture, which collectively and recursively poisons and corrupts Democracy and Capitalism worldwide in countless ways. The corrosive elements swirling within the Toxic Cloud have spawned every imaginable kind of pain and suffering, including:

Systemic financial crises; generational poverty; devastation of the Middle Class; stagnant incomes; a jungle of distorted and unevenly enforced regulations; a byzantine tax code; permanent structural unemployment; nationwide obliteration of human capital; political gridlock in Washington; insolvent public pension programs; perpetual government budget deficits;

skyrocketing private and public debt; wealth-destroying monetary policy; broken healthcare system; broken educational system; sprawling surveillance state; suffocating bank compliance apparatus; interventionist foreign policy; unjustified and immoral military conflicts; environmental catastrophes; job-killing bureaucracies; waste, fraud and abuse in the form of corporate welfare and cronyism-induced bank bailouts; among millions of other poisonous byproducts of our global economy and geopolitical institutions.

Is Your Country Heading in the Right Direction? Every major public opinion poll indicates a significant majority of Americans believe the United States is heading in the wrong direction economically and politically. Globally, Credit Suisse recently revealed that "the richest 1% have now accumulated more wealth than the rest of the world put together" and just eight people own more than 50% of Earth's entire population *combined*.[6] It seems everywhere we look, the Toxic Cloud is spreading and choking large portions of our planet. It's difficult for many people to determine who to blame or what to do about it because the Toxic Cloud and the Reality Distortion Machine blur the vision and awareness of everybody in their path.

Distorted Incentives Lead to Distorted Economies. When politicians and their special interest benefactors can control the democratic process, they invariably use the power of government as an instrument of their own political and financial gain. This fundamentally corrupts Democracy, distorts Capitalism, and diminishes the full economic potential of a country and its citizens. The size of corporations and the malfunction of Globalism 1.0 are the most significant factors that give special interest groups the power to inflict these distortions upon our global economic and political systems.

---

[6] Hardoon, Deborah, Ricardo Fuentes-Nieva, and Sophia Ayele. "An Economy For the 1%: How Privilege and Power in the Economy Drive Extreme Inequality and How This Can Be Stopped." Policy & Practice, January 18, 2016. http://policy-practice.oxfam.org.uk/publications/an-economy-for-the-1-how-privilege-and-power-in-the-economy-drive-extreme-inequ-592643.
"Oxfam Says Wealth of Richest 1% Equal to Other 99%." BBC News, January 18, 2016, sec. Business. http://www.bbc.com/news/business-35339475.
"World's Eight Richest People Have Same Wealth as Poorest 50%." The Guardian, January 15, 2017, sec. Business. https://www.theguardian.com/global-development/2017/jan/16/worlds-eight-richest-people-have-same-wealth-as-

It's Nearly Impossible to Reclaim Liberty After it's Lost. Politicians who have distorted incentives often exploit and perpetuate crises to increase the power of government over their constituents because the politicians know their constituents would never tolerate any erosion of their liberty during non-crisis conditions. Due to institutional inertia, it's very difficult for people to reclaim their liberty after it's lost, which is why fascist states never revert back to free states without bloody revolutions and wars.

The Convergence of Tyrants and Predators. After seeing the facts and evidence in this book, there should be no doubt that the U.S. Government has been creeping toward a state of tyranny. Intentional or not, the interests of tyrannical governments often converge with the interests of predatory corporations, making it easy for the most politically connected corporations to monopolize global markets and economic systems, thus inflicting a second dimension of tyranny on human populations.

Past Performance Does Not Guarantee Future Performance. The past performance of the U.S. economy gives many people a false sense of confidence in the future performance of the economy. When (not if) the U.S. Dollar loses its global reserve currency and petrodollar status, the U.S. economy will behave dramatically differently. When this happens, life in America will be very different for millions of people, especially if the politicians who control the government still have distorted incentives. The solutions in Part 2 of this book are designed to prevent economic disasters that would lead to nightmare scenarios like the one at the beginning of this chapter.

Everybody is Choking on the Toxic Cloud. The Toxic Cloud does not care if you're homeless or a billionaire. Everybody suffers in their own way. Yes, wealthy people can suffer from the Toxic Cloud, too, but of course they're not as vulnerable existentially. As you will see throughout this book, there is virtually no human on Earth today who is not directly harmed by the Toxic Cloud. This reality makes this book and the solutions in Part 2 deeply meaningful and relevant to every man, woman, and child living in the U.S. and around the world today. By the time you're finished reading this book, you will be an expert on the source of Broken Capitalism and you will be empowered with the specific tools and knowledge to fix it.

---

poorest-50.

The Meaning of Corruption

Special Interest Corruption. The issue of special interest corruption in politics is much deeper than many people imagine. Some of the most intelligent people I know were initially skeptical and thought I was exaggerating—until they learned how the game really works. They are often shocked by the level of sophisticated manipulation that occurs behind the scenes of the political process. Only recently have the Wikileaks revelations finally revealed publicly what I've been telling people for many years about the systemic corruption in the federal government and national security apparatus. Most people have no idea how the Regulatory Protection Racket works or how the symbiotic relationship between federal politicians, corporations, and special interest groups literally touches every community in America.[7]

Syndrome of Distortions. With the exception of economically destructive natural disasters, every financial or political crisis is caused by either a corrupt regulatory process, prodigal fiscal policy, short-sighted monetary policy, or all of the above. Distortions in any one of these three economic policy areas can cause great damage to a nation's economy and its political system. This book explores many dimensions of how the symbiotic relationship between politicians and their special interest benefactors creates what I call a "Syndrome of Distortions" in the economic and democratic processes of a nation.

Malignancy Spreads. The Syndrome of Distortions metastasizes into rampant, systemic malfunctions throughout entire economic and political systems. As this malignancy spreads, it imperceptibly but inevitably infects and corrupts the fundamental ethical purpose, structural integrity, essential character, and good intentions of a wide array of people and processes within these systems. Just as a malignant tumor hijacks the blood supply of neighboring healthy cells to spread its own corrupted DNA, the same is true of corrupted people and processes within a political system.

The Bouncy Castle. We have all seen examples of people who are

---

[7] The Regulatory Protection Racket is the phrase I use for a particularly nasty and common form of political corruption. This racket occurs when politicians shake down corporations, special interest groups, and wealthy individuals for election campaign donations in exchange for lenient regulatory oversight, tax loopholes, and other *quid pro quo* arrangements.

"corrupt" by any definition. These are the people whose names become news headlines and punchlines of jokes. The corruption of these people is usually obvious and does not require a book to understand. However, there is a much broader population of people who are not unusually corrupt by nature, but they are forced to work within a system that is itself highly corrupted by the Syndrome of Distortions. In this case, the system that exists all around them is continuously twisted, bent, and crushed like one of those air-filled bouncy castles in which rambunctious children love to play.

Everybody Falls Inside the Bouncy Castle. Being inside a bouncy castle can be a humbling experience for any adult. Flying human projectiles slam against the walls from every direction, causing shock waves to ripple throughout the castle. No matter how strong and well-balanced you are, you're very likely to fall down because the continuously shifting air pressure throughout the castle is too disruptive to maintain your balance.

Complexity Magnifies Distortions. As the *system of humans* flying around the castle increases in number and complexity, the castle itself is increasingly distorted in every direction, creating a Syndrome of Distortions all around you. From the inside, there's no easily discernible single source of these distortions, which is why it's a "syndrome," but these distortions become part of the very fabric of your existence while you're inside the castle. And while you're on the inside, you cannot avoid being twisted, bent and crushed because you have become an integral part of an environment that is itself twisted, bent and crushed.

Systemic Corruption vs. Moral Corruption. I metaphorically describe the U.S. political system and the boardrooms of large corporations as the "Bouncy Castle," but the Bouncy Castle is any institutionalized culture that incentivizes humans to undermine the integrity or health of their broader economic, political, or social ecosystems. For the purposes of this book, our definition of "corruption" is the following:

> *Any significant deviation from, or malfunction of, the intended purpose, spirit, structure, or character of an individual or process within a political, social, or economic system.*

The kind of "corruption" that I occasionally mention throughout this book should not be amplified with any significant emotional overtones. In other words, we are primarily concerned about the corruption of systems, processes, and institutions that result in widespread human pain and suffering, not the personal character flaws or the subjective moral corruption of individual victims and perpetrators within these systems.

Existential Pressures and Distortions. The distinction between systemic and moral corruption is important to keep in mind because it's not fair or accurate to say that "all politicians are corrupt" or that "all corporate executives are self-serving and greedy." If they appear that way, it's usually because they must operate within a system that distorts and bends their existence every day. They must adapt and continuously adjust within that undulating system; otherwise, the system will chew them up and spit them out and they will lose their jobs, their financial security, and they would have no way to support their families. Contrary to popular opinion, most politicians and corporate executives have some humanity in them, too.

The Victims Are Often the Perpetrators. We should remember that when humans are forced to live and work inside a Bouncy Castle that is continuously afflicted with a Syndrome of Distortions, the victims can sometimes be the perpetrators and vice-versa, depending on which aspect of the system we are observing at any given moment. So let's never forget this important human dimension as we explore the causes and solutions of Broken Capitalism.

Avoiding Common Mental Traps

Self-Deceptions and Ideological Boxes. Respectfully, to all the ideological purists out there: As you read this book, look at the world *that actually exists* today and vividly visualize the frightening world that is inevitably coming within your lifetime. While you read this book, assume everything you have been taught about economics and politics in school, the media, and corporate propaganda machines is either garbage or so distorted by ideological bias that it is useless. To see problems and solutions clearly, we can't be trapped in the same self-imprisoning deceptions and ideological boxes that have created the problems we're facing today.

Perfection Is the Enemy of Progress. We should not allow preconceptions about how the world *should work* to interfere with our ability to see opportunities to improve the way *it does work*. There will always be flaws in human systems because humans are inherently flawed by their self-interest, but improving human systems is possible when we come together in good faith to resolve problems. The despotism of the Soviet Union, sending humans to the Moon, inventing the Internet, reducing the lethality of AIDS, abolishing institutional slavery, giving African-Americans and women the right to vote, perfecting organ transplant surgeries to extend human life, and many others—these were all huge human problems that were overcome because enough people came together in good faith to make incremental progress until the problems were solved. Fixing Broken Capitalism is no different.

Is Systemic Collapse the Only Path Forward? The entire global economic and geopolitical system will collapse if it continues down the current path. This should be obvious to any conscious human, especially after reading this book. What is *not* obvious to many people is how to fix or replace the existing system. I've met a few people *who actually want* the entire system to collapse so that we can restart the system from a clean slate. By instantly dismissing solutions that do not conform to their desire for total systemic collapse, they become blind to practical and viable solutions that would avoid the unimaginable pain and suffering that will inevitably result from a total systemic collapse.

Government Intervention *Already Exists* and *Will Expand*. In the coming years, *governments will intervene on a massive scale in every country* because all the problems associated with Broken Capitalism are getting rapidly worse every year. So we should not be deluded into believing that there is any path forward that avoids government intervention. The only relevant questions are:

- Will governments *continue to intervene as they already do today* to distribute *and redistribute* wealth to the wealthy and politically connected elite; or will they intervene in the public interest to ensure the broad creation and broad distribution of wealth for all their citizens?
- Will governments *continue to intervene* to make it easier for *too-big-to-fail* goliaths to dominate our global economy; or will they intervene to make it easier for smaller companies to survive?

Remember these questions throughout this book because the fate of human civilization depends on the answers.

***Expert* Delusions and Fantasies.** The *solutions* to Broken Capitalism presented by virtually all economists, political commentators, and policymakers today boil down to the same fundamental strategy: Increase personal income taxes and execute trillions of U.S. Dollars in unproductive transfer payments to jobless populations. All these so-called *experts* are locked inside this *tax-and-transfer* policymaking box because they are taught in school and inside corporate propaganda machines that it's OK to allow corporations to cannibalize their home economies as long as they are willing to pay higher taxes to subsidize an ever-expanding welfare state. But this trade-off—like many other *expert delusions* examined throughout this book—is a fantasy because the largest corporations exploit tax loopholes, play income-shifting shell games, and deploy their political power to reduce their effective tax rate to nearly zero.

Don't Settle for Unsustainable Tax-and-Transfer Policies. Most policymakers say the only thing that can be done to fix Broken Capitalism is to fiddle with the tax system to squeeze more money from one group and give it to another. I strongly disagree. As you read this book, you will see that my nonpartisan solutions are economically sustainable and they eliminate the ideological and social obstacles that plague all other economic and social welfare policies. Most importantly, the solutions in this book *do not* depend on confiscatory personal income tax increases. This is one of the many differences between the solutions in this book and the ideas floating around in policymaking circles today.

Political Labels Conceal Ignorance, Insecurity, and Manipulation. Economic or public policy discussions should never be reduced to vague labels and buzzwords like "Keynesianism," "Austrian School," "Marxism," "Liberal," "Conservative," "Republican," "Democrat," "Libertarian," etc. These are conceptual labels which have meanings that are easy for politicians and special interest groups to manipulate, which often causes their meaning to arbitrarily change depending on the time and place they are used. These labels are basically mental shortcuts, which are often misunderstood and used by lazy thinkers who don't really know what they're talking about. Or worse, they might use these labels to intentionally push you into an ideological box to silence you or try to make you feel inferior so they don't have to answer your important questions about how their economic and political policies work (or fail) in the real world.

Demand Clarity at All Times. Anybody who claims to be an expert at anything should be able to explain their ideas in simple and clear language that a reasonably educated high school teenager can understand. There is nothing complicated about the fundamental principles of supply and demand or regulations to prevent reckless politicians and corporations from engaging in blatantly reckless behavior.

Liberty = Personal Power. Authentic leaders empower citizens with more liberty; career politicians and large corporations have incentives to dis-empower citizens with less liberty because they want to control and exploit the thoughts and behavior of large populations. The solutions in this book empower all authentic business owners and leaders, political officials, and everyday citizens by giving them knowledge and tools to help them achieve more liberty, more prosperity, and more control over their own lives.

"The Only Thing Necessary for the Triumph of Evil is for Good Men to Do Nothing." – Edmund Burke. The Toxic Cloud is a byproduct of Broken Capitalism, which is suffocating billions of people around the world today. It can seem all-consuming and inescapable, causing many people to feel hopeless about their future. But please, don't allow the failures of past reforms—instigated by politicians whose incentives were distorted by self-interest—to close your mind to the principles in this book. Apathy is a dangerous form of blindness. Please keep your mind open as you read this book. If you can do that, you will understand how, working together to implement the solutions herein, we can dramatically improve the lives of billions of people on Earth today and billions more for generations to come.

Key Points

- **Avoiding the Malthusian Nightmare.** If Broken Capitalism is not fixed before artificial intelligence substantially controls every major economy, we will see permanent *real* unemployment rates between 40-60% within the lifetime of nearly everybody reading this book.

- **The Government Will Never Voluntarily Fix Broken Capitalism.** The politicians who control the U.S. Government have too many conflicts of interest, which perpetuates Broken Capitalism. Unless the people reading this book push their elected government officials to implement the nonpartisan reforms described in Part 2 of this book, politicians are guaranteed to succumb to special interest pressures again and again. And unless they read this book, they will likely misdiagnose the problems, which means they will mismanage the reforms that are necessary to minimize the pain for all of us.

- **The Toxic Cloud is Choking Out All Human Life.** A growing population of Americans and citizens in many countries today are feeling totally powerless to escape the asphyxiating Toxic Cloud, which is caused by Broken Capitalism. This is why restoring trust and integrity in Capitalism is the most critical task for our generation.

- Chapter 2 -
What's Wrong with the Global Economic System?

"Let me issue and control a nation's money
and I care not who writes the laws."
— Mayer Amschel Rothschild (1744-1812),
founder of the House of Rothschild

The 2008 Wall Street Communist Revolution. The 2008 Wall Street bailout was the largest government intervention (as a percentage of GDP) in world history. It was even larger than Russia's 1917 Communist Revolution 100 years ago. In case anybody thinks I'm exaggerating, let's remember that Communism is fundamentally an economic system in which the people who control the government expropriate private property and give it to somebody else. That's exactly what happened in 2008 as the U.S. Treasury and global economy were plundered by the convergent interests and actions of a tiny group of people in Washington and Wall Street. In fact, since 2008, we have seen an orgy of corporate welfare and bank-bailout socialism amounting to approximately *$29 trillion*.[8] That's a level of wealth confiscation and redistribution that Vladimir Lenin and his Russian Bolsheviks could have never imagined.

Mass Confusion. Many people have a vague sense that the global

---

[8]   Carney, John. "The Size of the Bank Bailout: $29 Trillion." CNBC, December 14, 2011. http://www.cnbc.com/id/45674390.
Greenstein, Tracey. "The Fed's $16 Trillion Bailouts Under-Reported." Forbes. Accessed April 20, 2017.
http://www.forbes.com/sites/traceygreenstein/2011/09/20/the-feds-16-trillion-bailouts-under-reported/.

economic system is broken and corrupt, but they often don't know how to explain exactly what is wrong. This is understandable because there is so much noise, false information, and propaganda spewed by the self-serving mainstream media, politicians, and large corporations that feed at the trough of the status quo. Additionally, many politicians and their corporate overlords deliberately manipulate public perceptions of what they have done to the U.S. economy to avoid being held accountable.

The Broken ATM Machine. The phrase "Broken Capitalism" accurately describes the state of Capitalism today, but of course, the system works perfectly for certain special interest groups; so they pretend it's not broken at all. For this reason, it's useful to visualize Broken Capitalism like a broken ATM machine: The machine is broken because there is a glitch that causes it to spit out piles of money without accounting for who is taking all the money. As the money gushes out, the people who already have the most money can hire political thugs (lobbyists and politicians) to block everybody else from getting close to the malfunctioning ATM gusher. This enables the wealthiest people to fill their buckets with piles of cash while everybody else drowns in debt and slides into poverty.

Lack of Knowledge Leads to Exploitation and Tyranny. Inequitable access to the Broken ATM Machine is a big problem, but lack of knowledge within the general public about how the system really works is the fundamental cause of the problem. When the general public understands the actual mechanisms and technical language used by certain groups in society who undermine the functional integrity of Capitalism and make a mockery of Democracy, society is in a much stronger position to compel policymakers to stop playing games with our lives and hold the miscreants accountable. The Rothschilds understood these dynamics very well, which we can observe in their following quote.

> *The few who understand the system will either be so interested in its profits or be so dependent upon its favours that there will be no opposition from that class, while on the other hand, the great body of people, mentally incapable of comprehending the tremendous advantage that capital derives from the system, will bear its burdens without complaint, and perhaps without even suspecting that the system is inimical to their interests.* — The Rothschild brothers of London writing to their associates in New York in 1863.

What's Really Wrong with the U.S. Banking System?

Nearly every global economic trend and crisis in human history over the past 120 years has originated within the U.S. economy. There are many historical reasons for this, some of which are covered below and in the following chapters of this book. Yes, the Eurozone is a basket-case and creates some global economic tremors from time-to-time; and yes, in the future, Asian countries will be much more influential. But for now, if you understand how the U.S. economy works, you will understand nearly everything you need to know to comprehend what is happening in the global economy. So let's dive into the U.S. banking system now because it influences and distorts everything else in the U.S. and global economies.

1970: New York Stock Exchange Allows Member Firm IPOs. Prior to 1970, investment banks were structured as private partnerships, but earning public trust was essential for them to earn business. Most importantly, their profits were generated by risking *the partners' own money*, which ensured that they managed every transaction cautiously and responsibly. All that changed after 1970. The NYSE allowed investment banks to sell their own stock to the public. This gave them access to billions of dollars of cash and stock-swap value that they could parlay into ever-larger mergers and acquisitions. This fueled a deal-making bonanza that led to the hyper-consolidation of the banking industry, concentrating enormous amounts of capital, wealth, and political power into the hands of a tiny number of monopolistic banking behemoths with an aggressive culture of risk-taking *with other people's money*.

1980s: The God of Shareholder Value is Born. In the early 1980s, American Capitalism mutated into a religion that worships a god called "shareholder value." This religion was thrust upon all public corporations when corporate raiders started using junk bonds and leveraged buyout strategies to force public company executives to pray to the same god. In this religious environment, if a corporate executive refuses to pay tribute to this god—i.e., export American jobs to foreign countries and squeeze their customers for every possible penny to satisfy the clerics on Wall Street—they are crucified by the raiders and pushed off their thrones when the raiders invade their corporate temples. This fear of the raiders has been institutionalized and is the fundamental cause of the short-term, quarterly profit-driven mentality that dominates American public corporations today. Is is also the source of Transnational Economic

Cannibals, which we will cover in the next chapter.

1980s—Present: The Financialization of the Economy. The total compensation (profits, wages, salary and bonuses) of financial intermediaries is currently about 9% of U.S. GDP—*nearly $2 trillion per year.*[9] On top of that, over-financialization reduces U.S. GDP growth by an additional 2% every year—*another $400 billion per year.*[10] Too much financialization increases the frequency of economic booms and busts, leaving countries worse off and with lower real GDP growth. Too much financialization sucks talent and human capital away from productive industries. There's a direct relationship between the size of a country's financial sector and economic instability caused by moral hazard, increased rent-seeking, increased rent-extraction from other sectors of the economy, leading to economy-wide misallocation of resources. Even the Bank for International Settlements (BIS) has recognized the problem: "The financial sector grows more quickly at the expense of the real economy. . . . Financial [sector] growth disproportionately harms financially dependent and R&D-intensive industries. . . . By draining resources from the real economy, financial sector growth becomes a drag on real growth."[11]

1982: Garn-St. Germain Depository Institutions Act. This legislation almost completely deregulated savings and loans (S&L) institutions and significantly watered down S&L accounting standards, which allowed them to enter new and riskier markets to compete with money market mutual funds. Of course, this was never the purpose of savings and loans ("thrifts"), but that didn't stop short-sighted politicians from passing this legislation and blowing up the S&L industry between 1986 and the early 1990s. (High interest rates and inflation in the late 1970s and 1980s were problematic, too, but those factors did not cause the egregious fraud and risk-taking that could only occur after the 1982 Garn-St. Germain Act.)

---

[9] Philippon, Thomas. "Finance vs. Walmart: Why Are Financial Services so Expensive?" *Rethinking Finance," A. Blinder, A. Lo and R. Solow (Eds)*, 2012. https://www.russellsage.org/sites/all/files/Rethinking-Finance/Philippon_v3.pdf.

[10] Ms. Ratna Sahay, et al. "Rethinking Financial Deepening: Stability and Growth in Emerging Markets." International Monetary Fund, May 4, 2015. http://www.imf.org/external/pubs/cat/longres.aspx?sk=42868.0.

[11] "Why Does Financial Sector Growth Crowd out Real Economic Growth?" Bank for International Settlements, February 12, 2015. http://www.bis.org/publ/work490.htm.

1986—1990: "Section 20 Affiliates" Restriction is Abolished. Despite their monopolistic role as custodians of the core banking apparatus of the economy, their special access to Federal Reserve funds at discounted rates, and their special status as FDIC-insured institutions (all of which give commercial banks significant competitive advantages against money market mutual funds and other financial service providers), several commercial banks complained to Congress that they could not compete without repealing Section 20 of Glass-Steagall. Section 20 prevented commercial banks from owning or controlling non-bank affiliates that are "engaged principally" in investment-related activities. As a result of bank lobbying pressure, the Federal Reserve approved the request of those banks to participate in various investment banking and insurance underwriting schemes, trading of commercial paper, municipal bonds, and mortgage-backed securities. This was the proverbial camel's nose in the tent.

1989: The FICO Score is Invented. Fair Isaac Corporation invented the FICO score in 1989 to automate consumer credit evaluations. By 1995, Fannie Mae and Freddie Mac were using FICO scores to determine which Americans could qualify for homeownership. Shortly thereafter, FICO proliferated throughout the U.S. economy like an invasive, alien fungus. American mailboxes exploded with glossy credit card, home mortgage, and auto loan offers. Investment banks and other financial firms gorged themselves on Collateralized Debt Obligations (CDOs), exotic financial instruments that often contained junk assets passed off as AAA-rated bonds. As debt-fueled profits flowed into retail and investment banks, their greed fueled the systemic fraud, predatory banking culture, and corporate malfeasance that culminated into the 2008 sub-prime mortgage crisis. Today, the U.S. economy is a debtor's prison that has trapped nearly 90% of all American households.[12]

1991: CFTC Secretly Allows Banks to Act Like Commodities Producers. The Commodity Futures Trading Commission (CFTC) begins secretly issuing exemption letters to the biggest Wall Street banks, allowing them to trade futures contracts in the commodities markets as if they were actual producers of physical commodities. With a combination of depositor

---

[12] LaMagna, Maria. "Americans Are Now in More Debt than They Were before the Financial Crisis." *MarketWatch*. Accessed February 14, 2017.
http://www.marketwatch.com/story/this-is-how-much-credit-card-debt-americans-racked-up-in-2016-2016-12-20.

funds, exotic derivatives, massive debt leveraging, and many forms of financial engineering, the banks and their affiliates dramatically increased the size, volatility, and price levels of all commodities markets. This directly contributed to the astronomical price increases of oil and gasoline; metals like copper, iron, and zinc; and agricultural products like corn, wheat, and soybeans to unprecedented levels, which magnified the 2008 global financial crisis. These exemption letters were essentially waivers that allowed the banks to avoid all the rules that were in place to protect the markets from aggressive speculation. The result was trillions of dollars of highly speculative trading, resulting in hundreds of billions of dollars of wealth siphoned out of the global economy and into the coffers of the largest banks and their affiliates. This activity still continues to this day.

1996: Glass-Steagall is Gutted. The Federal Reserve "reinterpreted" the Glass-Steagall Act multiple times by the end of 1996, which collectively allowed consolidated bank holding companies (commingling retail banks and investment banks) to generate up to 25% of their revenues from investment-related activities. This was arguably the most significant action that set the precedent for the next decade of regulatory folly, leading directly to the 2008 catastrophe.

1998: Collapse of Long-Term Capital Management. The large hedge fund, Long-Term Capital Management (LTCM), collapsed from massive leverage and derivatives exposure, which demonstrated that complex trading of exotic derivatives (using over 100 times leverage in many cases) posed a catastrophic systemic risk to the entire global financial system. There were obvious lessons that should have been learned from this event, but they were substantially ignored by the most senior officials at the U.S. Treasury, Federal Reserve, and Congressional banking committees. Brooksley Born (Chairperson of the CFTC) and Sheila Bair (Chairperson of the FDIC) were laughed at and pushed out of their jobs when they tried to warn the Fed, Congress and Treasury that the same risks that destroyed LTCM were leading to an even bigger financial crisis in other sectors of the economy.

1998: Citicorp/Travelers Merger. Despite strong protest from many good-faith economists, financial industry analysts, and other industry stakeholders warning that this was a bad idea, Congress succumbed to relentless lobbying pressure and explicitly approved the Citigroup merger. Clearly illegal under the 1933 Glass-Steagall Act, this merger combined large retail banking, insurance underwriting, and investment banking operations into the world's largest financial services conglomerate. Naturally, after this precedent was established, all the other ambitious financial corporations wanted to create their own systemically dangerous conglomerates.

1999: Financial Services Modernization Act (aka, the Gramm-Leach-Bliley Act). After protecting the banking system from destructive banking practices for over 60 years, the Glass-Steagall Act was repealed by the deceptively labeled Financial Services Modernization Act. This was effectively a retroactive law to create the appearance of legal legitimacy for the Citigroup merger the previous year. It also *legalized* the Fed's and Congress' legally dubious previous "reinterpretations" of Glass-Steagall, which had been eroding the law's efficacy for years. After 25 years and $300 million worth of lobbying and political campaign donations from the banking industry, Congress officially capitulated. This "modernized" the U.S. economy by allowing retail and investment banks and other financial corporations to merge into giant conglomerates and commingle their assets in ways that increased the size, scope, and systemic risk of their operations. Shortly after serving on the Glass-Steagall demolition team, the U.S. Treasury Secretary was rewarded with a senior position at Citigroup and made $126 million while revolving between Wall Street and Washington.

2000—Present: Artificially Low Interest Rates. The Federal Reserve has maintained artificially low interest rates, which has fueled the debt-leveraged bonanza that has allowed financial corporations and the general public to accumulate massive, unsustainable amounts of debt. Officials at the Fed know artificially low interest rates create a strong economy-wide bias to consume rather than to save. They know artificially low interest rates have created a debtor's prison for nearly 90% of Americans today. They know too much debt creates too much risk for the entire economy and will dramatically decrease the quality of life for virtually all Americans. Despite knowing all of this, they continue to pursue the same toxic monetary policies for self-serving political reasons at the expense of the integrity and health of the entire global economy.

2000: Commodity Futures Modernization Act. This deceptively named legislation substantially repealed the regulation of derivatives, which enabled banks, commodities trading firms like the despised Enron Corporation, and other financial service companies to conceal the true size and risk of their debts and derivatives exposure from their counterparties and regulators. This legislation "modernized" the commodities trading industry by forcefully blocking effective regulations that would have prevented the credit default swap abuses that destroyed confidence in the entire financial system seven years later.

2001—2004: Net Capital Reductions & the "Consolidated Supervised Entities Program". A series of complex regulatory changes collectively reduced the net capital required by banks and their broker-dealer subsidiaries. These adjustments created a strong bias for banks to leverage up on mortgage-backed securities (MBSs) because the MBSs were arbitrarily granted a lower risk weighting in their risk models. These changes also allowed banks and brokerage firms to essentially regulate themselves across a broad range of risky activities. This created powerful incentives for banks to ignore widespread mortgage industry fraud and to engineer every aspect of their retail banking, investment banking, insurance underwriting, and broker-dealer operations in ways that maximized their ability to gorge themselves on risky sub-prime mortgage-backed securities.

2008: Boom. We all saw the riveting drama unfold in the media; so there's no need to rehash those familiar details here. However, *after* the financial crisis, many people optimistically hoped that these politicians would learn from their preceding egregious mistakes, but "learning" is not really what they care about. They're more interested in preserving their role at the center of the Regulatory Protection Racket that subsidizes their re-election campaigns. Now we continue into the post-2008 era of ongoing incompetence and planet-destroying negligence. . . .

2008: Emergency Economic Stabilization Act. This deceptively named legislation created the Troubled Asset Relief Program ("TARP") and used trillions of taxpayer funds to purchase toxic securities and inject capital into the big banks and other large corporations without any meaningful accountability. Of course, this does not "stabilize" anything over the long-run. Rather than forcing the banks to properly reorganize under existing bankruptcy laws so that they could shed their irresponsible management that engaged in excessive risk-taking activities and dispose of their toxic assets in an orderly fashion without putting innocent taxpayers on the hook, the politicians chose to waste trillions of taxpayer funds to prop up banks and their wealthy shareholders. Predictably, this made them even more powerful by eliminating competition from smaller companies that could not compete with the government-backed behemoths.[13]

2009: Public-Private Investment Program. Among a flurry of federal programs designed to prop up the biggest banks, the U.S. Treasury implemented the "Public-Private Investment Program" to purchase toxic assets from financial institutions backed by American taxpayer funds. As of today, this and many similar *banking relief* programs are part of an ongoing parasitic malignancy that is sucking all the life out of the U.S. economy while the biggest financial institutions balloon into even bigger and more systemically dangerous behemoths. These politicians continue to put ever-more taxpayer dollars at risk with these bailout programs, which of course inspires their special interest donors to continue financing their election campaigns.

2010: Dodd-Frank Act. The Dodd-Frank Act was pitched as the most ambitious financial reform legislation since FDR's New Deal Era reforms in the 1930s. Dodd-Frank was supposed to "lift our economy" and "end too big to fail" and "promote financial stability," all of which have been total fantasies at best, and deliberate lies more likely. Predictably, since 2008, too-big-to-fail financial corporations are much bigger today, large numbers of smaller community banks and asset management firms have been systematically destroyed, less competition has enabled the biggest banks to ratchet up their fees thereby hurting their customers, the entire financial system is much less stable, job growth is anemic, and the U.S. economy is in a permanent malaise.

2010—Present: Ongoing Fraud, Abuse, and Anti-Competitive Practices. Since 2010, the U.S. Department of Justice and other financial regulatory agencies have convicted the largest banks operating in the U.S. of the following unlawful activities:

- Toxic securities and mortgage abuses
- Manipulation of foreign exchange markets
- Manipulation of interest rate benchmarks
- Assisting tax evasion

---

[13] Despite the false doomsday propaganda from bad-faith politicians and special interest groups, bankruptcy does not destroy a company; it restructures it to operate more responsibly and/or facilitates the sale of its assets to more responsible management teams.

- Credit card abuses
- Failing to report suspicious behavior by Bernie Madoff
- Inadequate money-laundering controls
- Discriminatory practices
- Manipulation of energy markets
- "Other Major Cases"

Were the Banks and Their Senior Management Punished? The list above represents several hundred major cases, resulting in over $160 billion in fines.[14] That might seem like a lot, but in most cases, these fines were offset by special tax deductions and various deferral agreements that have reduced the actual fines paid to about 10% of the total amount. The net result: The fines are a small fraction of one year of revenue, no senior executives were criminally charged, they continue doing business as usual, they continue destroying smaller competitors, and they continue capturing and distorting ever-larger portions of the global economy.

Too Much Idiotic Bureaucracy; Not Enough Rational Regulation. Too much idiotic bureaucracy is killing smaller companies that can't afford to pay legions of lawyers, tax and compliance experts to manage the exploding bureaucracy. *Too much idiotic regulation* obscures the rules with endless gray areas, which makes it easier for the behemoths' to exploit compliance loopholes and easier for politicians to use regulation as a political weapon to extort campaign contributions from their corporate prey. (Recall in the previous chapter: The victims of the Regulatory Protection Racket are often also the perpetrators, and vice-versa.) Politicians habitually (and often deliberately) fail to address the most basic problems where rational regulation *would actually help*: Too much debt, too much financial risk-taking, too much fraud, too much predatory behavior, and too little personal accountability for the senior executives and political officials who are responsible.

Every Toxic Step was Predicted, Predictable, and Preventable. At every fateful step along the path to the 2008 financial crisis there were

---

[14] Based on the fantastic research tool and report provided by GoodJobsFirst.org. "The $160 Billion Bank Fee: What Violation Tracker 2.0 Shows about Penalties Imposed on Major Financial Offenders." Accessed April 13, 2017.
http://www.goodjobsfirst.org/sites/default/files/docs/pdf/160billionbankfee.pdf.

specific politicians responsible for each negligent decision to dismantle and block important regulations designed to protect the banking system from systemic collapse. Many people are on the record warning them long before each crisis occurred. In fact, if you look at the source of their campaign financing at the nonpartisan OpenSecrets.org site, you will see exactly how and why the integrity and actions of these politicians were distorted and corrupted. You probably won't be surprised to know that the top-10 largest donors to all these politicians (Republicans and Democrats) were the biggest U.S. banks and financial institutions.

Pain and Suffering. It's hard to ignore the pain and suffering that these politicians have caused 100s of millions of people around the world today because of their bad-faith legislation, political partisanship, and incompetent regulation of the financial services sector. The destruction and re-distribution of trillions of dollars of wealth from unsuspecting taxpayers, retirement account holders, and novice investors around the world into the pockets of a tiny number of well-placed politicians, political campaigns, banks, traders, and corporate executives certainly meets the definition of a crime against humanity. Of course, none of the people responsible for these crimes are ever held accountable because they hide behind various legal and institutional walls (which they often create) that are designed to shield them from personal accountability.

The Anatomy of a Financial Crisis

Conscious, Incremental, Ethical Compromises. "How could Maestro Greenspan have known the government's policies would lead to the 2008 crisis?" some people might ask. They *always* know they're manipulating the economy because they must make conscious choices and ethical compromises at every pivotal point along the path to a crisis, while secretly serving their special interest benefactors. Most of them probably *hope* the consequences of their fiscal and monetary manipulation won't be as bad as the warnings they receive from nonpartisan experts, but that's about as generous as we can be to politicians who succumb to fantasies that result in the loss of trillions of dollars and incalculable human pain and suffering.

Death by Design or Incompetence is Still Death. Some people wonder if politicians are deliberately killing their country or if they're just really incompetent. This is a reasonable question, but the answer is simple: Does it really matter? If the result of deliberate or incompetent behavior is exactly the same, do we really need to make excuses for them? If there's a big, fat, harry, smelly guy *accidentally* sitting on your face while you're gasping for breath, suffocating to death, do you really care *why* he's killing you?

Persistent, Systematic Deception. Let's be clear: *Most policymakers know or have good reasons to suspect* that their policies are destroying Capitalism, but they're trapped in the Bouncy Castle described in the previous chapter. To vividly illustrate this truth, let's reminisce about the period between 2000 to 2008. Virtually every major economic policy mistake that led to the stock market crash of 1929 and the Great Depression was substantially repeated in the years leading up to 2008. Let's now look at how the 2008 crisis unfolded from the perspective of Federal Reserve Chairman Ben Bernanke's propaganda compared to the reality of what *actually* happened at each phase of the crisis.

November 2002 – *The Chairman:* "The U.S. government has a technology, called a printing press (or today, its electronic equivalent), that allows it to produce as many U.S. dollars as it wishes at no cost."[15]

The Reality: The Fed's Ponzi money is only temporarily possible because of the once-in-human-history gift—the world's reserve currency—that the U.S. received at Bretton Woods, which is slipping away rapidly. And printing money is certainly not "at no cost." The costs are already accumulating within the Toxic Cloud and more severe costs are only temporarily hidden until China completes its ongoing decoupling from the U.S. economy, the U.S. currency, and U.S. debt.

July 2005 – *The Chairman:* "We've never had a decline in house prices on a nationwide basis. So, what I think what [sic] is more likely is that house prices will slow—maybe stabilize—might slow consumption spending a bit. I don't think it's gonna drive the economy too far from its full employment path, though."[16]

The Reality: The 2008 crisis came with a vengeance to prove the Chairman wrong on all points.

November 2005 – *The Chairman:* "With respect to their safety, derivatives, for the most part, are traded among very sophisticated financial institutions and individuals who have considerable incentive to understand

---

[15] "Speech, Bernanke --Deflation-- November 21, 2002." Accessed February 5, 2017. https://www.federalreserve.gov/boarddocs/speeches/2002/20021121/.
[16] PaulWilliamsWorld. *Bernanke: Why Are We Still Listening to This Guy?* Accessed February 5, 2017. https://www.youtube.com/watch?v=HQ79Pt2GNJo.

them and to use them properly."[17]

The Reality: With all due respect Mr. Chairman, anybody who has ever spent any meaningful amount of time on an actual derivatives trading floor knows that the moral hazards of the Fed's bailout policy, plus the high pressure in public companies to increase quarterly profits, plus the barely functional gambling addiction of most traders, plus flawed "Value-at-Risk" risk models previously used by virtually all major investment banks, plus the fact that the $700-800 *trillion* OTC swaps market has never been seriously regulated and has virtually no transactional transparency, plus numerous other structural and inter-personal incentives to engage in risk-taking among intra-bank trading teams—all of these factors *guarantee* that derivatives traders will blow up the financial world. How could you possibly make such a negligent statement?

February 2006 – *The Chairman:* "I don't think that Chinese ownership of U.S. assets is so large as to put our country at risk economically."[18]

The Reality: In 2006, China held $400 billion in U.S. Treasury debt and $1 trillion in U.S. currency reserves. As of early 2015, China held approximately $1.3 trillion in U.S. Treasury debt and $4 trillion in currency reserves. At any moment, China has the power to inflict immense damage upon the entire U.S. economy in numerous ways because of their control of all these assets. This castrates U.S. foreign and economic policy negotiations with China and reduces the U.S.' ability to economically compete in Asia, South America, Africa, and in every country in which China is rapidly expanding. These are all very significant risks.

March 2007 – *The Chairman:* "The impact on the broader economy and financial markets of the problems in the subprime markets seems likely to be contained."[19]

---

[17] Jones, Kristin. "Top Regulators Once Opposed Regulation of Derivatives." *ProPublica*, October 6, 2008. http://www.propublica.org/article/top-regulators-once-opposed-regulation-of-derivatives.

[18] Reuters. "U.S. Assets Safe in China, Fed Chief Says." *The New York Times*, February 17, 2006. http://www.nytimes.com/2006/02/17/business/worldbusiness/us-assets-safe-in-china-fed-chief-says.html.

[19] "Looking for Ways out of the Subprime Mortgage Crisis - CNN.com." Accessed February 5, 2017. http://www.cnn.com/2007/US/03/29/subprime.congress/index.html?_s=PM:US

The Reality: At that time the U.S. housing crisis is in full swing. Banks and hedge funds are forced to write down billions of dollars in worthless assets as foreclosures rise sharply. Mortgage giant Freddie Mac says it will no longer buy risky subprime loans, but it's already too late.

May 2007 – *The Chairman:* "We do not expect significant spillovers from the subprime market to the rest of the economy or to the financial system. . . . The vast majority of mortgages, including even subprime mortgages, continue to perform well."[20]

The Reality: Around this same time Bear Stearns has $13.4 *trillion* in derivatives exposure and two of its multibillion-dollar hedge funds collapse because of risky securities backed by subprime mortgage loans. New Century Financial slides into a "death spiral." American Home Mortgage Investment company goes bankrupt. Fitch Ratings gives one of its worst ratings to the largest mortgage lending company in the world, Countrywide Financial. The secondary mortgage-based securities market freezes up. Countrywide, with over $200 billion in assets and $5 *trillion* in mortgage-backed securities and loans, is on the brink of insolvency. Merrill Lynch and other institutions publicly suspect Countrywide may go bankrupt. Over 50 other mortgage lenders go bankrupt. The entire mortgage lending and mortgage banking industry is collapsing and industry insiders report widespread subprime fraud and abuse to FBI investigators.

October 2007 – *The Chairman*: "It is not the responsibility of the Federal Reserve – nor would it be appropriate – to protect lenders and investors from the consequences of their financial decisions."[21]

The Reality: But it's the Fed's responsibility "to protect lenders and investors from the consequences of their financial decisions" in the banking industry by providing them $29 trillion in corporate welfare since 2008?[22]

January 2008 – *The Chairman:* "The Federal Reserve is not currently forecasting a recession. . . . We will not monetize the debt. . . .

---

[20] "FRB: Speech, Bernanke--The Subprime Mortgage Market--May 17, 2007," May 17, 2007.
https://www.federalreserve.gov/newsevents/speech/bernanke20070517a.htm.
[21] "BBC NEWS | Business | Highlights of Ben Bernanke's Speech." Accessed February 5, 2017. http://news.bbc.co.uk/2/hi/business/6972767.stm.
[22] $29 Trillion: A Detailed Look at the Fed's Bailout by Funding Facility and Recipient – Levy Economics Institute

We're not printing money. . . . The money supply is not changing in any significant way."[23]

The Reality: The U.S. economy officially entered a recession the *previous month* before this statement and remained in the Great Recession for 18 months thereafter. The Fed has monetized, quantitatively eased, and provided a total of about *$29 trillion* in loans, bailouts, government guarantees, and corporate welfare to the banking industry since 2008.[24]

February 2008 – *The Chairman:* "Among the largest banks, the capital ratios remain good and I don't expect any serious problems of that sort among the large, internationally active banks that make up a very substantial part of our banking system."[25]

The Reality: The U.S. economy is officially in recession. The crisis in subprime mortgages infects all credit markets now. Credit begins to freeze up throughout the economy. The Federal Reserve prepares to announce its agreement to guarantee $30 billion of Bear Stearns' assets in connection with the government-assisted sale of Bear Stearns to JPMorgan.

June 2008 – *The Chairman:* "The risk that the economy has entered a substantial downturn appears to have diminished over the past month or so. . . ."[26]

The Reality: A few weeks later, one of the largest mortgage banks in the United States, IndyMac Federal Bank, collapses and is seized by the FDIC. A few additional weeks later the entire U.S. and global economies collapse into the greatest economic crisis in nearly 80 years.

July 2008 – *The Chairman:* "The GSEs [Fannie Mae and Freddie Mac] are adequately capitalized. They are in no danger of failing."[27]

The Reality: A few weeks later Fannie Mae and Freddie Mac, with

---

[23] Saul Loeb / AFP-Getty. "Bernanke: Fed Ready to Cut Interest Rates Again." *Msnbc.com*, January 10, 2008. http://www.nbcnews.com/id/22592939/ns/business-stocks_and_economy/t/bernanke-fed-ready-cut-interest-rates-again/.

[24] Ibid.

[25] "Banks Should Seek More Capital: Bernanke." *Reuters*, February 28, 2008. http://www.reuters.com/article/us-usa-fed-bernanke-banks-idUSWBT00848420080228.

[26] "FRB: Speech--Bernanke, Outstanding Issues in the Analysis of Inflation--June 9, 2008." Accessed February 5, 2017. https://www.federalreserve.gov/newsevents/speech/bernanke20080609a.htm.

[27] "Highlights: Bernanke Faces Questions from U.S. Lawmakers." *Reuters*, July 16, 2008. http://www.reuters.com/article/us-usa-fed-highlights-idUSN1638306220080716.

over $5 trillion in total mortgage-backed securities and debt are taken over by the government. Bank of America agrees to help Merrill Lynch avoid bankruptcy by purchasing the company for $50 billion. Lehman Brothers collapses with about $760 billion in debt and becomes the largest bankruptcy in world history.

September 2008 – *The Politicians:* For some tragicomic relief, let's recall Senator John McCain's unforgettable words on Black Friday, September 15, 2008: "The fundamentals of this economy are strong." Lehman Brothers declares bankruptcy a few hours later.[28] Shortly thereafter, several government officials tell Americans they won't be able to cash their paychecks and ATM machines will freeze up if they don't immediately pass the Troubled Asset Relief Program ("TARP") to bailout nearly 1,000 financial institutions and auto companies, including AIG, Bank of America, Bear Stearns, Citigroup, Lehman Brothers, Countrywide, Wachovia, Wells Fargo, Goldman Sachs, Washington Mutual, General Motors, and hundreds of others. Several other federal programs are launched and several of the taxpayer-subsidized bailouts are still ongoing as of today.

The Reality: Credit markets were almost completely frozen and several large banks were collapsing. Bank deposit customers already had FDIC insurance for the vast majority of deposits. Retirement accounts and other individual savings and money market accounts should have been saved; however, the Fed, FDIC, U.S. Treasury, SEC, Comptroller of the Currency, and Congress should have coordinated an orderly bankruptcy liquidation of *all* the failing banks. No private organization is "too big to fail" and they should have been forced into bankruptcy to clean out the toxic assets from the financial system. Whatever was left after bankruptcy could have been sold at their fair market value to new owners who would have continued commercially operating those assets much more responsibly and at more sustainable levels of profitability.

The Financial Crisis Inquiry Commission Show. Two years later, Congress orchestrated the Financial Crisis Inquiry Commission

---

28 "The fundamentals of the economy are strong." – quote from Senator John McCain, reprinted by Time Magazine's list of the "Top 10 Unfortunate Political One-Liners," available at:
http://content.time.com/time/specials/packages/article/0,28804,1859513_185952 6_1859517,00.html

("FCIC") theatrical show, which added 14,000 pages to the Regulatory Protection Racket. The FCIC preserved most of the toxic financial assets and they're still in the financial system in various forms today. Even worse, the FCIC consciously allowed the banks to get even bigger, which is even more systemically destabilizing to the financial system. And now we're careening toward another, bigger financial collapse.

December 2010 – The Chairman: "I wish I'd been omniscient and seen the crisis coming."[29]

The Reality: A central banker is obviously never omniscient, which is why central banks have destroyed fiat currencies and national economies literally every time they have existed since Kublai Khan introduced the first fiat currency in 13th Century China.[30] Regardless of whether the Chairman saw the crisis coming or not, he obviously knows that central banks can never completely predict and effectively control the long-term unintended consequences of their money supply and interest rate manipulation.[31]

The Fed is Controlled by the White House. Many people feel this is true instinctively, but until recently, there was no direct validation of this feeling publicly. Validation finally came in the form of a December 2015 interview, in which Ben Bernanke was asked several questions about why he failed to foresee and prevent the 2008 financial crisis when he was Chairman of the Federal Reserve. Bernanke replied, "Well, it was partly the

---

[29] "Fed Chairman Ben Bernanke's Take On The Economy," December 3, 2010. http://www.cbsnews.com/news/fed-chairman-ben-bernankes-take-on-the-economy/.

[30] Monograph on the History of Money in China (1881) – the author, Alexander Del Mar, former Director of the U.S. Bureau of Statistics, quotes the famous 13th Century explorer, Marco Polo: "Population and trade had greatly increased, but the emissions of paper notes were suffered to largely outrun both. . . . All the beneficial effects of a currency that is allowed to expand with a growth of population and trade were now turned into those evil effects that flow from a currency emitted in excess of such growth. These effects were not slow to develop themselves. . . . The best families in the empire were ruined, a new set of men came into the control of public affairs, and the country became the scene of internecine warfare and confusion."

[31] For a refreshing contrast, most of the policy statements from the St. Louis Federal Reserve Bank actually reflect rational economic reality. See: Thornton, Daniel L. "The Federal Reserve's Response to the Financial Crisis: What It Did and What It Should Have Done," 2012. https://papers.ssrn.com/sol3/papers.cfm?abstract_id=2171836.

result of the fact that *I was representing the administration. And you don't really want to go out and say, 'Run for the hills,' right?*[32] This rare glimpse of honesty confirms that the toxic influence of partisan party politics—and the politics within the White House in particular under all administrations—distorts the Fed's monetary policy. These distortions are specifically caused by individual politicians who manipulate Fed policies to advance and protect their own careers at the expense of the American people.

Globalism 1.0: A Brain-Rotting Neurotoxin

What is Globalism? "Globalism" can mean many things, but from an economic perspective, it's an economic ideology that spawns a pattern of worldwide commercial activity governed by a system of international trade agreements between nations. These agreements are all predicated upon an ideologically-driven theory that configuring Capitalism on Earth to maximize the total amount of international trade *automatically* maximizes the overall welfare of humanity. People who subscribe to this theory are often called "globalists."

Globalism 1.0 and the Blue Screen of Death. The version of globalism that exists today should be perceived as a very buggy 1.0 beta version that should never have been deployed in a live, production environment. Globalism today is the socioeconomic equivalent of the infamous "Blue Screen of Death" that historically plagued the Microsoft Windows operating system. Most people living today can relate to this dreaded experience: You're trying to work and be productive, then suddenly the Blue Screen of Death fills you with terror. You're paralyzed, unable to work or create any value because the system has crashed. All you can do is try to restart and pray that you haven't lost everything. That's exactly how the jobless American labor force feels today, along with a rapidly expanding population of economic refugees worldwide.

The Neurotoxin Embedded within Globalism 1.0. Globalism 1.0 cheerleaders promote free trade policies as the key to creating global prosperity, but they ignore many social, economic, and political factors that

---

[32] 2015 interview with Stephen J. Dubner, author of the best-selling book, Freakonomics. See: http://freakonomics.com/2015/12/03/ben-bernanke-gives-himself-a-grade-a-new-freakonomics-radio-podcast

actually determine the long-term welfare of human populations. Creating global prosperity is a worthwhile goal, but the way global Capitalism is configured today is creating much more long-term harm than good. I call this misconfigured form of global Capitalism "Globalism 1.0." Sadly, the ideology embedded within Globalism 1.0—variously called "Economic Liberalism" and "Neoliberalism" (which have nothing to do with political liberalism in the U.S.)—has become a powerful neurotoxin that blinds many people to reality and causes them to destroy their own economies.

Three Waves of *Globalization*. There have been three waves of *globalization*: The Age of Discovery ushered in an era of *partial* globalization when new navigation technologies like the mariner's compass and more accurate maps made it possible for the Portuguese, Spanish, and Dutch to dominate European, Asian, and South American trade between the 16th and 17th Centuries. Then there was Industrial Age globalization spawned by new methods of industrial ship-building combined with John Harrison's invention of the marine chronometer, which gave Britain (and later, the United States) the ability to dominate international trade during the 18th and 19th Centuries. And now, we are in the third wave of globalization— instigated by the Information Age—which has spawned a complete globalization of the mind. This third wave began with the collapse of the Soviet Union in 1991 and blossomed into a globe-gripping ideology when China joined the WTO in 2001. This is when Globalism 1.0 was born.

Globalization vs. Globalism. "Globalization" is a cyclical process; "globalism" is an ideology. Ideologies like Communism, Capitalism, Liberalism, Conservatism, Libertarianism, Globalism and all other *isms* take control of the human mind and shape the thoughts, perceptions, intentions and behavior of humans. The ideology of Globalism—as exemplified by Globalism 1.0 cheerleaders and so-called Neoliberal economists today—hijacks the human mind and squeezes out all other perspectives and possibilities regarding how Capitalism can be configured to achieve a more equitable and sustainable form of global trade. Unlike the process of cyclical globalization, *Globalism 1.0 is a new creature*, which has infected every country on Earth with its brain-rotting neurotoxin since the end of the 20st Century.

Globalism 1.0 Increases the Speed, Scope, and Magnitude of Crises. In one of their own reports, the IMF admits:

Indeed, the process of capital account liberalization appears to have been accompanied in some cases by increased vulnerability to crises. Globalization has heightened these risks since cross-country financial linkages amplify the effects of various shocks and transmit them more quickly across national borders.[33]

This amplification effect is what transformed the 1997 "Asian Contagion" and the 2008 Financial Crisis into global economic earthquakes when they would have been small tremors if more rational economic policies existed. What is the IMF's solution? From the same report, "The evidence presented in this paper suggests that financial integration should be approached cautiously, with good institutions and macroeconomic frameworks viewed as important." In other words, they have no idea how to make Globalism 1.0 work. In Part 2, we will explore how globalism can and should work.

Should We Maximize Industrial Output or Human Life? Should Capitalism be configured to incentivize humans to produce *stuff* like mindless robots merely for the sake of *production and profit;* or should Capitalism be configured to improve the quality of life for the greatest number of humans? One of the most persistent delusions in mainstream economics today is that maximizing industrial output is the highest priority of a free market. This delusion is caused by a deep systemic bias in favor of transnational corporations, which is embedded into our school system, our media, and our global economy. It is this bias that elevates the Profit Motive to a religion, appoints corporate executives as bishops over our economy, anoints Wall Street bankers as high priests over our society, and worships shareholder value as the merciless god to which they all pray.

The Betrayal of Our Economic Godfathers. Broken Capitalism is the culmination of over 200 years of manipulation and propaganda by powerful corporate interests who have strategically adopted the most myopic and extreme interpretation of the work of Adam Smith and David Ricardo, the godfathers of modern economics. Like every violent religion that deviates from its founder's virtuous message, Broken Capitalism is not what Smith and Ricardo intended. Anybody who has read their warnings about capital and wealth concentration knows this. And anybody who can

---

[33] International Monetary Fund. "Effects of Financial Globalization on Developing Countries: Some Empirical Evidence," March 17, 2003. http://www.imf.org/external/np/res/docs/2003/031703.pdf.

block out the buggy Globalism 1.0 brainwashing for just 10 seconds will probably conclude that an economy should be structured to maximize *human life*, not *industrial output*.

Our Economic Godfathers Had a Home Bias. Both Adam Smith and David Ricardo had a *home bias* perspective on global trade. Ricardo said that capitalists should "be satisfied with the low rate of profit in their home country. . . ."[34] Both Smith and Ricardo knew that industrialists who disregarded the interests of their home countries would destroy their home economies. It was in reaction to this observation that Adam Smith invoked his famous "invisible hand" phrase. Specifically, he hoped that capitalists would be guided by *an invisible hand* that would naturally compel them to build their *domestic economies*. Regarding capitalists, Smith said:

> *As every individual, therefore, endeavours as much as he can both to employ his capital in the support of domestic industry . . . . By preferring the support of domestic to that of foreign industry, he intends only his own security; and by directing that industry in such a manner as its produce may be of the greatest value, he intends only his own gain, and he is in this, as in many other cases, led by an invisible hand to promote an end which was no part of his intention.*[35]

Adam Smith also had a deeply idealistic assumption about the ability of free markets to distribute wealth equitably. In his 1759 book, *The Theory of Moral Sentiments*, Smith understood the critical importance of broad wealth creation and distribution when he said:

> *The rich . . . are led by an invisible hand to make nearly the same distribution of the necessaries of life, which would have been made, had the earth been divided into equal portions among all its inhabitants, and thus without intending it, without knowing it, advance the interest of the society. . . .*[36]

Despite his idealism, Adam Smith explicitly warned against

---

[34] Ricardo, David. On The Principles Of Political Economy And Taxation (1821). Kessinger Publishing, LLC, 2010.

[35] Smith, Adam, and Alan B. Krueger. The Wealth of Nations. Annotated edition. New York, N.Y: Bantam Classics, 2003.

[36] Smith, Adam. The Theory of Moral Sentiments. London: A. Millar, 1759.

squeezing the Middle Class and allowing wealth to concentrate into the hands of a few. In his own words:

> *No society can surely be flourishing and happy, of which the greater part of the members are poor and miserable. It is but equity, besides, that they who feed, cloath and lodge the whole body of the people, should have such a share of the produce of their own labour as to be themselves tolerably well fed, clothed, and lodged.[37]*

The Godfathers Did Not Want Globalism 1.0. Nearly 250 years later, Broken Capitalism today proves that Smith's assumption about free markets creating an equitable distribution of wealth was an idealistic fantasy.[38] However, it's clear that Smith's and Ricardo's *intention* was to develop an economic philosophy that promotes human welfare above the myopic Profit Motive that fuels the rapacious greed of transnational corporations today. So nobody can legitimately say the Broken Capitalism that exists today is what Adam Smith or David Ricardo intended. That means the self-serving corporate propaganda and biased curricula in the school system that collectively defends Broken Capitalism today is utter nonsense.

JFK on Globalism. Many people think that U.S. President John F. Kennedy was one of the greatest presidents in American history. His diplomatic skill and exceptional leadership ability were legendary. His handling of the Cuban Missile Crisis in 1962 is a model of international crisis management taught in virtually every Political Science program in the world today. And JFK was a sincere champion of minorities and the less fortunate members of American society. However, when he made the following statement in 1962, there was no way he could have predicted how devastating Globalism 1.0 would be to the country he loved and the people he died serving.

> *If we do not take action, those who have the most reason to be dissatisfied with*

---

[37] Smith, Adam, and Alan B. Krueger. The Wealth of Nations. Annotated edition. New York, N.Y: Bantam Classics, 2003.

[38] The belief that free markets can exist at all in a Presidential System of government without strictly enforced accountability for corruptible politicians and regulators is the biggest fantasy.

our present rate of growth will be tempted to seek shortsighted and narrow solutions—to resist automation, to reduce the work week to 35 hours or even lower, to shut out imports, or to raise prices in a vain effort to obtain full capacity profits on under-capacity operations. But these are all self-defeating expedients which can only restrict the economy, not expand it.[39]

A Society is Not Wealthy If a Majority of Its People Live in Poverty. The problem with JFK's statement, and many similar statements from politicians since 1962, is that they are theoretically true, but they paint an incomplete picture of reality. They completely ignore the most important factor in the prosperity and welfare of a nation: The prosperity and welfare of a nation's *actual people.* They also ignore the critical role of small- to medium-sized business communities, which must be healthy for widespread prosperity to exist. With the exception of a few lonely voices every generation, there has been no meaningful consideration given by American policymakers to ensure the gains from global trade at the corporate level *actually spread equitably throughout American society.* We will explore the important difference between "equity" and "equality" in a later chapter, but for now, remember that "equity" has nothing to do with "Socialism" or "income inequality" as many political operatives on both sides of the ideological divide like to claim.

Group-Think, Corporate Raiders, and a Convergence of Blinding Ideology. In 1962, the concept of laissez-faire global trade was still fresh and exciting. As always, Globalism 1.0 economic models all pointed in the same direction: *More global trade equals more prosperity for everybody!* At that time, very few people had any expertise or real-world experience analyzing the long-run impact of global trade policies. Even fewer people had a true understanding of how corporate governance would mutate in the 1980s under the relentless onslaught of hostile raiders who drove corporations to cannibalize their own people. And the fantasy of frictionless global trade logically supported the U.S. Government's ideological mission to destroy the economy of the Soviet Union. So we can forgive JFK and most policymakers before the 1980s if they did not have the economic expertise and foresight to see the seeds of the economic Armageddon that they were planting.

---

[39] President John F. Kennedy, New York Economic Club, 1962

Sincere Ignorance May Be Forgiven; Willful Blindness is Unforgivable. As the data and the sober reality of Globalism 1.0's impact on the American labor force began to emerge during the late 1980s and 1990s, it became clear that there was something wrong with JFK's vision of a free-trade utopia. The data summarized throughout this book has been available to American policymakers for decades. Knowing this, how should Americans interpret the intentions of their elected officials? At best, maybe we can say that *some* policymakers have been frozen between their political conflicts of interest (which compel them to pander to large corporations) and their ignorance about how global trade actually impacts real humans. At worst, we can say that there is no conceivable way that politicians could *accidentally* vote year after year for all the trade policies, labor policies, corporate tax policies, monetary policies, fiscal policies, and regulatory policies that have directly caused Broken Capitalism today.

The Logical Conclusion of Globalism 1.0: One Corporation to Rule Us All. Given the perpetually increasing returns to scale of every large corporation, here is the *logical but totally irrational* conclusion that Globalism 1.0 cheerleaders must embrace if they are intellectually honest with themselves: A single monopolistic firm producing all the goods and services for the entire planet is best for humanity because a single monopolistic firm will have the maximum possible returns to scale and economies of scale, which means the monopoly firm can produce its goods at the lowest possible price and sell at the highest possible profit. Of course, most humans in the real world can instantly recognize that this kind of logic confuses optimal production with quality of life by ignoring the real-world geopolitical factors that determine quality of life in every society.

The Antidote to Globalism 1.0 Propaganda. The chart below is a powerful defense against Globalism 1.0 policymakers, their self-serving corporate cheerleaders, and the legions of brainwashed economics students who mindlessly regurgitate the so-called *virtues of globalism*, "comparative advantage," and their illusory "benefits to society." For my non-U.S. readers: If you research the economic data from your own countries for the same categories depicted in my chart, you will see that this chart illustrates what is happening in nearly *every Western economy* today. And over the long-run, it will also destroy all economies in the East and throughout the entire world for all the same fundamental reasons.

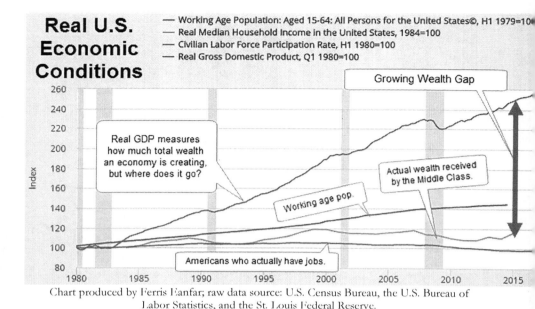

Chart produced by Ferris Eanfar; raw data source: U.S. Census Bureau, the U.S. Bureau of Labor Statistics, and the St. Louis Federal Reserve.

Dealing with Globalism 1.0 Propaganda. If you show that chart to a Globalism 1.0 cheerleader, you will usually see one of two responses: (1) "Wow, I didn't realize it was that bad." or (2) "Yes, it's bad for many Americans right now, but these things take time and Americans just need to be patient for the benefits of global trade to reach them." If you get the first response, you know you're dealing with a sincere human whose brain has not been fully colonized by aliens. If you get the second response, you know you're dealing with a zombie who is so blinded by the fantasy of Globalism 1.0 dogma that they literally cannot see the real world anymore. In that case, just wish them well and move on with your life because they have totally lost control of their brains and they will never escape the blinding effect of this neurotoxin until they, too, are chewed up and spit out by Broken Capitalism.

Globalism 1.0 is a Powerful Neurotoxin. I don't usually give up on people if I believe they are truly open-minded, but Globalism 1.0 is a particularly powerful neurotoxin that rots the brain and destroys the mind's capacity to see and accurately interpret reality. If you're still on the fence about this issue, let's be clear: Stare at the previous chart for a while. Look at every aspect of it. If you really understand what you're looking at, you will know that there is no conceivable scenario in which Globalism 1.0 will ever truly benefit the majority of humans on Earth over the long-run. In

Part 2 of this book, we will cover what I call "Globalism 2.0," which is part of the solution to Broken Capitalism.

Automation & Globalization Amplify Gains to Capital and Losses to Labor. Throughout most of the 20th Century, the general rule of thumb in economics was the ratio of Gross Domestic Income (GDI) flowing to workers ("Labor") and owners of capital ("Capital") was relatively constant.[40] However, aside from two short blips in the data caused by the late-1990s Dot-Com and mid-2000s Housing Bubbles, the portion of GDI flowing to Labor compared to the portion flowing to Capital has been consistently falling for decades.[41] The following chart illustrates this trend.

Source: U.S. Bureau of Economic Analysis, Shares of gross domestic income: Compensation of employees, paid: Wage and salary accruals: Disbursements: To persons [W270RE1A156NBEA]; Federal Reserve Bank of St. Louis.

---

[40] Many economists still use GDP instead of GDI in this analysis, but GDP measures domestic output, not income, which makes GDP a much less reliable metric. Theoretically, GDI should equal GDP, but GDP is measured based on expenditure accounts, not income accounts. This often creates significant statistical discrepancies between the value of domestic income (GDI) versus the value of domestic production (GDP), which results in frequent errors in GDP reports that must be corrected. GDI is less prone to these types of errors.

[41] This blip occurred because corporations in the mid-1990s were racing to hire the first generation of newly skilled IT workers--paying them unusually high wages--to help the corporations implement all the new software and computer systems necessary to automate many IT tasks, which was never possible before. After the Dot-Com Bubble popped, the short-term gains to high-skilled Labor reverted back to the downward trend. See also: "Labour Pains." *The Economist.* Accessed February 19, 2017. http://www.economist.com/news/finance-and-economics/21588900-all-around-world-labour-losing-out-capital-labour-pains.

Debt Mountain

A Once-in-Human-History Gift to the Banks. The primary reason the 2008 Wall Street Communist Revolution has not already resulted in widespread food shortages and starvation similar to the Soviet Union is because the U.S. Dollar's reserve currency status has artificially and temporarily propped up the U.S. economy. This has allowed the U.S. banking system to gorge on a mountain of consumer debt, which the banks create and profit from, of course. Without the once-in-human-history gift of a planetary reserve currency, the U.S. banking system and U.S. economy would have completely collapsed decades ago.

Poverty Whitewashed with Debt. Broken Capitalism is crushing citizens in nearly all Western countries with mountains of debt. In the U.S., the Middle Class is desperately trying to preserve the standard of living that they had prior to the 1990s, but with Broken Capitalism, the only way for them to do this is to drown themselves in debt. In the chart below, you can see the perfect synchronization of an increasing mountain of debt with a simultaneous loss of the American Middle Class' wealth, both of which correspond to the full implementation of Globalism 1.0 trade policies. Without a mountain of debt, over 50% of the entire American population would be living below the poverty line today.

U.S. Economy
Total Consumer Debt vs. Real GDP vs Median Household Income

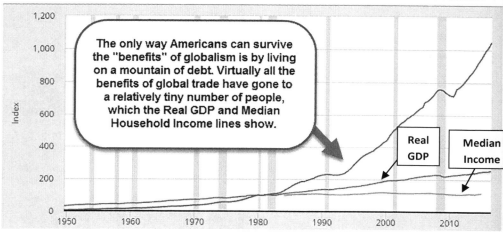

Raw data source: U.S. Census Bureau, the U.S. Bureau of Labor Statistics, and the St. Louis Federal Reserve; chart produced by Ferris Eanfar.

Abuse of the USD Creates Crisis. From the oil and currency crises in the 1970s, to the Latin American debt crises in the 1980s *and* 1990s, to the Asian Contagion in the 1990s, to the tech and housing market crashes in the 2000s, the U.S. Dollar's (USD) reserve currency status has been a major catalyst for every global financial crisis in modern history. And this once-in-human-history gift has been subsidized directly or indirectly by the involuntary generosity of nearly every human on Earth due to the distortions it has created and the wealth it has extracted from the entire global economy.

The Global Revolt Has Begun. Most people outside the United States know that their countries are adversely impacted by the profligacy of U.S. politicians and their abuse of the U.S. Dollar. This is why there has been a quiet global revolt against the U.S. Dollar since 2008. This revolt has led to the rapid increase in bilateral trade agreements between countries that deliberately exclude the United States and bypass the U.S. banking system. All the largest developing nations, including China, Russia, India, Brazil, and many others, are working relentlessly to liberate themselves from the economic oppression that the U.S. Dollar has inflicted upon their populations for generations.

Wall Street Communism Is Hanging by a String. When the U.S Dollar is no longer the world's reserve currency, the Federal Reserve and the U.S. banking system will no longer be able to print money to inject mountains of debt into the U.S. economy. When that happens, the 90% of Americans living on Debt Mountain today will be transformed into economic refugees virtually overnight. Like a gilded palace hanging over a cliff by a string, the entire U.S. economy will come crashing down as soon as that gift is fully withdrawn. When—*not if*—that happens, Wall Street's habitual privatization of profits and socialization of losses that has occurred since the 1980s will plunge the U.S. economy into widespread deprivation and destruction just like the Soviet economy.

Missing Good-Faith Business and Political Leadership. For decades, American politicians and so-called business *leaders* have been well aware that their economic and labor policies would be disastrous for the U.S. economy. The data in the charts above have been available to them for decades, but they have chosen to ignore and suppress the data because it doesn't serve their personal interests. Instead of preserving America's leadership as the most productive labor force in the world, they chose the self-serving path, which channeled profits and political power into the hands of a very small number of people at the expense of the American economy and labor force. We'll cover this in more detail in later chapters.

Wars and Economic Policies Based on Lies and Half-Truths. At every step of America's descent into its current economic swamp, there were specific economic policies that should have been implemented and specific public statements that American political *leaders* should have clearly communicated to the American business community and general public. Just like the wars in Vietnam, Iraq, and others around the world, if these so-called political *leaders* would have been honest with the American people about the true consequences of globalism-mutated-into-unabashed-corporatism, the American people would have never gone along with it.

Who Should We Blame? I'm asked this question frequently. It's human nature to want to focus our anger on a single source. And it's often doubly frustrating when the source of the problem seems so amorphous and systemic—like the blame is simultaneously everywhere and nowhere. Nevertheless, there is a clear focal point for our anger: Without the incompetence, gross negligence, and abuse of government power and taxpayer resources perpetrated by certain politicians over the past several decades, the banks and corporations would never be able to perpetuate their frauds and predatory behavior. Corporations are expected to be greedy because they represent their shareholders, but democratically elected government officials are supposed to represent their nation's citizens, not corporations. That's why citizens should blame their politicians much more than the banks and corporations, while simultaneously demanding economic reforms that eliminate the abuses of corporate power.

This is Only the Tip of the Iceberg. I've compressed many of the most important facts and events from the past several decades of U.S. economic history into this chapter, but this is by no means an exhaustive account of all the deliberate and toxic decisions that a small number of politicians have made, which have unleashed an ongoing economic catastrophe upon our world. From the Savings and Loan, Treasury Bond rate manipulation, and junk bond scandals in the 1980s and 1990s; to the LIBOR and swaps rates manipulation, money laundering, fraudulent customer accounts, and accounting scandals in more recent years; to the ocean of debt that is drowning nearly 90% of the American population today—nearly every global economic crisis since the 1970s can be traced to one or more of the events I've summarized in this chapter.

However, all these events are merely symptoms of a much more fundamental problem at the heart of Broken Capitalism that has spread worldwide. In the following chapters, we will take a deeper dive into the essence of what Capitalism actually is and what happens when predatory corporations are allowed to destroy the essential engines of value creation and prosperity within a society.

Key Points

- **Broad Peace and Prosperity Cannot Coexist with Broken Capitalism.** The worst consequences of the 2008 Wall Street Communist Revolution are coming. Many countries are already devolving into violent protests as I type because of the consequences of Broken Capitalism, but this is nothing compared to what is coming if we don't fix this problem soon.

- **Economic Crises Are Predictable and Preventable.** All the economic crises in modern history have been predictable and preventable, but when corporations hijack governments and prevent rational regulations from being enforced, economic catastrophe is the inevitable consequence.

- **Adam Smith Would Be Disgusted with Broken Capitalism.** Everything in Smith's writings indicates he would be revolted by Globalism 1.0, Debt Mountain, and the too-big-to-fail monsters that dominate Earth today. Broken Capitalism spawns countless market distortions, frauds, and predatory behaviors on a planetary scale that Smith never intended and could have never imagined.

- Chapter 3 -
Warning: Risk of Death to Your Economy

"Economics is not an exact science.
It's a combination of an art and elements of science."
— Paul Samuelson, First American Nobel Prize Winner in Economics

What is Economics?

Socioeconomic Meteorology. The field of economics should be perceived like the field of meteorology. Like meteorologists, economists use various technical tools and measuring techniques to try to predict the weather of an economy. Economic weather is determined by the forces of human nature, Mother Nature, and geopolitical events, none of which are within an economist's ability to control or predict with any significant level of accuracy. Nevertheless, measuring the *consequences* of economic weather enables economists to develop theories about how economic weather works under specific conditions, how it can impact humans, and how human societies *might* be able to mitigate those impacts in the future. Perceiving the field of Economics this way is a more accurate way to understand its role in human societies.

　　What's the Socioeconomic Forecast? Just as people check the weather to see if a storm might interfere with their daily lives, policymakers should consult economists to see if their economic and social policies might encounter stormy economic weather. But just as a meteorologist's forecast is not a *law of nature*, an economist's forecast is not a *law of economics*. Their forecasts are merely *guesstimates* about what *could* happen under highly specific conditions, but it's up to policymakers to implement and maintain the most appropriate policies to ensure that dangerous economic weather is minimized and the intended benefits of public policies are maximized.

The Consequences of Flawed Models. *Unlike* the field of meteorology, when economic models and theories are taken out of context and exploited by politicians and politically connected corporations, they actually *create* dangerous economic weather. A flawed meteorological forecast can sometimes lead to devastating consequences for a relatively small number of people if a hurricane path is incorrectly predicted, but most of the time, the worst that can happen is getting wet in an unexpected rain storm. In contrast, a flawed economic model can cause your life savings to evaporate, your job to be blown away to a sweatshop country, and your community to be decimated by an economic typhoon—economic storms whipped up by the same people elected to serve you.

Dangerous Products Should Have Warning Labels. Products that come with plastic bags that can suffocate and kill children have warning labels. Economic policies that can suffocate and kill a country's economy should also have warning labels. For example, "Warning: Risk of Death to Your Economy" should be the label on all macroeconomic policies. And like all products that are manufactured for human consumption, the product packaging of macroeconomic models and policies should also include a prominently displayed list of ingredients and usage instructions. This list should include all the economic and political assumptions, conditions, and their consequences for a country that will likely occur if those assumptions and conditions are not perfectly valid for any reason.

The Plague of Economic Ignorance in Government. One of the biggest problems that exists in the world today is the ignorance that many politicians have about the way their economies work and how international trade works in the real world. They have no idea how to differentiate between a good or bad economic policy unless at least one the following two conditions exist:

> (1) They have real-world experience building companies that operate in global markets; or
> (2) they have taken advanced college courses in economics and international trade to learn the vocabulary and analytical tools that economists use to create their global trade models, upon which all global economic policy prescriptions are constructed.

Without at least one of these two conditions being true, politicians are forced to depend on the *business expertise* of self-serving multinational corporations and the *objective analysis* of economists with no real-world business experience, many of which are tainted by deep ideological bias and/or captured by corporate interests. The result is a circus of the blind leading the blind as the ambition of politicians, the greed of multinational corporations, and perpetually insecure economists feed off each other to produce economic policies that distort reality to achieve their own interests.

Absurd Assumptions

Our Duty to Protect Society from Harm. This book is intended for the general public, not for ivory tower academics, but don't get me wrong; I love learning, I respect the value of higher education, I did very well in college, and I have many technical and professional certifications. So I'm not one of those people who says, "Don't go to college because it'll destroy your mind." College is necessary for many reasons in the modern world. However, sometimes a college curriculum can become so disconnected from reality that it causes harm to society by promulgating false facts and assumptions about how the real world works. And if those false facts and assumptions become institutionalized in the form of self-destructive government policies, I think we all have an ethical duty to protect our society from that harm.

Distinguishing Between Fact and Fantasy. To protect our society from harm, this chapter occasionally gets a little bit technical to draw attention to some of the most egregious false facts and assumptions that exist in advanced economics college curricula today. We will cover specific false facts and assumptions that I was spoon-fed when I was in college, which are still being taught today to all our future political and business leaders. The existing and future leaders of our world will never be able to connect the dots between why Capitalism is broken and the fantasies they are learning in school if they don't read books like this that help them distinguish between fact and fantasy.

Economic Policies Based on Autarky vs. Globalism. The basic principles of supply and demand, marginal utility, and even comparative advantage within the context of a single national economy are all useful and valuable to understand. These basic principles alone are usually sufficient to guide policymakers when it comes to *domestic* economic policies. This is because these basic principles are generally all that is needed to effectively model and understand the reality of how *domestic* markets generally work in "autarky," i.e., without any international trade.

The Deep, Murky Oceans of International Trade. In contrast to the basic economic concepts above, when policymakers start wading into deeper economic principles of international trade like General Equilibrium Models, the Ricardian Theory of Comparative Advantage, Heckscher-Ohlin Model, Stolper-Samuelson Theorem, and all their corresponding unrealistic assumptions, policymakers are often deceived by an illusion of scientific rigor. They don't realize that these economic models are incapable of capturing the reality of real-world global economic phenomena. The result is false confidence in their models, which leads to false confidence in their policies.

The Unproven Peace Dividend of Global Trade. One of the most significant *theoretical benefits* from global trade is the creation of social and political relationships between nations, which *can* help to reduce tensions that might otherwise escalate into war. If two nations are economically co-dependent, they are not very likely to destroy one another's export markets and sources of GDP. However, prior to WWI, there was free trade worldwide at nearly the same trading partner density that exists today; and yet, humanity still suffered through two world wars for geopolitical reasons and global trade did nothing to stop it. Nevertheless, the peace dividend is a *theoretically meaningful benefit*; so it's still a rational reason to embrace global trade, *but only under the right conditions.*

Globalism Can Work for All Nations Under the Right Conditions. A global trade policy that destroys a nation's labor force and dramatically reduces the quality of life for most of its citizens is an even more powerful catalyst for war than no trade at all! So the "peace dividend" of global trade is not a sufficient benefit without a corresponding *real wealth dividend* to the majority of a nation's people. In Part 2 of this book, we will meet Globalism 2.0, a much more sustainable version of globalism that doesn't suffer from all the flaws and fantasies of the bug-infested 1.0 version.

Examples of Reasonable and Rational Assumptions. Economists make many assumptions to make their models work. Some of these assumptions are reasonable and rational because they make it possible to predict certain types of economic phenomena without catastrophically distorting the policy outcomes of their models and disconnecting themselves from reality. These benign assumptions include things like:

- limiting the scope of analysis to a narrowly defined set of products or economic actors to analyze the impact of economic policies on those particular products and actors;

- limiting the scope of analysis to a particular market or factor of production to analyze policy impacts on those particular variables;

- assuming most people prefer more of a good than less;

- focusing on a narrow area of economic activity while holding other variables constant to test the impact that a change in one variable might have on one or more other variables, among others.

Those are all examples of reasonable and rational assumptions that simplify narrowly defined aspects of the real world so that economists can develop insights that may be useful in developing targeted economic policies specifically for particular segments of a *domestic* economy.

Examples of *Unreasonable* and *Irrational* Assumptions. In contrast to the reasonable and rational assumptions above, economists, politicians, and multinational corporations that promote Globalism 1.0 trade policies make many *unreasonable* and *irrational* assumptions that egregiously distort reality and destroy the credibility of their economic models and policies. For example, consider the following list of dangerous and absurd assumptions ("AA"s) that are explicitly required by nearly all Globalism 1.0 economic models. All these assumptions in the list are extracted directly from a popular college economics textbook, "Advanced Economics: International Trade."[42] I've made only minor edits to condense each statement down to their essential meaning because economics textbook authors are notoriously *uneconomical* with their words, often filling several pages to explain a simple concept that could be communicated in a

---

[42] I won't disparage the author here so I've slightly adjusted the textbook title and omitted the author's name. However, every advanced economics and international trade textbook that I've ever seen includes all the same assumptions. There are several curriculum development committees around the world that control what ideas are included in the major university and college economics degree programs. They influence what to include in these textbooks. So you can easily read any textbook that covers advanced economics and international trade to verify that they really do make all these absurd assumptions.

couple sentences.

1. **AA:** There will always be more winners than losers from global trade.

2. **AA:** A country can never be made worse off from global trade.

3. **AA:** When global trade eliminates jobs in one industry those workers will always find jobs in another industry within a reasonable amount of time.

4. **AA:** Significant unemployment cannot exist because an efficient labor market will always shift labor to a country's competitive export industries and away from its uncompetitive import industries.

5. **AA:** Unemployment is a *domestic business cycle phenomenon*; therefore, it's not possible to measure the impact of global trade on the unemployment rate.

6. **AA:** Wage rates are determined by the value of the marginal product of labor, i.e., as workers become more productive, their wages will rise at approximately the same rate as their productivity.

7. **AA:** Price inflation throughout an economy will not substantially impact workers' real wages. (Based on the assumption above.)

8. **AA:** All economic agents (corporations, consumers, governments, etc.) act rationally at all times; thus, all markets behave rationally, too, and converge toward equilibrium.

9. **AA:** All people act independently based on perfect information.

10. **AA:** Markets allocate resources efficiently.

11. **AA:** Groups of individuals behave the same as individuals.

12. **AA:** There is no power imbalance between market participants in an economy.

13. **AA:** Manufacturing is no more important to an economy than services.

14. **AA:** Consumer surplus is more important than producer surplus; thus, consumption is more important than production.

15. **AA:** Consumer spending is more important than consumer saving.

16. **AA:** Factors of production are immobile; i.e., *labor and capital cannot move between countries*. (Some models remove this assumption, but then they ignore the real-world reality that labor is almost

completely immobile in most non-Eurozone countries due to political and cultural barriers.)

17. **AA:** Factors of production are perfectly mobile between industries *within* a country; i.e., *labor and capital can easily move between industries within a country.*

18. **AA:** There are no barriers to free and fair trade, i.e., *domestic and international politics and special interest groups do not exist.*

19. **AA:** There are no negative externalities associated with production or consumption, i.e., there are no negative consequences from environmental pollution, resource depletion, social and cultural destruction, moral hazards, national security risks, or any other negative consequences.

20. **AA:** Community preferences reflect collective individual preferences and can be sufficiently modeled with community indifference curves.

21. **AA:** Trade between countries will always be balanced because *exports must pay for imports*; thus, exports will always be equal to imports.

22. **AA:** The flow of wealth between countries will always be balanced over the long-run. (Based on the previous assumption.)

23. **AA:** Inflationary monetary stimulus and government borrowing to balance trade deficits will not significantly offset workers' real wages.

24. **AA:** Per-capita GDP reasonably reflects the distribution of wealth within a country (even though every economist and statistician knows that median metrics are more realistic and accurate than per-capita metrics).

25. **AA:** Production gains from specializing in a country's comparative advantage industries result in more per-capita GDP, more per-capita wealth, higher per-capita consumption, and higher per-capita quality of life for everybody in all countries over the long-run. (Based on the previous assumption.)

26. **AA:** The concept of "money" is irrelevant and ignored.[43] This may

---

[43] Money is typically only discussed as a component of "International Finance" courses, but very few Economics students are required to take courses in Finance to obtain their degrees in Economics. This severely limits their understanding of

seem unbelievable for a field like *Economics*, which many people assume is the study of *money*, but it actually has almost nothing to do with money. Most economists treat money as just another commodity, but money is much more than that. The reason they ignore the more complex characteristics of money is because economic models can't handle the reality that "money" is actually a sociological and political concept, not an economic concept. Ironically, this disregard for the concept of money leads to many questions about the *utility* of the field of Economics.

Who Really Believes All Those Absurd Assumptions? For any Globalism 1.0 policy to work *for the majority of people in all countries*, all the assumptions above must hold true. Yet, for anybody with real-world business experience, the assumptions above are so absurd that it's difficult to believe any American who truly understands how Globalism 1.0 works today *would ever* publicly associate their name with a Globalism 1.0 economic policy.

Distorted Analysis. If all those absurd assumptions were not enough to make you laugh, even when the textbook authors cite statistics *that prove* Globalism 1.0 has been destroying jobs and real wages throughout the U.S. economy for decades, the authors put the best possible spin on the data. For example, in these textbooks you will often see references to trends in manufacturing and service sector employment with charts visibly illustrating the precipitous decline of total jobs and real wages across industries. Instead of pointing out the obvious reality—*American jobs and real wages are falling rapidly, which strongly suggests that global trade policies are not working for the majority of Americans*—the authors say, and I quote: "The earnings of those displaced in the service sectors do not suffer as much as the earnings of workers displaced from manufacturing." These authors are either blinded by the Globalism 1.0 neurotoxin, or there's a real conspiracy to whitewash the textbooks to *re-interpret* all the data in the best possible light in favor of Globalism 1.0.

Most Students Can't Distinguish Between Fact and Fantasy. One of the biggest problems in the typical college economics degree program today is that, what you learn is often *true* only within a very narrow context.

---

real-world Economics and gives them a false sense of confidence in their economic models.

This makes it difficult for students to recognize the difference between fact and fantasy unless they already have significant business experience and political awareness within the broader context of the real world. Since most students are young when they go to college, they don't have any meaningful real-world business or political experience. So when they learn from their textbooks that "there are always more winners than losers from global trade" without understanding that economics in the real world is driven by government policy, *not the free market*, they become emotionally attached to the fantasy of a planet full of *winners* prancing around cornucopias of abundance.

Humanity's Distorted Happiness Curve. In some cases, students are aware of political corruption and economic injustice in the abstract, and they might even have a sincere desire to use their education and skills to create more peace and prosperity in the world, but they usually don't realize that what they're leaning in school is not going to help them achieve those goals. They don't realize that what they're learning is one of the most significant causes of the problems. They don't understand that government policy is distorted and often corrupted by special interest groups. They don't understand that their neat graphs and perfectly balanced economic models don't reflect how dirty politics and distorted government policies get in the way of optimizing humanity's happiness curve.

Their Fantasies Control Our Lives. Students naturally carry an emotional attachment to the fantasies they learn in school beyond the classroom and into their daily lives. These fantasies become deeply embedded into everything they do. Their entire perception of reality is filtered through this lens, which causes them to make professional and personal decisions based on these fantasies. They vote for politicians who believe their fantasies. They ascend to powerful positions in corporations, banks and governments, managing trillions of dollars of pension funds and legislating public policies that impact billions of people. Their fantasies control our lives. Then when their fantasies blow up the world, they say things like former Federal Reserve Chairman Alan "The Maestro" Greenspan said in his congressional testimony after the 2008 Financial Crisis:

> *Those of us who have looked to the self-interest of lending institutions to protect shareholders' equity, myself included, are in a state of shocked disbelief. . . . Yes, I've found a flaw. . . . Flaw in the model that I perceived is a critical*

functioning structure that defines how the world works, so to speak. . . . This modern risk-management paradigm held sway for decades. The whole intellectual edifice, however, collapsed in the summer of last year. . . . This crisis has turned out to be much broader than anything I could have imagined. It has morphed from one gripped by liquidity restraints to one in which fears of insolvency are now paramount.[44] [45]

Don't Worry, Humans Can Swim. Think about all the absurd assumptions that we've seen so far. What would happen if we all made assumptions of the same magnitude in our daily lives? Imagine sitting next to an economist on an airplane over the Atlantic Ocean halfway between Europe and North America. Suddenly the plane hits some bumpy turbulence and starts to nose-dive. The economist says, "Don't worry, humans can swim." Now, that is a *true* statement, but should you feel any comfort from such a statement? Should you take any significant action based on that statement? You are human, you can swim; so the economist must be right! Now, should you assume that you would survive a plane crash in the middle of the Atlantic Ocean? Based on the economist's *true* statement, *you don't even need to worry about gravity* because gravity was ignored in his analysis. So you can safely assume that you have many viable options available to you, including jumping out the airplane without a parachute.

Magnitude of Stupidity. Does that scenario seem absurd to you? It illustrates the same magnitude of stupidity as most of the absurd assumptions that politicians and large corporations have been making about Globalism 1.0 and the global banking system over the past several decades. It's not sufficient to study Economics or to make statements about economic policies that could only be true under the most narrowly defined conditions. Anybody who uses Globalism 1.0 economic theories to justify a country's monetary, fiscal, labor, tax, banking, and trade policies is just like the myopic economist on the airplane. They can make *true* statements about the *theoretical* outcomes of their policies, but they almost never give you the

---

[44] Andrews, Edmund L. "Greenspan Concedes Error on Regulation." *The New York Times*, October 23, 2008.
http://www.nytimes.com/2008/10/24/business/economy/24panel.html.

[45] Andrews, Edmund L. "Greenspan Concedes Error on Regulation." *The New York Times*, October 23, 2008.
http://www.nytimes.com/2008/10/24/business/economy/24panel.html.

complete picture about how their policies will *actually* work when their assumptions crash and burn in the real world.

Defective Economic Products. Globalism 1.0 policies and the economic models used to support them are the *defective products* that transnational corporations, their captured economists, and their self-serving political patrons in Washington have been selling to the American people for decades. An entire chapter could be written about each of the absurd assumptions covered in this chapter, why they erode the credibility of Globalism 1.0 economic models, and how each assumption leads to serious adverse consequences by ignoring crucial socioeconomic and geopolitical realities. But this book is intended to be relatively short; so let's move on.

The 5-Minute Advanced Economics Course

To truly understand the deep flaws in the Globalism 1.0 ideology and to respond to them effectively, it's useful to learn a few of the basic concepts in the field of Economics. This will also help you to visualize what they're trying to accomplish, why it's naive and impossible to achieve, why it's destroying the sovereignty of every nation worldwide, and why it's destroying Capitalism and Democracy on Earth. I promise, this section will be brief and relatively painless.

Modeling the World. The following chart illustrates the essence of Economic Neoliberalism and the ideology of Globalism 1.0. Our world is infinitely complex, but Neoliberal economists reduce the world down to charts like this to visualize how their mathematical models interact with arbitrary data inputs and outputs. This process can reveal some useful insights about an economy, but it doesn't take a Nobel Laureate to understand that a grossly simplified model can never explain or predict all the complex behaviors in an infinitely complex world.

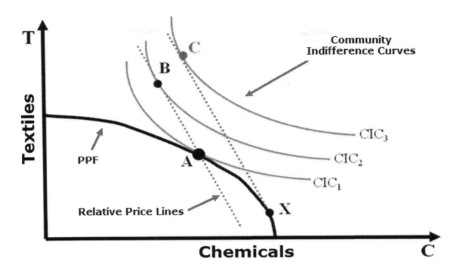

The chart might look complicated to some people who have not taken an International Trade economics class, but the underlying principles are straight-forward. I will explain what each part of the chart means below. Let's break down the chart into its individual parts:

The Vertical and Horizontal Axis. In this chart, we have two products: Textiles on the vertical axis and Chemicals on the horizontal axis. If you recall your high school math classes, plotting dots on a chart represents the intersection (or combination) of two quantities. Connecting all the dots creates the lines in the chart. In the field of Economics, this is a convenient way of visualizing the trade-off between two goods in a world of finite resources—a.k.a., scarcity.

"PPF" = Production Possibilities Frontier. The PPF represents all the possible combinations of goods that a country can theoretically produce given a certain amount of resources. All economic models must simplify these combinations to a tiny number of goods so that they can all fit on a neat chart. Nevertheless, in International Trade Theory, the PPF represents the total productive capacity of a country.

Relative Price. If you understand the general concept of an opportunity cost, then you already have some intuition about relative prices. The concept can be clearly understood with a simple question: How many units of product X are you willing to sacrifice for one more unit of product Y? In this case, we would say, How many units of Textiles are you willing to give up for one more unit of Chemicals? Because scarcity of time, space, and resources exists, if we want more Textiles, we need to give up some

Chemicals, and vice-versa. Relative price is one of the most important concept in the field of Economics.

Relative Price Lines. Similar to the PPF, price lines represent all the possible combinations of goods that can be theoretically *purchased* given a certain amount of money. All economic models must simplify these combinations to a tiny number of goods so that they can all fit on a neat chart. Nevertheless, in International Trade Theory, the price line represents the theoretical consumptive capacity of a country, in contrast to the theoretical productive capacity represented by the PPF.

Community Indifference Curves ("CICs"). A CIC represents all the possible combinations of goods that will make *consumers happy* or *satisfied* at a given level of consumption. Do you want 20 units of Textiles and 20 units of Chemicals or 10 units of Textiles and 30 units of Chemicals? Your preferences can be plotted on the chart; and connecting all those dots creates the curved CIC line. The *higher* the CIC line is on the chart, the *better* it supposedly is for consumers and the economy. This concept can be applied to many interesting aspects of life, including personal satisfaction and fulfillment of any kind, which can yield some useful insights.

Can CICs Predict Your Behavior? Like the PPF and Price Lines, the CIC is a gross simplification of the infinitely diverse influences that affect consumer choices at any given moment. And CICs completely ignore externalities and costs to society caused by destructive corporate, consumer, and government behaviors. Nevertheless, in International Trade Theory, CICs are the gold standard that economists and policymakers use to predict how economies and individual humans will respond to their policies.

GDP is Driven by Government Policy, Not the Free Market. If you talk to a Globalism 1.0 cheerleader, you will often hear them say things like, "The natural pressures of supply and demand force producers in each country to focus on their comparative advantage, which means they will specialize in the goods and services that they can deliver at the lowest opportunity cost." That sounds quite logical, which is why Globalism 1.0 is such a powerful neurotoxin, but in the real world, supply and demand between countries is overwhelmingly driven by government policy, not the fantasy of unfettered free markets assumed in their theoretical models.

Supply and Demand Still Rules the World. If they're being honest, every economist will confirm that all the tools, mathematical models, and techniques that they use to study global economics can be reduced to one principle: the relationship between supply and demand.

Everything economists do is designed to analyze how supply and demand respond to changes in the price of goods in relation to one another. None of them are intended to analyze how supply and demand respond to geopolitical and sociological changes, which are the most significant factors that determine the price of virtually everything in every economic environment. The reason they don't include those factors is because those factors are messy, resistant to reductionism, often based on illogical human behavior, and impossible to perfectly predict over any significant period of time. In other words, they can't be effectively modeled; and what can't be modeled does not exist, from the perspective of mainstream Economics.

Congratulations: You've Passed the 5-Minute Advanced Economics Course! There are many other aspects of macroeconomics and global trade that we could explore, but everything boils down to supply and demand. It may be hard to believe, but now you know everything that really matters in Economics. Virtually everything else that economists do can be summed up as a masturbatory orgy of mathematical theorizing. Mathematical masturbation is fun and interesting from the perspective of stimulating our brains, but mathematical masturbation is still masturbation, which means it can be addictive and it can fool us into believing it's the real thing. But ultimately, it's almost completely useless for real-world economic policymaking.

Now do you see why Globalism 1.0 cheerleaders and policymakers are so frequently wrong and so terribly destructive when their absurdly unrealistic models are used to control the lives of billions of people on our planet?

The Difference Between a Model and a Map

Economic Models <u>Are Not</u> Like Roadmaps. Economists often defend their economic models, absurd assumptions, and Globalism 1.0 policies by saying things such as, "Like roadmaps, economic models are not intended to capture the full reality of any economy; they are only intended to be abstractions of reality to serve as guides to help predict economic phenomena." Most economists say this with good intentions, but the comparison between roadmaps and economic models is far too benign and falls far short of capturing the destructive capacity that bad economic models have on the countries that follow them. To put this into perspective, let's examine a few of the most significant differences between a roadmap and the Globalism 1.0 economic models that have guided American policymakers for generations.

- **Roadmaps <u>Do</u>:** Simplify reality by ignoring geographical features of the planet that are *irrelevant* to the traveler because those features do not interfere in any way with the traveler's ability to travel from point A to point B on the map. Roads that are straight on the map are straight in reality; roads that are curved on the map are curved in reality. Thus, we can reasonably and rationally assume that calculating the time and distance between each point on a roadmap will enable us to effectively navigate the real world. This enables us to make highly accurate predictions about the best path to take between point A and point B on the map and the corresponding locations in the real world.

- **Roadmaps <u>Do Not</u>:** Depend on dozens of *unreasonable* assumptions that reduce the reality of human existence to a nonsensical fantasy that renders them useless and dangerous in the real world. Mountains, oceans, roads, and lakes on a roadmap don't irrationally and unexpectedly shift their position based on the ideology and political ambition of each new government administration. No matter how powerful they are, multinational corporations can't use a roadmap to secretly re-route an interstate freeway across the Grand Canyon to serve their corporate shareholders. The politically tainted glory of a Nobel Prize in Economics does not suddenly make one roadmap more accurate than all the others. Roadmaps do not impose themselves upon our communities, destroy our wealth, decrease our quality of life, and ignite violent revolutions when they occasionally fail to capture an important feature of reality (e.g., a new construction zone that causes us to be 20 minutes late for an appointment).

- **Globalism 1.0 Economic Models <u>Do</u>:** Distort reality by *ignoring the most consequential features of human existence that actually produce economic reality.* This makes it virtually impossible for a country to safely travel from economic point A to economic point B unless the country is cheating and defying World Trade Organization rules at every possible point along the country's growth curve; or, unless the country is the beneficiary of transnational structural monetary policies that give the country an unfair competitive advantage by enabling the country to manipulate the terms of international trade and/or avoid the consequences of dangerous bank debt accumulation. Examples of these unfair structural advantages are the U.S. Dollar's reserve currency status and the European Union's monetary policies that result in huge EUR surpluses in Germany's banks because none of the other EU countries can adjust their currency exchange rates to make their products and services more competitive.

- **Globalism 1.0 Economic Models <u>Do Not</u>:** Provide benign, simplified, nonpartisan versions of real-world economic reality. They *do not* take into account the most influential geopolitical and socioeconomic factors that actually produce economic outcomes in the real world. They *do not* reliably predict quality-of-life outcomes for the vast majority of humans in any country. They *are not* used as *objective* tools by policymakers to make complex decisions about how to allocate scarce resources in any country. They *do not* reasonably or consistently predict real-world outcomes in international trade beyond the most simplistic national level of analysis. And even then, the accuracy of predicted outcomes is severely limited to only the most rudimentary predictions of supply and demand of basic goods and services, which reveals virtually nothing about the actual distribution of wealth, the quality of life of a country's citizens, stability of a given society, or the health of a given economy in the real world.

Unlike Roadmaps, Economic Models Can be Used as Weapons. Economic models are only useful to the degree that they can predict real-world economic phenomena to help government policymakers make decisions that enhance the quality of their citizens' lives. If an economic model has obvious flaws, is based on absurdly unrealistic assumptions, or can be used in ways that violate its intended purpose, then the model can easily become a weapon that destroys wealth and human life. This is no different than a bazooka: A bazooka is a dangerous tool that can be used for defensive or offensive purposes. When bazookas are used offensively in non-combat zones, it's a crime when people and property are destroyed. The same should be true for economic policies and their underlying economic models whenever they are revealed to be destructive to the health and welfare of a nation and its citizens.

Now you understand what's really wrong with the global economic system. See you in the next chapter.

Key Points

- **Economists Are Socioeconomic Meteorologists.** Like many weather forecasters, the predictions of mainstream economists are frequently wrong or incomplete. This is usually because their models are filled with absurd assumptions that ignore the geopolitical and socioeconomic factors that trigger real-world economic events.

- **Globalism 1.0 is the Mutant Child of Broken Capitalism.** The "globalism" that exists today is based on dozens of false and absurd assumptions, bad-faith propaganda, and economic imperialism perpetuated by flawed economic theories that are used to dominate human populations in every country on Earth.

- **Economic Models Ignore the Complexity of Money.** Most economists ignore the concept of money because it's too difficult to model the complex dimensions of money. But without taking into account all the sociological and geopolitical characteristics of money, economic models will inevitably produce false predictions and flawed interpretations of economic events.

Your Country Needs You Now.

If you understand why it's important to fix Broken Capitalism, please give this book a positive rating online and tell at least 10 people about it today.

Home: Eanfar.org | **Facebook:** Facebook.com/Eanfar
Twitter: @FerrisEanfar | **AngelPay:** AngelPayHQ.org

- Chapter 4 -
Size Kills

"A government big enough to give you everything you want is a government big enough to take from you everything you have."
— Gerald R. Ford, former U.S. President

Do Corporations Maximize Human Life?

Engines of Creation or Destruction? Corporations can be engines of positive or negative change in a society. When they produce positive change, technological innovation and broad-based prosperity are the result. When they produce negative change, the result is anti-competitive market domination, economic oppression, anti-creative destruction, political distortions, ecological destruction, widespread health crises, and humanitarian crises. Distinguishing between positive and negative change can sometimes be difficult because the process of creative destruction creates winners and losers in every economy. But from a public policy perspective, there is only one question needed to cut through all the noise: Are corporations collectively creating a world that maximizes human life by broadly creating and broadly distributing wealth and human health?

A Parade of Criminal Activity. Prior to the 20th Century, multinational corporations often behaved like government-sponsored land and sea pirates, exploiting and plundering colonial lands and people with their government's official support. In Part 2 of this book, we will briefly explore the historical evolution of the idea of a "corporation." In the meantime, just within the past few decades, we have seen a parade of well-documented criminal corporate activities, including: fraud, bribery, money laundering, embezzlement, grand larceny, murder, manslaughter, reckless trading, obstruction of justice, environmental disasters, among many others.[46]

Size Determines Destructive Potential. Many millions of deaths and cases of disease have been caused by products containing lead, asbestos, mercury, PCBs, and other toxic and carcinogenic chemicals.[47] In every case, the corporations that produced these deadly products deliberately concealed and suppressed the evidence of the harm that their products inflicted upon large populations. They also systematically hijacked the political system to block regulations that would have saved lives. When corporations are small, the destruction caused by their malfeasance is limited to small populations. When they grow to the economic size of entire countries, their destructive behavior can impact millions or billions of people. Thus, size is the most significant factor that determines the destructive potential of every corporation.

Size Kills Economic & Political Independence

10 Shocking Facts About the Distribution of Economic Power. Consider the following facts.

1. In the year 2000, the 100 largest economic entities on Earth were 51 corporations and 49 countries. In 2017, 69 are corporations and 31 are countries.[48] At the current rate, approximately 100 corporations will substantially control every material aspect of

---

[46] "Mankind: Death by Corporation." Truthout. Accessed April 14, 2017. http://www.truth-out.org/news/item/17178-mankind-death-by-corporation. "10 Evil Corporations You Buy From Everyday." Listverse, February 21, 2013. http://listverse.com/2013/02/21/10-evil-corporations-you-buy-from-everyday/. "Killer Pharmacy: Inside a Medical Mass Murder Case." Newsweek, April 16, 2015. http://www.newsweek.com/2015/04/24/inside-one-most-murderous-corporate-crimes-us-history-322665.html. See "List of Corporate Collapses and Scandals." Wikipedia, March 26, 2017. https://en.wikipedia.org/w/index.php?title=List_of_corporate_collapses_and_sca ndals&oldid=772310821. Note: These sources represent only a tiny fraction of corporate criminal activity because it is U.S.-centric. I'm aware of dozens of other cases of criminal activity outside the U.S.

[47] Ibid.

[48] All data is derived from the CIA World Factbook and the Fortune Global 2000 List for the years indicated.

human life on Earth by 2045.

2. The 10 largest corporations have more combined economic power than 92% (180) of all the countries on Earth *combined.*[49]

3. The revenue of the 200 largest corporations is approximately 25% of Earth's GDP. In other words, less than 0.0002% of the corporations on Earth control 25% of humanity's income. The largest 2,000 (0.002%) corporations control 50% of humanity's income.[50]

4. While consuming 50% of Earth's income, these 2,000 corporations employ less than 1% of Earth's labor force.

5. The 50 largest financial corporations on Earth control over $70 trillion in assets, which was 91% of Earth's GDP in 2014.[51] (This concentration is certainly higher today.)

6. The richest 1% of humans now have more wealth than the rest (99%) of the world combined. And within that 1% group, the top-1% of 1% (the top-0.01%) own approximately 90% of all the 1%'s wealth. That means the majority of the 1% has more in common with the 99% than most people realize.[52]

7. The eight richest people own more than the bottom 50% of Earth's entire population.[53]

8. Despite being one of the most natural resource-rich countries on

---

[49] In this case, "financial power" is measured by annual corporate revenue for corporations and tax revenue for countries.

[50] Derived from the 2014 Forbes Global 2,000 list and based on global GDP of $77 trillion. All the preliminary 2016 data indicates the concentration is even higher today.

[51] Ibid.

[52] Hardoon, Deborah, Ricardo Fuentes-Nieva, and Sophia Ayele. "An Economy For the 1%: How Privilege and Power in the Economy Drive Extreme Inequality and How This Can Be Stopped." Policy & Practice, January 18, 2016. http://policy-practice.oxfam.org.uk/publications/an-economy-for-the-1-how-privilege-and-power-in-the-economy-drive-extreme-inequ-592643.
"Oxfam Says Wealth of Richest 1% Equal to Other 99%." BBC News, January 18, 2016, sec. Business. http://www.bbc.com/news/business-35339475.
"World's Eight Richest People Have Same Wealth as Poorest 50%." The Guardian, January 15, 2017, sec. Business. https://www.theguardian.com/global-development/2017/jan/16/worlds-eight-richest-people-have-same-wealth-as-poorest-50.

[53] Ibid.

Earth with at least $21 trillion in mineral resource wealth, the Democratic Republic of Congo (DRC) consistently ranks at the bottom of the Global Hunger Index.[54] The DRC is one of many natural resource-rich countries that have been exploited by large corporations and collusive governments, which use their wealth and power to manipulate indigenous political systems, perpetuate wars and institutional corruption, suppress the growth of indigenous industries, and extract obscene amounts of wealth.[55]

9. More than 3 billion humans live on less than $2.50 per day. Approximately 5.5 billion humans (80% of the global population) live on less than $10 per day.[56]

10. Approximately 50% of all children on Earth are living in poverty.[57]

The Essence of Broken Capitalism. With such enormous economic and political power concentrated in the hands of less than 0.01% of Earth's corporations and less than 0.0000001% of Earth's human population, is it any surprise that political systems worldwide are imploding, humanitarian crises are exploding, and 80% of the global population lives in poverty? Is this the "free market" that Globalism 1.0 cheerleaders and Neoliberals talk about? All the problems discussed throughout this book are only possible when corporations become "too big to fail" and "too big to jail." This is the essence of Broken Capitalism.

Corporate Influence. Large corporations today influence every aspect of human life. When their financial resources reach the level of a small- to medium-sized country, their economic, political, and market power gives them supreme power *inside every country*. This enables them to influence and control: the media through their advertising budgets; the political system,

---

[54] The Global Hunger Index measures food and nutrition availability within each country. See "Global Hunger Index | IFPRI." http://www.ifpri.org/topic/global-hunger-index.

[55] "Apple: Time to Make a Conflict-Free iPhone." The Guardian, December 30, 2011, sec. Technology.
https://www.theguardian.com/commentisfree/cifamerica/2011/dec/30/apple-time-make-conflict-free-iphone.

[56] If you want to learn more about global poverty, see the Global Issues website, which has aggregated poverty statistics from many primary sources:
http://www.globalissues.org/article/26/poverty-facts-and-stats

[57] Ibid.

international trade agreements, and public policies through their lobbying and political campaign financing; their industries through their marketing and operating budgets; culture, public opinion, and even a population's perception of reality through their secret funding of think tanks, captured economists, and paid endorsements from authority figures in society who promote their commercial agendas.[58] Nearly every society on Earth today is substantially controlled by the strategic coordination of all these financial resources and ecosystem cogs that collectively amplify the messages of large corporations, while crowding out all other messages.

Concentration of Power Leads to Oppression. When former U.S. President Gerald Ford said that big governments can "take from you everything you have," he had national governments in mind. However, as the economic power of transnational corporations grows to the size of entire countries, President Ford's warning is also applicable to unelected corporate boardroom governments today. Indeed, the size of corporations *and* national governments determines the level of control and destruction they can inflict upon human populations.

The Destructive Fantasy of Perpetual Growth. The structural incentives that shape public company behavior today require them to perpetually increase shareholder value by perpetually increasing the size of their operations. This often serves their shareholders' interests at the expense of the public interest. Of course, perpetual growth is physically impossible, which is why, no matter what corporate cheerleaders may claim, a company dominated by the god of shareholder value will inevitably slide into corruption. The reason their corruption is inevitable is because the only way they can keep growing beyond the limitations of physics and fair and *free markets* is to hijack the power of government and engage in anti-competitive behavior. This is fundamentally what is destroying the small- and medium-sized business community worldwide.

Size Spawns Selective Corporate Welfare

The Selective Corporate Welfare State. Selective corporate welfare costs

---

58 Lipton, Eric, and Brooke Williams. "How Think Tanks Amplify Corporate America's Influence." The New York Times, August 7, 2016. https://www.nytimes.com/2016/08/08/us/politics/think-tanks-research-and-corporate-lobbying.html.

U.S. taxpayers at least $100 billion per year.[59] Of course, this doesn't include trillions of dollars in loans, federal loan guarantees, special tax breaks, special access to valuable geopolitical information, discounted asset sales, and other sweetheart deals that politicians dole out to their favorite corporate donors. This selective corporate welfare provides the biggest corporations with prejudicial protection from foreign *and* domestic competition, which increases the price of consumer goods and services and transfers wealth from smaller companies and the Middle Class to a tiny group of politically connected corporate behemoths. All these resources are a direct form of taxpayer-funded government welfare to the biggest corporations on Earth.

The Fortune 500 Gets the Most Corporate Welfare. Nearly 100% of the top-100 federal subsidy recipients are Fortune 500 companies; and an overwhelming majority of all federal subsidy funds go to multi-billion-dollar companies.[60] Among many other reasons covered in this book, selective corporate welfare is one of the most significant reasons that already-large corporations grow into systemically destructive "too big to fail" monsters. Selective corporate welfare is also one of the biggest reasons that small- to medium-sized companies are dying, jobs are being destroyed, and the Middle Class is being eviscerated. Is this the "free market" that Neoliberals and Globalism 1.0 cheerleaders talk about?

Taxpayers Subsidize Their Own Demise. It's no accident that U.S. exports are dominated by huge corporations selling huge airplanes, heavy equipment, petrochemical products, military weaponry, and pharmaceuticals. Airplanes and heavy equipment are supported by taxpayer-subsidized federal loans to foreign customers from the U.S. Export-Import Bank.[61] Petrochemicals are subsidized by massive tax breaks, the DoD's

---

[59] See: "Corporate Welfare in the Federal Budget" on the Cato Institute website. Yes, Cato is a right-leaning group, but the report was also cited by the left-leaning CommonDreams.org group.

[60] To learn more about federal subsidies, see the fantastic report and corporate subsidy database provided by GoodJobsFirst.org. "Uncle Sam's Favorite Corporations: Identifying the Large Companies That Dominate Federal Subsidies," 2015. http://www.goodjobsfirst.org/sites/default/files/docs/pdf/UncleSamsFavoriteCorporations.pdf.

[61] "Ex-Im Funds Flow to Few States, but All Bear the Risks." *Mercatus Center*, July 30, 2014. https://www.mercatus.org/publication/ex-im-funds-flow-few-states-all-

taxpayer-subsidized global appetite for petroleum products, and U.S. Military protection of oil and gas facilities worldwide.[62] Pharmaceuticals are funded by massive tax breaks, taxpayer-subsidized R&D throughout the public university system, an anti-competitive patent system, FDA regulations that are hostile to foreign and natural alternatives, and never-ending price inflation throughout the broken U.S. healthcare industry, which is directly caused by government manipulation of the *free market*.[63] And the U.S. military-industrial complex sells over 50% of Earth's military weapons thanks to generous taxpayer-subsidized gifts to the biggest defense companies.[64]

The Perpetual Cycle of Corporate Welfare. Naturally, corporate welfare is appreciated by the recipients. In fact, they're so grateful that they reward their loyal political patrons with large financial donations to various PACs and SuperPACs, which produce persuasive get-out-the-vote campaigns tailor-made just for their favorite politicians. This helps the politicians get elected year after year. The cycle of gratitude continues, and while the politicians are in power, they create or influence the development

---

bear-risks.

[62] Carrington, Damian, and Harry Davies. "US Taxpayers Subsidising World's Biggest Fossil Fuel Companies." *The Guardian*, May 12, 2015, sec. Environment. https://www.theguardian.com/environment/2015/may/12/us-taxpayers-subsidising-worlds-biggest-fossil-fuel-companies.
Kocieniewski, David. "Oil Companies Reap Billions From Subsidies." *The New York Times*, July 3, 2010.
http://www.nytimes.com/2010/07/04/business/04bptax.html.
"The Surprising Truth About Oil and Gas Tax Breaks." *US News & World Report*. Accessed February 4, 2017. http://www.usnews.com/opinion/economic-intelligence/2014/08/06/the-surprising-truth-about-oil-and-gas-company-corporate-tax-rates.
[63] Angell, Marcia. "The Truth About the Drug Companies." *The New York Review of Books*. Accessed February 4, 2017.
http://www.nybooks.com/articles/2004/07/15/the-truth-about-the-drug-companies/.
Herper, Matthew. "Can Anything Stop Drug Companies From Fleeing The U.S. Tax System?" *Forbes*. Accessed February 4, 2017.
http://www.forbes.com/sites/matthewherper/2014/07/19/can-anything-stop-drug-companies-from-fleeing-the-u-s-tax-system/.
[64] "America's Arms Exports Dominate Despite Global Competition." US News & World Report. Accessed April 4, 2017.
https://www.usnews.com/news/articles/2016-12-27/americas-arms-exports-dominate-despite-global-competition.

of legislation that benefits the corporate welfare recipients even more. This perpetual cycle of gratitude and selective corporate welfare goes on year after year.

Time = Money = Life: Corporate Welfare Nickels & Dimes You to Death. Whenever politicians raise your taxes or spend your money on something that does not benefit you in any meaningful way, always remember the most important existential equation of human existence: "Time = Money = Life." When governments take your money to pay for selective corporate welfare and special interest programs, they're consuming the time that was required for you to earn that money. If you work 2,000 hours per year and the government takes 50% of your income, you've lost 1,000 hours of your time each year. Since you only have a finite number of hours during your life on Earth, that means the government is literally taking your life one hour, dollar, nickel and dime at a time. Depending on your state and tax bracket, government taxes may take 50% or more of your life. This is why it's so important to hold politicians accountable for how they consume and spend your Time = Money = Life.

Thousands of Selective Corporate Welfare Programs. As of 2017, there were over 2,000 selective federal corporate welfare programs.[65] Each of these programs creates multiple entry points for politicians to penetrate deeper into every community in America. Each of these programs takes money from private citizens in one area of the country and gives it to corporations in another area of the country without the citizens' consent or knowledge. In the overwhelming majority of cases, this selective corporate welfare does not benefit you, me, or anybody other than a very small number of special interest groups.

The Catalog of Selective Corporate Welfare. The 3,200-page U.S. Catalog of Federal Domestic Assistance ("CFDA") is an official list of all federal aid and subsidy programs for state and local governments, corporations, and non-profit organizations. The programs include grants, loans, insurance, and various other types of cash and non-cash benefits. People can also visit the CFDA website to download the official 3,200-page PDF catalog, which I recommend to anybody who doubts that the mission creep of the U.S. federal government has grown way beyond the scope of its constitutional parameters.

---

[65] Source: U.S. Catalog of Federal Domestic Assistance (2014)

Accountable Policymakers Would Nurture (Not Kill) Competition. If they were truly accountable for their performance, policymakers would implement specific policies that would minimize the influence and negative impact of corporate power. These policies would enable the government to create and enforce rational tax policies and industry regulations that make it easy for companies to get started and grow, but very hard for them to grow into systemically dangerous behemoths that destroy their communities, ecosystems, labor markets, and countries. Today, we have *unaccountable policymakers* who exploit the convergence of state and corporate interests to maximize their combined coercive power over their customers and constituents. In Part 2 of this book, we will explore specific solutions to this problem.

Drawing the Line Between Corporate Welfare and Public Welfare. Before we continue to the next section, let's be clear about an important point: This book is not about bashing corporations for exploiting people and the environment. Yes, there are some corporations that are guilty of blatant exploitation, but most corporations are guilty of nothing more than being economic sharks that simply consume more wealth and resources than their ecosystem can support. They are not trying to hurt people deliberately in most cases, but their size, market power, and profit motive drive them to cannibalize their ecosystem, leaving too few resources and opportunities for everybody else. At some point, a society must draw a clear line between corporate welfare and public welfare. This book is about identifying where and how to draw *and* enforce that line.

Size Kills Justice

In March 2013, the U.S. Congressional Committee on Financial Services (the Committee) initiated a review of the U.S. Department of Justice's (DOJ's) decision not to prosecute HSBC Bank, its affiliates, or any of its executives or employees for, according to the report:

> . . . *serious violations of U.S. anti-money laundering (AML) and sanctions laws and related offenses. The Committee's efforts to obtain relevant documents from DOJ and the U.S. Department of the Treasury (Treasury) were met with non-compliance, necessitating the issuance of subpoenas to both agencies. Approximately three years after its initial inquiries, the Committee finally obtained copies of internal Treasury records showing that DOJ has not been*

forthright with Congress or the American people concerning its decision to decline to prosecute HSBC.[66]

The Committee's report included, among others, the following specific findings, as quoted from the report:

- *Senior DOJ leadership, including Attorney General Holder, overruled an internal recommendation by DOJ's Asset Forfeiture and Money Laundering Section to prosecute HSBC . . .*

- *HSBC appears to have successfully negotiated with DOJ for significant alterations to the DPA's [Deferred Prosecution Agreement's] terms . . .*

- *DOJ and federal financial regulators were rushing at what one Treasury official described as "alarming speed" to complete their investigations and enforcement actions involving HSBC in order to beat the New York Department of Financial Services.*

- *In its haste to complete its enforcement action against HSBC, DOJ transmitted settlement numbers to HSBC before consulting with Treasury's Office of Foreign Asset Control (OFAC) to ensure that the settlement amount accurately reflected the full degree of HSBC's sanctions violations.*

- *Attorney General Holder misled Congress concerning DOJ's reasons for not bringing a criminal prosecution against HSBC.*

- *DOJ to date has failed to produce any records pertaining to its prosecutorial decision making with respect to HSBC or any large financial institution, notwithstanding the Committee's multiple requests for this information and a congressional subpoena . . .*

- *Attorney General Lynch and Secretary Lew remain in default on their legal obligation to produce the subpoenaed records to the Committee.*

- *DOJ's and Treasury's longstanding efforts to impede the Committee's investigation may constitute contempt and obstruction of Congress.*

- *The Committee is releasing this report to shed light on whether DOJ is making prosecutorial decisions based on the size of financial institutions and DOJ's belief*

---

[66] Committee On Financial Services, U.S. House Of Representatives. "Too Big To Jail: Inside The Obama Justice Department's Decision Not To Hold Wall Street Accountable." Congressional Report. U.S. Congress, House of Representatives, July 11, 2016.
http://financialservices.house.gov/uploadedfiles/07072016_oi_tbtj_sr.pdf.

that such prosecutions could negatively impact the economy.

In the Committee's report, a senior Treasury Department attorney summarized the reasons why the DOJ and Treasury refused to prosecute HSBC, which became the official reason that Attorney General Holder gave to the Committee. Specifically:

> *. . . a felony plea or conviction could have very serious collateral consequences for the bank, including a possible revocation of its charter authorizing it to do business in the United States.*[67]

Too Big to Jail. "Collateral consequences" is code for "they will be forced out of business and their shareholders would suffer." Yes, that's what *should have happened* because that's exactly what happens to smaller companies and individuals when they commit serious crimes. But HSBC and most other behemoth corporations get away with their crimes, suffering only slap-on-the-wrist fines because they're conveniently classified as "too big to fail." This effectively means that they're *too big to jail*. When organizations become that big, they're obviously a menace to society. A *legitimate* government would stop at nothing to prevent any private organization from becoming *too big to fail*.

The Problem is Much Bigger than HSBC. HSBC acted atrociously and they certainly should have had their banking charter revoked, their senior management should have been fired, and the employees directly responsible should have been sent to prison, but the problem is bigger than HSBC. It's even bigger than the atrocious behavior of all the largest banks in the world in recent years. This congressional report is a rare *official* indictment on the entire Regulatory Protection Racket that enables politicians to feed corporate welfare to gargantuan corporations, deliberately fail to enforce *existing regulations* that would prevent bad corporate behavior, and block criminal prosecution in exchange for campaign financing support. This is another example of how politicians, serving their own interests at the expense of the public interest, are directly causing Capitalism and Democracy to collapse in the U.S. and around the world.

---

[67] Ibid.

Size Kills Liberty

The Centrally Planned U.S. Economy. Most people today believe that Communism and centrally-planned economies are doomed to self-destruction, but many people conveniently ignore that an economy controlled by a central bank and dominated by a tightly coordinated banking cartel is fundamentally no different than the central planning that occurs under the label of Communism. Whatever we call it, the end result is similar because the essence of their activities is the same: Arrogant policymaking, delusions about their ability to control the economy, unbridled self-interest, and grossly false assumptions all lead to a long-term decent into corporate and governmental authoritarianism. Thomas Jefferson understood this when he said: "I believe that banking establishments are more dangerous to our liberties than standing armies."[68]

Size Creates Distortions of Reality. A year before the 2008 Financial Crisis, at a time when the U.S. financial sector already dominated 8% of the entire U.S. GDP, an infamous McKinsey & Company report was commissioned by senior government officials in response to relentless Wall Street lobbying pressure.[69] The report was based almost exclusively on surveys and interviews with Wall Street executives. Predictably, the report indicated that derivatives trading was *too regulated*, capital requirements were *too high*, Wall Street firms needed to be *protected* from lawsuits, it was *too difficult* to replace American workers with foreign workers, and all these problems were causing U.S. banks *to lose their competitive edge* against banks in other financial centers like London and Hong Kong. Just a year later, Wall Street blew up the world and every single one of these findings was proven to be totally out of touch with reality.

Size Creates Hubris. Here's the real insight that policymakers *should* have learned from the McKinsey report: Asking Wall Street what Wall Street wants is like asking a group of kids what they want to eat, then

---

[68] The Papers of Thomas Jefferson, Retirement Series, vol. 10, May 1816 to 18 January 1817, ed. J. Jefferson Looney. Princeton: Princeton University Press, 2013, pp. 86–90.] Note: This version is commonly used and attributed to Jefferson, but some historians believe this is a paraphrase of a much longer quote, which can be found in the cited source.

[69] City of New York, and U.S. Senate. "Sustaining New York's and the US' Global Financial Services Leadership," January 22, 2007.

declaring, "candy and ice cream is what's best for the kids!" In her book, *Bull by the Horns*, Sheila Bair, the Chairperson of the FDIC during the 2008 crisis, commented on the regulatory hubris on Wall Street:

> *"By November [2008], the supposedly solvent Citi was back on the ropes, in need of another government handout. . . . Citi had not had a profitable quarter since the second quarter of 2007. Its losses were not attributable to uncontrollable 'market conditions'; they were attributable to weak management, high levels of leverage, and excessive risk taking. It had major losses driven by their exposures to a virtual hit list of high-risk lending: subprime mortgages, 'Alt-A' mortgages, 'designer' credit cards, leveraged loans, and poorly underwritten commercial real estate. It had loaded up on exotic CDOs and auction-rate securities. It was taking losses on credit default swaps entered into with weak counterparties, and it had relied on unstable, volatile funding—a lot of short-term loans and foreign deposits. If you wanted to make a definitive list of all the bad practices that had led to the crisis, all you had to do was look at Citi's financial strategies. . . . What's more, virtually no meaningful supervisory measures had been taken against the bank by either the OCC or the NY Fed. . . . Instead, the OCC and the NY Fed stood by as that sick bank continued to pay major dividends and pretended that it was healthy."*[70]

The Financialization of the Economy. Today, the financial sector dominates approximately *11% of U.S. GDP—3% more than it did in 2008*—which amounts to $2.2 trillion as of 2017. The financial sector sucks talent and human capital from other productive industries, which distorts and skews the entire economy toward unproductive debt-fueled consumption. Predatory corporations and traders exploit the banking system by pumping up stock market and debt bubbles, which enables their financial engineering scams to extract the most wealth from the real economy. The damning report from the relatively non-predatory Bank for International Settlements confirms this:

> *The financial sector grows more quickly at the expense of the real economy. . . .*

---

http://www.nyc.gov/html/om/pdf/ny_report_final.pdf.

[70] Bair, Sheila. *Bull by the Horns: Fighting to Save Main Street from Wall Street and Wall Street from Itself.* Reprint edition. New York, NY: Simon & Schuster, 2013.

Financial [sector] growth disproportionately harms financially dependent and R&D-intensive industries. . . . By draining resources from the real economy, financial sector growth becomes a drag on real growth.[71]

Size Kills Savings. When bad companies and executives are caught and convicted, their companies sometimes go bankrupt, which can harm thousands or millions of shareholders who are indirectly invested in the company through their pension funds, mutual funds, insurance funds, endowments, and other collective investment vehicles. This is tragic, but this tragedy only occurs because of the moral hazard that policymakers have created by refusing to convict senior executives for their serious crimes and criminal negligence. By allegedly seeking to avoid "collateral consequences" that might hurt a *too-big-to-fail* corporation's shareholders, government officials are creating catastrophic consequences for the entire global economy, which destroys the wealth and quality of life of *billions of stakeholders* worldwide during every major crisis and criminal scandal.

Casino Capitalism. The economic activity that led to the 2008 Financial Crisis was not the result of Capitalism. In this particular case, a more precise description is "Casino Capitalism" because behemoth banks in the U.S. and their European counterparts have literally transformed the global economy into a global casino. This is not just a metaphor; it is the *actual reality* of the global financial markets. The poker chips and slot machine tokens of Casino Capitalism are Credit Default Swaps, Repo Contracts, and derivatives contracts. Every day *fiduciary* gamblers around the world insert these casino tokens into their flawed risk models, pull the debt lever, and watch the daily trading numbers spin and spin while the noise makers and talking heads in the government-media complex perform distracting magic tricks for the crowd. It is a debt-fueled extravaganza more elaborate than any Las Vegas show. And it's the direct cause of the European sovereign debt crisis that hundreds of millions of humans are still suffering from today.

Actual Casinos Are Praised as a Benefit of Globalism. Ironically, one of the biggest "success stories" that you will see in several popular global trade college textbooks is the conversion of a steel mill in

---

[71] "Why Does Financial Sector Growth Crowd out Real Economic Growth?" Bank for International Settlements, February 12, 2015.
http://www.bis.org/publ/work490.htm.

Pennsylvania into a large casino. This casino is presented *as proof* that global trade has benefited the United States. The author claims that the casino, which generates about $1 million per day by exploiting gambling addicts, is an example of how the principle of comparative advantage and global trade help countries increase the quality of life for their populations. Since Capitalism in America has been transmogrified into Casino Capitalism, I guess we should not be surprised that an *actual casino* is praised as a shining example of the benefits of globalism.

Banks Are Not "Institutions." Casino Capitalism is not possible unless banks are allowed to grow into systemically dangerous "institutions." Notice that word: "institution." Even the language used in the media today to describe banks as "institutions" is designed to subtly make banks *appear* to be so systemically important that taxpayers have no choice but to open the corporate welfare spigot and bail them out when their casino bets go bust. "Banking" in the abstract is obviously necessary to any modern society, but no single bank or collection of banks is so indispensable that the bad ones can't be dismantled and reformed into smaller and more responsibly managed "corporations." That's what they are: "corporations." They are not "institutions" of higher learning or "institutions" of government—they are profit-driven "corporations," just like any other for-profit corporation. And they should never be granted any special status in our economy. Calling them "institutions" merely plays into their game and sucks more victims into their casino.

How Big Is Too Big?

In Part 2 of this book, we will explore specific and straight-forward ways to optimize the competition within every industry, which automatically resolves the corporation size problem. In the meantime, a recent IMF study about the financial sector revealed:

> *. . . once the [financial] sector becomes too large—when private-sector credit reaches 80% to 100% of GDP— it actually inhibits growth and increases volatility. In the United States in 2012, private-sector credit was 184% of GDP.*[72]

---

[72] Ms. Ratna Sahay; Martin Cihak; Mr. Papa M N'Diaye; Mr. Adolfo Barajas; Ms.

In other words, the U.S. financial sector is already far beyond the ideal level of financialization, as illustrated in the IMF's Financial Development (FD) Index below. The FD Index quantifies the ideal ratio between the size of a country's financial sector relative to the size of its national economy. Countries on either side of the bell curve either do not have mature enough financial sectors (see Gambia) or have too much financialization (see the U.S.A.).

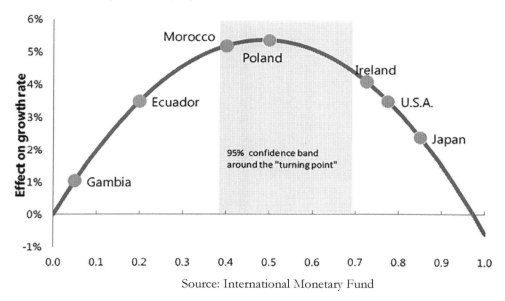

Source: International Monetary Fund

The Cost of Too Much Financialization. The IMF study indicates the direct cost to U.S. economic growth caused by over-financialization is 2% of GDP per year. In other words, the U.S. economy should be generating 3% to 4% GDP per year instead of the paltry 1% to 2% that we've seen in recent years. Additionally, the rise of financialization parallels the gutting of the U.S. manufacturing sector and the collapse of the Middle Class. Financialization is not the only factor, but it's clear that the

Diana B Ayala Pena; Ran Bi; Miss Yuan Gao; Ms. Annette J Kyobe; Lam Nguyen; Christian Saborowski; Katsiaryna Svirydzenka; Mr. Reza Yousefi. "Rethinking Financial Deepening: Stability and Growth in Emerging Markets." International Monetary Fund, May 4, 2015.
http://www.imf.org/external/pubs/cat/longres.aspx?sk=42868.0.

banking sector has diverted massive amounts of capital away from capital-intensive sectors like manufacturing to focus on get-rich-quick schemes in the stock, commodities, real estate, insurance, and derivatives markets. How much more competitive would capital-intensive American industries be today if Wall Street had not transformed the U.S. banking system into a casino?

Rising from Servant to Master. Before the 1980s, Wall Street had very little power over the U.S. and global economies. The "3-6-3 Rule" (borrow at 3%, lend at 6%, and be on the golf course by 3 PM) generally characterized the safe and conservative way that banks made money during the post-WWII economic boom until the early 1980s. In fact, Wall Street was a quiet and faithful servant to manufacturing industries, which produced widespread wealth throughout the American population. The traditional retail and investment banking functions of capital aggregation, lending, and deposit safekeeping were the reasons Wall Street existed. Then, after the financialization of the economy began to take root in the 1980s, Wall Street's power rapidly grew far beyond anyone could have imagined just a decade earlier.

The Real Adam Smith

Adam Smith Understood the Dangers of Big Business. When Adam Smith published *The Wealth of Nations* in 1776, he was enamored with the extraordinary productivity and wealth that the division of labor and Capitalism could achieve, but he was acutely aware of the dangers of corporate self-interest harming the public interest. He observed how corporations would frequently conspire against the public to promote their own interests, which naturally requires citizens to push back and protect the public interest. In Smith's own words:

> "People of the same trade seldom meet together, even for merriment and diversion, but the conversation ends in a conspiracy against the public, or in some contrivance to raise prices. . . ."[73]

Smith also observed how corporations hijack the regulatory and

---

[73] The Wealth Of Nations, Book IV Chapter VIII, p. 145, para. c27.

law-making apparatus of national governments to serve their interests and "to deceive and even oppress the public." In his own words:

> To widen the market and to narrow the competition, is always the interest of the dealers. . . . The proposal of any new law or regulation of commerce which comes from this order, ought always to be listened to with great precaution, and ought never to be adopted till after having been long and carefully examined, not only with the most scrupulous, but with the most suspicious attention. It comes from an order of men, whose interest is never exactly the same with that of the public, who have generally an interest to deceive and even oppress the public, and who accordingly have, upon many occasions, both deceived and oppressed it.[74]

Smith also observed the free-riding and rent-seeking behavior that capitalists demonstrate whenever they hijack political institutions to extract more resources from society than they deserve.

> As soon as the land of any country has all become private property, the landlords, like all other men, love to reap where they never sowed, and demand a rent even for its natural produce. . . . Whenever the legislature attempts to regulate the differences between masters and their workmen, its counsellors are always the masters. . . . All for ourselves, and nothing for other people, seems, in every age of the world, to have been the vile maxim of the masters of mankind. . . . Civil government, so far as it is instituted for the security of property, is in reality instituted for the defence of the rich against the poor, or of those who have some property against those who have none at all.[75]

Adam Smith on Corporate Accountability. The idea that any corporation could operate recklessly and not suffer terminal consequences would have never occurred to Smith. His entire philosophy of Capitalism was based on the assumption that competitive, free markets naturally eliminate the bad apples within an economy. That's why he said:

---

[74] The Wealth Of Nations, Book I, Chapter XI, Conclusion of the Chapter, p.267, para. 10.
[75] Smith, Adam, and Alan B. Krueger. The Wealth of Nations. Annotated edition. New York, N.Y: Bantam Classics, 2003.

The real and effectual discipline which is exercised over a workman is that of his customers. It is the fear of losing their employment which restrains his frauds and corrects his negligence.[76]

Adam Smith Never Envisioned a "Too Big to Fail" Corporation. During Smith's time, the concept of "too big to fail" would have seemed laughable. And Smith could not have imagined any legitimate government protecting corporations from their own repeated incompetence, fraud and negligence, as many of the largest corporations on Earth have been protected in recent years. The 2008 government bailout of nearly 1,000 corporations would have been inconceivable to him.[77] Smith believed that poorly managed and customer-unfriendly corporations would *always* collapse to make room for more effectively managed firms. This is why Smith was so confident in his philosophy of free markets, but if he could see how corporations have grown today into massive systemic time-bombs, protected from their own mistakes, it's likely that his *Invisible Hand* would be replaced with visible disbelief and disgust.

Adam Smith Would Not Recognize Broken Capitalism Today. It should be clear by now that Adam Smith was not the greedy capitalist mastermind that many people mistakenly envision when they hear his name today. To the contrary, Adam Smith was thoughtfully and strongly opposed to anything that harmed the public interest or disturbed the harmonious balance between Capital and Labor within a society. In fact, the Broken Capitalism that corporate raiders and Wall Street denizens have spawned over the past 40 years to justify their ongoing rape of the global economy is not what Adam Smith intended when he developed the philosophy of Capitalism and gave birth to the field of Economics.

Adam Smith, Thomas Jefferson and Their Egalitarian Spirit. Thomas Jefferson was a contemporary of Adam Smith. Jefferson and all the U.S. Founding Fathers were familiar with Smith's books. In fact, Smith's body of work was a source of inspiration and guidance for Jefferson, Alexander Hamilton, James Madison, John Jay, John Adams and all the

---

[76] Smith, Adam, and Alan B. Krueger. The Wealth of Nations. Annotated edition. New York, N.Y: Bantam Classics, 2003.

[77] For the complete list of corporate welfare recipients, see: "Eye on the Bailout | ProPublica." Accessed March 30, 2017.
https://projects.propublica.org/bailout/list/simple.

Founding Fathers during the development of the U.S. Constitution and the early U.S. economy. During his final years on Earth, Jefferson reflected on the social and economic progress of the United States. His instinctive awareness of the delicate balance between Capital and Labor combined with his deep egalitarian spirit inspired him to say:

> *We have no paupers . . . . Most of the laboring class possess property, cultivate their own lands, have families, and from the demand for their labor are enabled to exact from the rich and the competent such prices as enable them to be fed abundantly, clothed above mere decency, to labor moderately and raise their families. . . . Can any condition of society be more desirable than this?*[78]

Classical Libertarians Were Opposed to Concentrated Wealth and Power. Smith, Jefferson, and the Founding Fathers of the United States were also the founders of the philosophy of Libertarianism; yet, they all understood that national and corporate governance policies should be designed to ensure that wealth and power are broadly created and broadly distributed to avoid many forms of tyranny. They all understood that when a relatively tiny number of private corporations own or control a large portion of our planet's economic activity, economic and political systems will malfunction, inevitably leading to the collapse of all the societal institutions that make human civilization possible.

Wealth Aggregates Until the Republic is Destroyed. The following quote has been attributed to Abraham Lincoln, but there is substantial controversy over whether Lincoln actually said it or somebody else during the same time period. Regardless, whoever said it gave us a prescient and ominous prediction that should be heeded by all political, business, and community leaders today.

> *I see in the near future a crisis approaching that unnerves me and causes me to tremble for the safety of my country . . . corporations have been enthroned and an era of corruption in high places will follow, and the money power of the country will endeavor to prolong its reign by working upon the prejudices of the people until all wealth is aggregated in a few hands and the Republic is*

---

[78] The Papers of Thomas Jefferson, Retirement Series, vol. 7, 28 November 1813 to 30 September 1814, ed. J. Jefferson Looney. Princeton: Princeton University Press, 2010, pp. 649–655.

destroyed.

Key Points

- **Obscene Wealth Concentration Is Leading to Civilizational Collapse.** When the 10 largest corporations have more combined economic power than 92% (180) of all the countries on Earth *combined*, the 50 largest financial corporations control wealth equal to over 90% of Earth's GDP, the richest 1% of humans have more wealth than the rest (99%) of the world *combined*, and the eight richest humans have more wealth than the bottom 50% of Earth's entire population *combined* . . . it's safe to say humanity is in trouble.

- **Should We Maximize Industrial Production or Human Life?** Maximizing *production and profit* is not the same as maximizing human life. In the past, these were symbiotic goals, but the law of diminishing returns erodes the benefits of efficient production when corporations grow to the same economic size and political power of entire countries.

- **Time = Money = Life.** This is the most important equation in human existence. That's why selective corporate welfare for too-big-to-fail corporations steals much more than our money and liberty . . . it steals our life. Given the obscene wealth concentration that already exists in the world today, every conscious human should be outraged at the size and scope of the U.S. corporate welfare state.

- Chapter 5 -
Why is the Government So Broken?

"Bad laws are the worst sort of tyranny."
— Edmund Burke

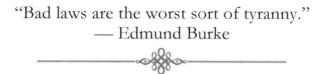

Any book that attempts to diagnose the disease of Broken Capitalism should devote some space to how political systems cause or impact the disease. To keep this chapter as short as possible, I've provided a condensed, nonpartisan summary of several chapters that I've written in one of my other books. This should help people understand the political dimension of Broken Capitalism. Although focused on the U.S., many of these systemic political problems are also destroying Capitalism in other countries.

Distorted Incentives Create Distorted Outcomes

Presidential Governments Attract *Political Investors.* "Presidential governments" like the United States, Afghanistan, Nigeria, Eritrea, Venezuela, Brazil, Congo (DRC), Sierra Leone, Argentina, and virtually all other corruption-plagued nations incentivize special interest groups to perceive national elections as *an investment*. Private interest groups in these countries are willing to *invest* millions or billions of dollars into elections or engage in deadly coups and destructive sabotage because they know that as soon as their favorite congressperson, senator, or president wins, they will have two-to-six years or more to exploit that politician's power over the entire country. In contrast, "parliamentary governments" like Canada, Norway, Denmark, Sweden, Luxembourg, Netherlands, New Zealand, United Kingdom, among others, can form and dissolve their governing coalitions without waiting years for the next election cycle; so there is no incentive for special interest groups to spend millions or billions of dollars trying to help any particular politician to get elected.

Presidential Governments Encourage Corruption and Oppression. Given the many ways that government officials within a presidential system can manipulate legislation and regulations to reward their most loyal donors, this creates many opportunities for their donors to receive a valuable *return* on their *investment* in the form of preferential tax breaks, lenient or non-existent regulations, and various forms of social and corporate welfare. Of course, all these kickbacks can only come at the expense of other citizens who are forced to suffer the economic and social consequences associated with the government's largess to special interest groups. This results in capital and income imbalances throughout the economy, which leads to large income disparities between the rich and poor and many other political, social and cultural consequences.

The Vicious Cycle. Politicians in presidential systems have far more incentives than their parliamentary system counterparts to exploit the consequences of their own incompetence and corruption, often with the intent of magnifying the divisions within society. This incentivizes special interest groups throughout the society to donate to influential politicians, hoping to position themselves closer to the levers of governmental power to achieve an incremental advantage over their competitors. This creates a vicious cycle of corruption, political oppression, social upheaval, and economic instability, which has nothing to do with the normal gyrations of a "business cycle"; it is the boom-and-bust vortex of a hijacked economy. This vicious cycle is the fundamental problem with the U.S. political system and it's the same problem that plagues all presidential governments, which have much higher levels of systemic corruption compared to their parliamentary government counterparts.[79]

The Fallacy of the Responsible Voter. I've heard several thoughtful and well-intending people argue that governments should limit their citizens' right to vote based on more restrictive criteria, such as property ownership, income, marital status, education level, or some other

---

[79] For extensive empirical data on the comparative virtues and vices of presidential vs. parliamentary systems, see the Swedish report by Bo Rothstein: "The Quality of Government Institute. Report for the first ten years of a Research Programme at University of Gothenburg."

factor. This premise is based on the assumption that citizens will feel a greater feeling of accountability to the political process if they have more to lose, which would lead to higher quality governance. This is actually how the Founder's originally designed the U.S. voting system—only white, male, property owners were allowed to vote. Aside from the cultural impossibility of implementing such a system in today's world and all the ethical questions, restricted suffrage does absolutely nothing to fix the fundamental cause of political corruption.

Restrictive Suffrage Does Not Fix Corruption in a Presidential System. No matter how restrictive the voting process is, if the voting occurs within the context of a presidential government, there will always be a self-serving subset of *eligible* voters who will be able to *invest* in politicians who are eager to exchange their power over legislation for campaign financing. This inevitably results in the same degeneration of institutional integrity that all presidential governments on Earth suffer from today.

It's Not the Money; It's Distorted Incentives in the Congress & Presidency. Please don't misinterpret my statements above as merely another argument for campaign finance reform. Campaign finance reform alone will do absolutely nothing to fix the problem. I'm making a much deeper point about the fundamental incentives that politicians have while serving in public office within the context of a presidential system and the length of time that politicians have to exploit their elected office for personal gain. This dynamic can only be truly understood after understanding the profoundly different systemic incentive structures that exist between presidential and parliamentary systems of governance.

Fixing a Broken Presidential Government. The only way to *fix* a presidential government is to impose unavoidable, fear-inducing mechanisms of personal accountability so that politicians feel truly accountable for their actions. At the very least, these mechanisms of accountability should include: term limits, severe financial penalties for verifiable gross negligence, severe ill-gotten wealth disgorgement penalties, felonious convictions and prison time for bad-faith legislation and regulation, and meaningful restrictions on the revolving door that enables politicians to exploit their taxpayer-funded public service for private gain after completing their term in public office.[80]

What's Wrong with "Representative Democracy"? This is like asking, "What's wrong with Capitalism?" There's nothing fundamentally "wrong" with either of these systems—they're simply social frameworks for allocating scarce human and material resources. However, problems begin when these systems cease to conform to their *actual* definition and purpose. For example, Capitalism ceases to be Capitalism when special interest groups capture a government's legislative and regulatory processes. When that happens, the economy devolves into Crony Capitalism, a Kleptocracy, Plutocracy, or some other economic system, but it's certainly no longer Capitalism. Blaming *Capitalism* because it has been degraded by corrupt, incompetent, or impotent politicians into some other economic creature is illogical.

The same is true of Representative Democracy: The moment a governmental body is no longer *representative* of the people being governed, it's no longer Representative Democracy. At that point, the government has devolved into something that feels increasingly authoritarian, alien, and punitive to the people being governed, while a small number of special interest groups feel the government is working fine for their narrow interests.

Nations Don't Collapse Because of Excessive Representation. I'm not aware of any empirical evidence of any nation throughout human history that has collapsed because its government was *too representative* of its citizens' wishes. In contrast, the collapse of *every* nation that I've studied can be directly traced to the self-serving ambition, hubris, and specific bad-faith actions of a tiny number of politicians, kings, emperors, and dictators who expropriated wealth from the general public to preferentially distribute it to a tiny number of private special interest groups. And there is a growing body of empirical evidence today from several nonpartisan research groups that demonstrates Democracy—*even Direct Democracy*—works just fine when the integrity of the structure of government itself (i.e., the legislative, regulatory, and judicial

---

[80] In my other nonpartisan book about the political system, I've written much more about the specific technical mechanisms that are necessary to fix the U.S. electoral system, which is the root of all political dysfunction in the U.S. To the surprise and delight of many, the solution does not require a Constitutional amendment or any new laws.

processes) is not degraded into a *commodity* that self-serving politicians can exploit and sell to their favorite special interest groups for private gain.[81]

Switzerland's Direct Democracy: The Most Effective Government on Earth. Switzerland's Federal Council and Federal Assembly have term-based federal election cycles, but their legislative system is directly accountable to a system of Direct Democracy. This system empowers Swiss citizens to efficiently repeal dubious laws that do not serve their interests. Direct Democracy eliminates the incentive for special interest groups to spend large sums of money on elections because they know they can't control the federal government or cram toxic laws down the collective throat of the Swiss citizenry. The Swiss system provides more continuity in the administration of government than a parliamentary system without reducing the power of the citizens to hold their elected officials accountable. Given that the Swiss Government has enjoyed the most stable political and economic environment on Earth since 1848 and has delivered the highest quality of life for the broadest number of its citizens for decades, I believe the Swiss have the best national governmental system on Earth today.

Who Has the Most Power Over Your Neighborhood Drug Market? Let's assume for a moment that crack cocaine is bad. Your neighborhood is filled with crack addicts. Hundreds of crack zombies are stumbling down your street, convulsing from painful withdrawal symptoms. They have no money to pay for food or shelter because they can't break their expensive physiological addiction. Maybe you're one of them, but at least one of them is in your family. Who do you blame for this tragic state of affairs: the users or the suppliers? Who has more power over your neighborhood drug market: your addicted child or the drug dealers?

Who Should We Blame: Political Drug Users or Political Drug Suppliers? Now, replace "drug dealer" with "politician" and "drug user" with "corporation." Who should we blame for governmental dysfunction and corruption: politicians (the "suppliers" of government

---

[81] See the inspiring and pioneering work by the Quality of Government (QoG) Institute, which was born at the University of Gothenburg, Sweden. Their quantitative and comparative measurements of national policy outcomes and the quality of governance across dozens of countries and hundreds of discrete governance quality metrics is providing new and profound insight into many age-old questions associated to the nature and performance of governments and their relationship with their citizens.

dysfunction and corruption) or corporations (the "users" of government dysfunction and corruption)? Yes, we should blame politicians who exploit their power to *sell* dysfunction and corruption to special interest groups (corporations, rich people, poor people, etc.) in exchange for the campaign donations and votes that keep their illicit racket going. Once you understand this reality, which I call the "Regulatory Protection Racket," there is no longer any mystery about what is wrong with the U.S. Government and how it can be fixed.[82]

Entry Points into Our Lives. The politically-driven expansion of the federal government is what enables special interest distortions to penetrate deeper and deeper into every aspect of a society. Each new special interest issue creates an *entry point* for federal politicians to penetrate deeper into our communities and into our homes. As the physical and financial size of government grows, more and more frequent opportunities emerge for federal politicians to abuse their political power, empower corporations to abuse their market power, and tinker with citizens' lives at ever-more granular levels within a society.

Regulations Are the Easiest Entry Points. The incentives that politicians have to expand their regulatory regime, and the proliferation of federal agencies to administer their regulatory regime in every industry, have a profound impact on the integrity of the democratic process. More regulations (entry points) produce more manufactured reasons for special interest groups to seek a politician's *support* on a perpetually increasing number of special interest issues. "Support" from a politician always comes at a price, typically in the form of a contribution to their election campaigns.

Politicians Are Incentivized to Create Endless Government Programs. Politicians must showcase their power and influence to their special interest benefactors to raise enough money to survive each political election season. They have learned that the easiest way to get campaign financing is to draw attention to their ability to *get things done* for their benefactors. They accomplish this by the number of government programs they create, the number of committees they're on that manage ever-more programs, and the size of the total budgets allocated to all these programs.

Self-Spawning Despotism. The *survival* of a politician in today's

---

[82] I've written extensively about this particular topic in my other nonpartisan book about the political system.

dysfunctional U.S. political system spawns a pernicious, self-perpetuating cycle of government expansion, more regulation, deeper government penetration into our lives, more expansion, more regulation, deeper penetration into our lives, *ad infinitum*. As this process continues, the reach of government inevitably becomes all-encompassing; nothing in society is free from the manipulation and distortions of politicians and the legions of corporate lobbyists and consultants that effectively control their decisions. These profit- and politically-driven legions fiddle endlessly with the DNA of the communities they increasingly control through the financial dependence they consciously or unconsciously thrust upon their constituents. The history of all despotic governments is the history of politicians who habitually fiddle until a free society is no longer free at all.

Human Nature & Power Concentration

The Fantasy of the Philosopher King. Winston Churchill famously said, "Democracy is the worst form of government, except for all the others." The Greek philosopher Plato also believed Democracy was inherently flawed. This sentiment leads many well-intending people to yearn for a "philosopher king" who can efficiently rule over a nation with perfect discernment, perfect knowledge, and perfect humility, without the complexity of a representative government. But why stop there? Why not yearn for a philosopher *emperor* to rule over the entire planet? The fantasy of the philosopher king is a delusion for the same reasons that Communism is a delusion: Any centralized authority with ultimate power over every citizen will be overwhelmed with the sheer volume of decisions that need to be made; and the system will succumb to the flaws in human nature that corrupt even the best human intentions.

Operating Systems for Human Civilization. With all due respect to Plato, Churchill, and many others today, they are mistaken when they confuse human-spawned institutional corruption with flaws in Democracy. There is no inherent flaw in Democracy for the same reason that there is no inherent flaw in Capitalism—they are both highly flexible sociological frameworks that streamline the process of structuring human affairs. Functionally, they are operating systems for human civilization. Like any tool, they are what we make of them. They need to be configured for the specific values and needs of each society that implements them. And the policymakers in charge of configuring them should know what the hell they're doing; otherwise, financial crises and bloody revolutions are the inevitable result.

Misconfigured Operating Systems Lead to Systemic Malfunction. If you don't configure your computer system correctly, it will malfunction and destroy your data. If you don't configure your Democracy correctly, it will malfunction and destroy your liberty. If you don't configure your Capitalism correctly, it will malfunction and destroy your prosperity and doom your society to tyranny and economic slavery. When people think they see flaws in Democracy and Capitalism, what they are really seeing is the inherent flaws in the human nature of policymakers whose incentives and intentions become corrupted by the concentration of power and wealth in small areas of the system. This is just like the concentration of static electricity in a computer that overwhelms and destroys a small circuit, which destroys the entire system's capacity to function as intended.

Power Concentration Risk. The only way to inoculate a society from the intrinsic flaws in human nature is to diffuse and diversify the power of corporate and national governance across the largest possible number of governing units. This is called "mitigating concentration risk," which is the same risk that investment portfolio managers easily avoid when they diversify a portfolio across multiple asset classes. Through diversification, no single component of the portfolio is large enough to catastrophically impact the rest of the portfolio. The Founding Fathers understood this principle very well. This is why they adopted federalism, which was intended to spread the majority of government power across all the states; it's also why they adopted the three-branch structure of government to create checks and balances between the Executive, Legislature, and Judiciary branches. The integrity of those checks and balances has been substantially compromised since our nation's founding, which is one of the reasons that our political system is so dysfunctional today.

Constant and Unavoidable Accountability is Required. When powerful private interests hijack the policymaking apparatus of government, it is like overwhelming a computer circuit with too much power and destroying the intended functionality of the entire system. Human nature will corrupt and destroy *every system* if a society does not structurally diversify its corporate and political power concentration risk. In addition to spreading governance power across as many governing units as possible, mitigating concentration risk requires holding each governing unit accountable to clearly defined standards of performance. Imposing constant and unavoidable accountability on political and business leaders in the form of severe penalties for proven malfeasance is the only way to restore institutional integrity to corporate and political governance systems.

Noose of Regulations

Large Quantities of Small Rules Are Lethal. Individually, each discrete government rule may seem logical and benign to the casual observer, just like each little leech in a pond is benign to a human. However, a bucket full of leeches will suck all the blood from an adult human in about five minutes. This same principle applies in many areas of our lives. For example, bacterial and viral infections are usually non-lethal when small numbers of these microscopic creatures invade our bodies, but they can kill any living creature within hours if they're allowed to grow into life-sucking swarms.

Sucking All the Life Out of the U.S. Economy and its Citizens. Anybody who has ever suffered from a computer virus knows how a bunch of small programs running in the background can suck up a computer's resources until it crashes or becomes so sluggish that it can no longer do anything productive. The reason large quantities of small things are so lethal is because they devour all available resources—one microscopic slurp at a time—until there is no longer sufficient resources to sustain life. This is exactly how the federal laws of the U.S. Government are sucking all the life out of the U.S. economy and its citizens.

"The More Corrupt the Republic, the More Numerous the Laws." – Ancient Historian, Tacitus. Politicians and federal regulators *officially claim* they are working to reduce social and economic risks to the U.S. economy and make Americans safer whenever they enact each new law and regulation. However, the available evidence reveals four disturbing realities that contradict this official claim: (1) the impossible challenge of complying with the overwhelming complexity of government regulations is actually making Americans *less safe*; (2) the cost of regulatory compliance to the U.S. economy severely cripples its global competitiveness; (3) the burden of regulatory compliance on each American household now exceeds the total cost of food, healthcare, and transportation *combined*; and (4) Congress, the White House, and legions of lifelong bureaucrats throughout the federal regulatory apparatus have many conflicts of interest and distorted incentives to pile on thousands of new regulations *every year* to serve their own special interests.[83]

A Little Bit of Regulation Goes a Long Way. To put the current regulatory insanity into perspective, the provisions within the federal Banking Act of 1933 that established the Federal Deposit Insurance Corporation (FDIC) required *only 18 pages*. Those 18 pages clearly defined the rules and regulations that banks must follow to protect Americans from the reckless banking activities that had wreaked havoc on the U.S. economy during the 1800s and early 1900s.[84] As a result of that 18-page act of Congress, today the FDIC provides relatively strong assurance that retail bank runs and panics will never threaten the stability of the U.S. banking system ever again.

What Does "Rational Regulations" Mean? If you're a politician, it means creating, funding, and staffing at least 13 financial regulatory agencies, including:

The Securities and Exchange Commission (SEC), the Commodities Futures Trading Commission (CFTC), the Municipal Securities Rule-making Board (MSRB), Comptroller of the Currency, Federal Reserve, National Credit Union Administration (NCUA), Consumer Financial Protection Bureau (CFPB), Federal Housing Finance Agency (FHFA), Financial Industry Regulatory Authority (FINRA), Federal Deposit Insurance Corporation (FDIC), Office of Thrift Supervision (OTS), Financial Accounting Standards Board (FASB), and the Internal Revenue Service (IRS).

A Blizzard of Laws and Regulations. Politicians also think "rational regulations" means creating a bureaucratic blizzard of laws, including the 74,000-page U.S. Tax Code and the 15,000-page Dodd-Frank Act.[85] There were about 175,000 pages of federal laws and regulations as of 2014, which has probably surpassed 200,000 pages by today.[86] With such a byzantine maze of compliance and legal requirements, no company or human really knows if they're ever fully compliant with all the laws and

---

[83] "Regulatory Overload"; Richard Williams, Mark Adams; Mercatus Center, George Mason University; (February 2012).

[84] TITLE 12 - BANKS AND BANKING; CHAPTER 16 - FEDERAL DEPOSIT INSURANCE CORPORATION; hosted online by Cornell University.

[85] 50,000 – 100,000 pages of financial regulation, depending on how you count and whether you include the huge body of case law that must taken into account, too.

[86] Source: "Ten Thousand Commandments 2015" – Competitive Enterprise Institute

regulations that control their lives. This creates constant confusion, fear, hesitation, and dramatically higher transaction costs, which wastes an enormous amount of time, energy, and money at every point throughout the entire U.S. economy.

A Time When American Laws and Regulations Were Rational. The Federal Reserve Act of 1913, which established the entire Federal Reserve System and numerous features of the U.S. economy, was only 31 pages. The Glass-Steagal Act of 1933 reformed the entire banking system during the Great Depression and it was only 35 pages. *In their original forms* (not the corrupted forms that came later), these two laws were very effective at protecting Americans from predatory financial institutions for generations. So we know it is certainly possible for the federal government to create rational laws and regulations that protect Americans without the overwhelming, rapidly growing complexity, cost and minutia that exists within the Federal Register of laws and regulations today.

Virtually All American Professionals are Now *Criminals*. Because of all the bureaucratic complexity, even the most experienced attorneys, bankers, accountants, doctors, and other professionals inadvertently commit approximately *three felonies per day*, according to *Three Felonies A Day: How the Feds Target the Innocent,* a book written by Harvard Law professor Alan Dershowitz and Harvey Silverglate, a nationally renowned attorney.[87] They investigated the egregious abuses of power wielded by the U.S. Department of Justice. Their conclusion: Unintentional regulatory non-compliance is transforming millions of unsuspecting American citizens into *felonious criminals.*

When Ambitious Humans Have Power, They Will Use It. The systemic assault on American civil liberties revealed in *Three Felonies A Day* gives regulatory bureaucrats and politicians *Gestapo power* at any time to control every aspect of our professional lives. When you give that kind of power to virtually any human, you will inevitably get the highly dysfunctional and systemically corrupt political system that we have today.

The Regulatory Black Hole Sucks America's Time = Money = Life. Between 2009 to 2012 alone, the U.S. federal bureaucracy manufactured over 13,000 new regulations, which is over 4,000 new regulations per year on average. Every one of these regulations has the

---

[87] Three Felonies A Day: How the Feds Target the Innocent; Harvey Silverglate (Author), Alan M. Dershowitz (Foreword); (June 2011)

gagging force of law on all Americans. According to the Competitive Enterprise Institute's widely respected "Ten Thousand Commandments" annual report, "Federal regulation and intervention cost American consumers and businesses an estimated $1.88 trillion in 2014 in lost economic productivity and higher prices." And "the cost of federal regulation exceeds half of what the U.S. federal government spends annually" and "economy-wide regulatory costs amount to an average of $14,976 per household. . . this *cost* of regulation exceeds the amount an average family spends on health care, food and transportation" combined. It's also about $160 billion more than all the combined personal and corporate income taxes collected by the IRS in 2014.[88]

Squeezing Maximum Donations from Every Special Interest Loophole. Why do you think it requires tens of thousands of pages to *regulate* an industry? Because politicians and their army of staffers and lobbyists literally write every sentence of every page of every law with the primary purpose of meticulously squeezing every possible special interest consideration into the law. Then, only after they've figured out how to accommodate as many special interest considerations as possible, they try to include language to discourage the latest reckless behavior that caused the latest easily predictable and preventable industry crisis.

Rational Regulations in Switzerland vs. the Regulatory Protection Racket in the U.S. How many pages do you think should be necessary to regulate the lending and borrowing activities within the financial services industry? Unless you're a politician running a Regulatory Protection Racket, there is no rational reason to write tens of thousands of pages to *regulate* an activity that could be effectively regulated with simple, plain language. If anybody doubts my characterization of the legislative or regulatory processes in the U.S. federal government or thinks I'm being too hard on politicians, tell them to study the financial regulations and Code of Obligations in Switzerland. Swiss financial regulations are simple, clear, logical, thoughtfully considered, (generally) evenly applied and enforced, and more fair and equitable than the regulatory regime in the United States.

Virtually No Major Scandals in Switzerland. When was the last time you heard of a financial crisis or political scandal in Switzerland? The most famous political "scandal" in Switzerland's modern history only

---

[88] Source: "Ten Thousand Commandments 2015" – Competitive Enterprise Institute

occurred because Swiss banks justifiably fought against the intrusive U.S. Foreign Account Tax Compliance Act ("FATCA") law, which U.S. politicians have been trying to inject into other sovereign countries since 2010. Despite the fear-mongering propaganda promulgated by the U.S. Government to discourage rational Americans from placing their assets in the safer Swiss banking system, the reality is that the Swiss have very few scandals in their political and banking systems. This is because Swiss laws are structured to eliminate most of the temptations and conflicts of interest that exist in the U.S. political and banking systems. And they actively cultivate a political culture that respects Democracy and the rule of law at every level of their political system.

The Compliance Jungle

Massive Compliance Backlog. To get a sense for how the U.S. financial regulatory jungle works in daily practice, consider this: I spoke to a compliance manager at one of the largest global banks in late 2013 who told me that they have over 400 compliance cases under investigation *at any given moment*. Each of these cases may require a few days to six months or more to resolve because of all the lawyers, tax issues, and governmental bureaucracy that is involved. In the vast majority of cases, the bank eventually releases the funds to the client without finding any client misconduct at all.

The Trauma and Opportunity Costs of Intrusive Bank Interrogation. When a client's funds are frozen, their lives are significantly disrupted by what can feel like a never-ending intrusion into their personal lives. The opportunity costs associated to not having timely access to their own money to execute their own legitimate personal or business activities is an extremely traumatic experience for clients who get inadvertently trapped in the compliance jungle. These costly delays accumulate throughout the banking system, which significantly increases economic friction throughout the U.S. economy. And it's only getting worse as each phase of the FATCA regime is implemented.

The Compliance Jungle Chokes the Life Out of Small Businesses. What does all this mean? It means misguided politicians are transforming the U.S. economy into a bureaucratic wasteland with sprawling regulations that cover the economic landscape like slimy-green kudzu, choking out all forms of human life, making it technically and financially impossible for small- to medium-sized companies to compete against the too-big-to-fail goliaths. Given that the goliaths and their lobbying apparatus are funding the politicians' political election campaigns, do you think it's an accident that the regulatory regime in the U.S. primarily benefits the largest financial institutions and solidifies their dominance and multi-generational torment of the entire U.S. economy?

Regulatory Protection Racket Helps Goliaths and Pushes Entrepreneurs Out of the U.S. The noose that is the U.S. financial regulatory system is the primary reason that many American entrepreneurs and citizens from around the world today will no longer establish their company headquarters in the United States. It's not because they don't want to live and work in the U.S.; it's because U.S. politicians and their Regulatory Protection Racket make it so difficult for small- to medium-sized companies to compete with the *too-big-to-fail* goliaths that are able to influence legislation to give themselves unfair, anti-competitive advantages in the marketplace. The result: Most of the smaller companies are dying and their unemployed owners and employees are becoming victims of the same Toxic Cloud that is choking the American labor force into extinction.

Suicidal Corporate Tax Policy

Big Business Benefits from Tax Complexity. The U.S. tax system is by far the most complicated tax system on Earth. No human has ever read the hundreds of thousands of pages of U.S. state and federal tax laws and compliance rules, which means no human understands more than a small fraction of the U.S. tax system. The reasons for this complexity are obvious to anybody who understands how special interest groups and the Regulatory Protection Racket distort U.S. tax policy by drilling an endless number of loopholes into the U.S. Tax Code. Since the largest corporations have the biggest influence over economic policies, we can be certain that the complexity of the U.S. tax system today benefits Big Business significantly more than it benefits the small- to medium-sized business community.

Loopholes and Tax-Breaks Are Expensive. Many people have no idea how expensive and anti-competitive the U.S. tax system is; so here's a succinct summary from the nonpartisan Mercatus Center at George Mason University.

The tax code, far beyond simply collecting revenue to fund the operations of the federal government, attempts to perform policy and political functions as well. This paper does not examine the normative value of these provisions, but instead examines the hidden costs of today's tax code: time and money spent submitting tax forms, foregone economic growth, lobbying expenditures, and gaps in revenue collection. These problems grow larger as the Internal Revenue Code becomes more complicated and temporary. Based on the studies reviewed in this paper, we estimate that hidden costs range from $215 billion to $987 billion and that the tax code results in a $452 billion revenue gap in unreported taxes. The economic costs are substantial relative to the $2.45 trillion in revenues raised by the federal government in 2012.[89]

Supporting an Army of Tax Mercenaries is Expensive. Corporations can reduce their taxes substantially by exploiting various loopholes and tax-breaks, but they are costly to exploit. Supporting the army of lawyers, tax experts, and lobbyists required to effectively understand and exploit the complex tax system year after year is not cheap. And the Regulatory Protection Racket is essentially another layer of direct and indirect taxation when politicians extort campaign financing from corporations through political action committees (PACs) and SuperPACs, among other corporate donation channels. All these costs add up to hundreds of billions of dollars every year, which is why only the biggest corporations can afford to benefit from the complexity. And even the corporations that can afford it are often tempted to move their corporate headquarters to less hostile and less expensive offshore jurisdictions.

Anti-Competitive Tax Policies Magnify Corporate Disloyalty. One of the most frequent excuses that large corporations give to justify their corporate disloyalty to the United States is the U.S. Government's anti-competitive corporate income tax policy. In addition to being the most complex tax system in the world, the U.S. has the second-highest average statutory combined state and federal corporate income tax in the developed world.

---

[89] "The Hidden Costs of Tax Compliance." Mercatus Center, May 20, 2013. https://www.mercatus.org/publication/hidden-costs-tax-compliance.
Note: Tax policy in general can be an interesting topic with many philosophical implications, but for our purposes in this book, we must limit our scope to corporate tax policy.

Hostile Policies Breed Corporate Hostility and Disloyalty. Regardless of whether we want corporations to pay more or less, they certainly will not pay more if they can reduce their tax burden by 80% simply by incorporating in another country. That's just too big of a gap for them to ignore, especially within the broader context of all the other anti-competitive features of U.S. labor policy and asphyxiating, minutia-laden federal regulations. Without more rational and less hostile business conditions, nothing short of National Guard tanks with their guns aimed at corporate offices is going to compel disloyal corporate executives to keep their headquarters and tax dollars in the U.S.

We Need Less Minutia and More Enforcement of Rational Rules. Given the U.S. Government's infamous waste and abuse of American taxpayer resources, it's a waste of time to demonize corporations of any size for their tax shenanigans—they're simply responding rationally to what they correctly perceive as an out-of-control federal tax monster. To support U.S. business competitiveness for companies of all sizes, the U.S. needs to eliminate all the complexity associated to the tax and regulatory system. Less minutia and more enforcement of a smaller number of rational rules will give companies of all sizes more incentives to remain loyal to the U.S.

Short-Sighted Policies Create Black Markets. As we've seen with the so-called *War on Drugs* and the Prohibition Era between 1920 to 1933, when it comes to commercial activity of any kind, the brute force of idiotic policies inevitably drives the regulated activity underground and to other jurisdictions. So what can we do to ensure that the U.S. corporate income tax promotes the growth of small- to medium-sized companies, is more attractive to companies of all sizes, while also ensuring that the U.S. Government is properly funded? We will explore the specific answer to this question in Part 2 of this book.

The Fourth Branch of Government

An unofficial branch of government has emerged to compete with the Executive, Legislative and Judicial branches of the U.S. Government. This newest branch of government voraciously consumes taxpayer resources, competes relentlessly for power and primacy within the federal budget, is comprised of career-minded bureaucrats with ideologically driven agendas, and exerts enormous influence over our daily lives. Americans feel the impact of this branch of government every day through a tangled web of powerful, centralized federal agencies including the IRS, EPA, NSA, SEC, CFPB, FDA, USDA, DOJ, DHS, DHHS, FTC, NLRB, DVA, FCC, FEC, HUD, SSA, DEA, DOT, DOC, DOE, DOI, and dozens of others. Many, if not most, of these agencies have been caught several times performing illegal and unconstitutional acts of fraud, violating American civil liberties, using their law enforcement power as a weapon against political opponents, and wasting billions of dollars of taxpayer resources. Welcome to the Fourth Branch of your federal government.

Can We Legitimately Call it the "Fourth Branch of Government"? The Fourth Branch is a sprawling bureaucracy that did not come into existence all at one time, which causes some people to doubt that it is really a separate branch of government. But just as a spider's web is a singular structure woven together over time by hundreds of strands of interconnected sticky threads, the tangled web of the U.S. federal bureaucracy has expanded, and continues to expand, into a collective source of concentrated, sticky federal control and power. This web of control and power is specifically engineered to trap as many Americans as possible to suck as much of their time=money=life as possible. This power is exercised and controlled by a very small group of unelected political appointees who dominate the lives of all Americans far more directly than any other branch of the U.S. Government. That's why we can legitimately call it the unofficial "Fourth Branch" of the federal government.

The Fourth Branch is a Political Weapon. As we've seen already, there are many ways that the Fourth Branch negatively impacts Americans every day. Just when it seems like it couldn't get any worse, it does. Decades of investigations by various nonpartisan groups, political scholars, and Freedom of Information Act disclosures have revealed that the IRS has been repeatedly used as a weapon against political opponents of U.S. presidents since at least the time of Franklin Delano Roosevelt in the 1930s. "My father may have been the originator of the concept of employing the IRS as a weapon of political retribution," said Elliot Roosevelt, FDR's son, but he certainly wasn't the last to use the IRS as a weapon.[90] Many other well-documented abuses of IRS power have been

---

[90] Jr, Burton W. Folsom. New Deal or Raw Deal?: How FDR's Economic Legacy Has Damaged America. 10/18/09 edition. New York, NY: Threshold Editions, 2009.

observed during the presidential administrations of John F. Kennedy, Richard Nixon, Bill Clinton, George W. Bush, and Barrack Obama.[91] And we have seen abuses of IRS power during virtually all presidential administrations since the IRS was created in 1862.[92]

The Fourth Branch Kills Free Speech. In government and nonprofit circles it's well known that using IRS power to block an organization from obtaining official tax-exempt status can be devastating to its growth and long-term success. Failing to obtain an official nonprofit exemption also creates an unjust stigma, which sends a signal to society that there must be something illegal or wrong with the organization. Many donors will not donate to an organization unless they can get a tax deduction for their donation. Without donations, nonprofit organizations don't have the resources to operate, which destroys their ability to communicate and spread their message. When the Fourth Branch unjustly withholds an organization's tax-exempt status, it is a direct violation of the First Amendment of the U.S. Constitution.

Tea Party in the Coalmine. Incumbent federal politicians and Fourth Branch bureaucrats have often used their power and control of taxpayer resources to slow down the progress of their political opponents. This reality, in addition to all the evidence made available to the public in recent years, is why Democrats and Republicans alike have acknowledged that the Tea Party was systematically harassed and substantially blocked by the IRS on 100s (possibly 1,000s) of separate instances prior to the 2012 presidential election. Just like the fate of the proverbial canary in the coalmine, the same toxic fumes emanating from the Fourth Branch that suppressed the Tea Party's momentum can choke off the life of any liberal or conservative group who opposes the federal government.

Forget About Partisan Ideology; the Fourth Branch Hurts All Americans. I've often seen a visceral response from liberals who want to dismiss any sentence that contains the words "Tea Party." Please remember it doesn't matter whether we're talking about the Tea Party, Democrats, Republicans, or the Muppets Party. Every party is guilty of using the Fourth Branch as a weapon. In this case, the IRS was unleashed on the Tea Party to help an incumbent president get reelected. How do we know this?

---

[91] "History of IRS Abuse"– Real Clear Politics (2013)

[92] "Misuse of the I.R.S.: The Abuse of Power" by David Burnham; New York Times; September 3, 1989

Among other sources, Harvard University and Stockholm University researchers analyzed the rate of the Tea Party's growth before it was targeted by the IRS.[93] Their conclusions reveal that if the Tea Party had not been blocked by the IRS and had been allowed to grow as fast as it was growing between 2009 to 2010, the Tea Party would have generated enough votes for Mitt Romney to win the 2012 presidential election.[94]

Totalitarian States Make and Enforce Laws Selectively Against Enemies. Regardless of whether we vote for Democrats or Republicans or some other third-party, we have learned that at the highest levels of both dominant political parties, there is no hesitation to violate the Constitution and use taxpayer resources to attack and destroy anybody who might try to challenge their dominance of the U.S. political system and the American people.[95]

Is the U.S. a Totalitarian State? Setting aside patriotism and nationalistic sentimentality for a moment (Remember, I'm a U.S. Air Force veteran; so I have plenty of patriotism.), when we look at the police-state environment that Americans—and especially American business owners— live in today, it's not an exaggeration to say that the United States *has already become* a totalitarian state. Some Americans may object to this characterization based on some vague feeling of patriotism or blind loyalty to the historical ideal of a free America, but what do you call it when a country is ruled by a tyrannical bureaucracy, is in a perpetual state of war and gunboat diplomacy, and is governed by a corrupt political system that controls all meaningful aspects of public and private life wherever and whenever possible? That's literally the definition of "totalitarianism."

Bureaucrats Move Fast When They're Trying to Cover Up Their Own Incompetence. We have seen examples of federal officials moving very quickly when the U.S. Treasury Department and Federal Reserve crammed the infamous Troubled Asset Relief Program (TARP) down the collective throats of the American people in 2008. TARP was a $700 billion program—more than the cost of FDR's New Deal, the

---

[93] "Do Political Protests Matter? Evidence from the Tea Party Movement" by Andreas Madestam from Stockholm University, Daniel Shoag and David Yanagizawa-Drott (both from the Harvard Kennedy School); December 2012.

[94] Remember: this was from two universities widely regarded as politically left of center; so they likely did not have any incentives to interpret the data favorably for the Tea Party.

[95] Bernie Sanders is the latest victim of party corruption in the 2016 U.S. pres. election.

Marshall Plan to rebuild Europe after WWII, and all the foreign wars combined prior to 2003—and it was *only three pages long*. The list of bureaucratic high-speed cover-ups by both Democrats and Republicans just within the past 10 years is long, including but not limited to:

- The Department of Veterans Affairs scandal in which federal bureaucrats tried on many occasions to conceal their gross incompetence in managing deadly hospital care for military veterans.[96]

- Constitutionally illegal NSA privacy violations revealed by Edward Snowden.[97]

- Deliberately delayed disclosures and blame games in response to multiple computer network breaches at the IRS and Office of Personnel Management (OPM) that enabled Chinese hackers to steal the personal records of at least 21 million Americans, which contained highly personal and confidential information.[98]

- Numerous hasty and collusive activities between members of the FDA, USDA, Congress, and special interest groups, which have led to the deaths of millions of Americans from pharmaceutical drug side-effects, household chemical poisoning, and chronic diseases like diabetes, heart disease, metabolic syndrome, Alzheimer's, and others, caused by politically distorted USDA recommendations, politically distorted healthcare policies, and unjustified "Generally Regarded as Safe" ("GRAS") government approvals.[99]

- The U.S. Treasury Department used AIG as a money laundering vehicle and sent emails instructing AIG to withhold critical information from the SEC to cover up the full scope of secret bailout activities during the 2008 crisis; and the paternal arrogance of senior Treasury officials was on full display in the text of their three-

---

[96] "Obama Accepts Resignation of VA Secretary Shinseki"; Washington Post; (5/30/2014)

[97] "NSA Spying on Americans Is Illegal" – American Civil Liberties Union; accessed on 8/9/2015; Available at: https://www.aclu.org/nsa-spying-americans-illegal.

[98] "Chinese breach data of 4 million federal workers" – Washington Post; (6/4/2015)

[99] Minger, Denise. *Death by Food Pyramid: How Shoddy Science, Sketchy Politics and Shady Special Interests Have Ruined Our Health*. 1 edition. Malibu, Calif: Primal Nutrition, Inc., 2014.

page bailout legislation: "Decisions by the [Treasury] Secretary pursuant to the authority of this Act are non-reviewable and committed to agency discretion, and may not be reviewed by any court of law or any administrative agency."[100] In other words, the Treasury Secretary was literally promoted to Dictator of the U.S. Economy without any accountability whatsoever.

- Senior State Department officials covered up their disclosure of classified information over unsecured, non-governmental channels, deliberately intended to avoid mandatory government surveillance systems during and after the "Arab Spring" Middle East revolutions in 2010-2011.[101]

- The "Richard Windsor" scandal in which senior EPA officials used fake names to conceal thousands of secret emails, letters, and other communications with private special interest groups to coordinate illegal and politically motivated enforcement actions, in addition to EPA collusion with the IRS to illegally disclose personal information about private American citizens to their political adversaries.[102, 103]

- The Department of Interior scandal in which staffers were taking gifts, having sex and using illegal drugs with employees of the oil companies they were responsible for regulating.[104]

And I've only scratched the surface. If you follow all the nonpartisan external references I've provided in this book, you will discover many other examples of bureaucrats who were highly motivated to act quickly to conceal their gross incompetence and misconduct from the millions of Americans whose lives they control every day. So there is no question that

---

[100] "Treasury's Bailout Proposal: The legislative proposal was sent by the White House overnight to lawmakers." – CNN (9/20/2008).

[101] "Benghazi Emails Put Focus on Hillary Clinton's Encouragement of Adviser" – New York Times (6/19/2015)

[102] "The Obama administration embraces secrecy and stonewalling." – National Review (1/5/2013)

[103] "The EPA's 'Richard Windsor; Email Scandal" – comprehensive report conducted by the Competitive Enterprise Institute, including a collection of media references and interviews. Available at https://cei.org/richard-windsor.

[104] Savage, Charlie. "Sex, Drug Use and Graft Cited in Interior Department." The New York Times, September 10, 2008.

http://www.nytimes.com/2008/09/11/washington/11royalty.html.

politicians and bureaucrats can move quickly when they really want to.

Negligent and Incompetent Bureaucrats Usually Die Before They Are Fired. Despite abundant and extremely costly examples of incompetence and misconduct all throughout the Fourth Branch, several nonpartisan studies have revealed that unelected government bureaucrats are more likely to die or retire before they are fired for incompetence or misconduct.[105] Did you vote for any of these people? Did you vote for this out-of-control bureaucracy? It's safe to say that none of the American people have voted for this. Who do we blame? The politicians in Congress who refuse to reform their lucrative Regulatory Protection Racket.

The Convergence of State & Corporate Power

Authoritarians Are Compelled to Censor Global Consciousness. The challenge to authoritarianism that the Internet represents is leading to escalating actions by governments to censor the free flow of information to control global consciousness. This is also true for large corporations who seek to control the wealth extraction apparatus of government. The largest corporations behave similarly to state governments in this regard: Both governments and large corporations seek to control global consciousness because they both depend on the wealth extraction power of the state to perpetuate their control and exploitation of large populations.

Large Corporations Emulate State Power. When the financial power of a corporation grows to the size of a small- to medium-sized country, their incentives invariably deviate from the incentives of their customers. Large-scale financial power carries within it the seed of coercive state power because it is financial power that gives both public and private organizations the ability to deploy propaganda and weapons of all types. Only with these instruments of mass coercion can states and corporations control global consciousness and the physical behavior of large populations to serve their particular agenda. And their agenda is controlled by the preferences of a tiny number of humans who wield that power. Every corporate monopoly and cartel demonstrates this phenomenon.

The Convergence of State and Corporate Interests. The

---

[105] "Some federal workers more likely to die than lose jobs" – USA Today online (7/19/2011)

convergence of state and large corporate interests often brings them together for the purpose of controlling the general public's perception of reality. Policies of every kind, including food and drug safety, energy policy, foreign policy, education policy, healthcare, housing, monetary policy, banking regulation—every public policy you can imagine is functionally distorted by this convergence of state and corporate interests. These distortions result in joint government-corporate censorship campaigns, which are led by governments and supported quietly by the largest corporations. This reality reveals the weak commitment that large corporations have to free-market capitalism, i.e., what large corporations really want is corporatism, fascism, mercantilism—any socioeconomic system that can be co-opted by financial power to thwart true representative government and free-market capitalism. This enables them to control the flow of wealth throughout an economy and channel public and private resources to their shareholders.

Small Government is a Big Part of the Solution. The principle of "small government" is not merely a partisan platitude embraced by Libertarians and Anarchists; a desire for small government reflects an authentic understanding of how the temptations that corrupt human nature and the destabilizing effects of large, complex systems inevitably lead to systemic corruption and collapse. The citizens of every country must consciously, vigorously, and continuously resist and trim the size of government with steadfast determination if they wish to live in a free society. Supporting public policies that minimize the size of government is the only political vaccine available to a citizenry to arrest the virulent mission creep that infects every aspect of a society within the ever-expanding reach of politicians and their special interest benefactors.

Fixing Broken Capitalism is the Most Critical Task of Our Generation. To restore trust and integrity in American Democracy, we must first chip away at the source of Democracy's decay: The influence of gargantuan corporations that rampage through our communities, our economies, and our political systems. That's why fixing Broken Capitalism is the most critical task of our generation.

Key Points

- **The Source of Virtually All Political & Economic Problems.** Virtually every conceivable malfunction in the U.S. economy and political system today can be traced to the systemic corruption of the electoral and regulatory processes that control the lives of all Americans and influence the lives of billions of humans worldwide.

- **The Regulatory Protection Racket.** It's not special interest groups' fault that they're forced into the Regulatory Protection Racket created and consciously perpetuated by politicians. The addicts will continue buying as long as the suppliers continue selling.

- **Too Many Laws; Not Enough Justice.** The American people are over-regulated, over-litigated, and under-represented in Washington. When corporations and their lobbyists control the legislative process, an endless river of bad laws is the result.

Your Country Needs You Now.

If you understand why it's important to fix Broken Capitalism, please give this book a positive rating online and tell at least 10 people about it today.

Home: Eanfar.org | **Facebook:** Facebook.com/Eanfar
Twitter: @FerrisEanfar | **AngelPay:** AngelPayHQ.org

- Chapter 6 -
Transnational Economic Cannibals

"In a country well governed, poverty is shameful.
In a country badly governed, wealth is shameful."
— Confucius

The Mechanics of a Global Wealth Transfer

Rapid Global Wealth Transfers Do Not Occur Spontaneously. One thing that is rarely discussed by Globalism 1.0 cheerleaders is the fact that "Ricardian Comparative Advantage" is not why Asian countries have dominated the West in manufacturing over the past few decades. In reality, the massive transfer of wealth from West to East did not just happen spontaneously through the natural free-market mechanism of supply and demand. It was promoted relentlessly by American corporate executives, corporate raiders, and politicians who were seeking to increase their wealth and political power by eliminating the domestic labor force.

    Rise of the Transnational Economic Cannibals. To accomplish the 14,000% growth in Chinese capital and wealth illustrated in the chart below, large American transnational corporations invested many billions of dollars into Chinese manufacturing capacity, providing technical assistance, intellectual property, valuable training, deeply discounted loans, political campaign funding to pro-corporatist American politicians, and other sources of value and propaganda to help launch offshore manufacturing facilities. By devouring and redirecting the wealth that was previously flowing into the American labor force and manufacturing sector, these *American* transnational corporations have cannibalized the value creation engine and economic life force of their own country. As a result, from this point forward, I will refer to them as "Transnational Cannibals."

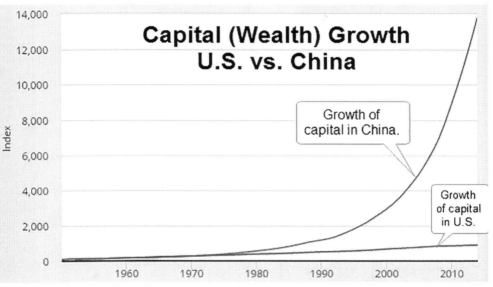

Raw Data Source: St. Louis Federal Reserve; University of Groningen and University of California, Davis; chart indexed to 1952 and illustrates % change in total capital stock in China vs. U.S. between 1952-2014; chart produced by Ferris Eanfar.

America's Flat Capital (True Wealth) Growth. Many people believe China's Communist Party can direct the Chinese economy relatively efficiently, which is why China has grown so quickly. That's only a tiny part of China's success story. The chart above illustrates how the U.S. capital stock growth rate has remained almost completely flat compared to China's capital stock growth rate. Given that capital stock represents accumulated wealth, this is a very troubling indication of the U.S. economy's true health.

Uncoordinated Alignment of Interests or Deliberate Conspiracy? Since the 1980s, American politicians have deliberately or unwittingly delivered their side of the toxic deal: distorted government regulations that favor Transnational Cannibals, uncompetitive tax and labor policies that push loyal American companies offshore and choke the life out of small- to medium-sized companies, and self-destructive trade policies that make it impossible for the small- to medium-sized business community to compete globally. This was a tremendous, multi-decade suicide mission that could not have been accomplished without persistent and highly self-interested American corporate executives and politicians disregarding the long-term health of the American economy and labor force. [106]

How Did a Communist Country Produce More Real Wealth Than the U.S. in Only 30 Years? American Transnational Cannibals have been working fast and furious with their patrons in Washington to pump China (and other sweatshop countries) full of American capital to supercharge China's industrialization and wealth accumulation. Rather than investing their capital in the U.S. economy and supporting American workers to increase U.S. capital stock and wealth, U.S. Transnational Cannibals and their patrons in Washington have transferred America's engine of prosperity (capital, jobs, intellectual property) to China to enrich their shareholders at the expense of the entire U.S. economy. The chart below confirms this.

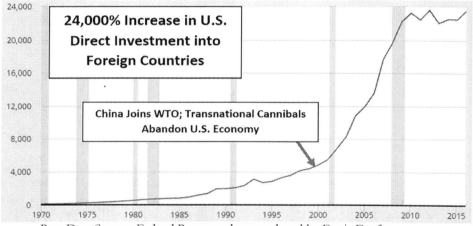

Raw Data Source: Federal Reserve; chart produced by Ferris Eanfar.

The Economic Consequences of Disloyalty. U.S. Transnational Cannibals have actively and systematically worked to transfer U.S. capital, technology, and manufacturing skills to foreign countries to increase their corporate shareholders' wealth. This means they have actively and systematically destroyed the comparative advantages that would have

---

[106] Of course, corporations and politicians in other Western countries jumped on the gravy train, too, after they saw what the Americans were doing. But the U.S. had an opportunity to set the tone for a more sustainable form of globalism, which they chose not to pursue because they were more interested in short-term riches. We will discuss a more sustainable form of globalism in a later chapter.

allowed the U.S. and all its citizens to compete globally in a far greater number of industries than they can today. This is another huge flaw in Globalism 1.0 economic models: They completely and conveniently ignore the catastrophic impact of disloyal multinational corporations, which undermines one of the most absurd assumptions (immobile factors of production) of most Globalism 1.0 economic models.

Capital is Wealth. To understand how a global wealth transfer works, we need to understand the basic relationship between capital and wealth. Capital accumulation is the ultimate form of wealth accumulation because capital is essential to the development of every economy. "Capital" is all the physical, financial (*not* stocks and bonds), and intellectual property assets that are required to produce something of value. Without capital, nothing can be produced and an economy can't exist. It took the United States (a capitalistic economy) nearly 250 years to achieve its current level of capital stock and corresponding national wealth. In contrast, only about 30 years after the political rise of Deng Xiaoping in China and his "socialist market economy" reforms, China's total capital stock rocketed past the United States' capital stock in 2011. That means *China has surpassed the U.S. in total wealth*, too, because a country's capital stock is a far more realistic measure of wealth than all the *paper wealth* of stocks, bonds, and derivatives peddled on Wall Street.

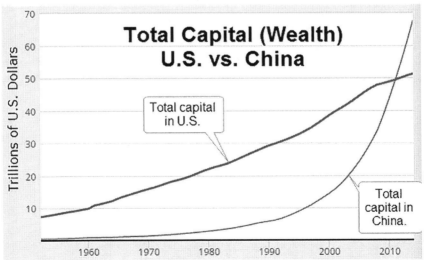

Raw Data Source: St. Louis Federal Reserve; University of Groningen and University of California, Davis; chart illustrates the real change in total capital stock in China vs. U.S. between 1952-2014; chart produced by Ferris Eanfar.

The Chinese Scapegoat. Until the late 1980s, the U.S. had the most productive labor force on the planet. Virtually nobody could compete with American labor in most industries. But by aggressively transferring their expertise, capital, and other forms of value to sweatshop countries, the largest *American* Transnational Cannibals essentially forced those countries to rapidly industrialize and cannibalize the American labor force. That enabled American corporate executives and politicians to rapidly eliminate the American labor force's share of American wealth and power while blaming it on the "cheating Chinese."

Irrational Economic and Labor Policies. A combination of federal fiscal accountability, rational monetary policy in the form of attractive interest rates to nurture savings, capital investment and the avoidance of moral hazard-inducing bailouts, rational corporate governance like Germany's co-determination policy (more on this in Part 2 of this book), along with a more globally competitive corporate tax regime like Switzerland's would have ensured that American manufacturing remained the most prolific and efficient in the world. With rational economic and labor policies, even the sweatshops in Asia would not have been able to match American technological prowess and productivity.[107]

Rising Out of Poverty; Descending into Slavery and Sorrow. Governments commit their greatest atrocities when their citizens have been stripped of their economic and political liberties. Sadly, that is what is happening today all over the world. A small fraction of humanity is rising out of poverty, but many more humans worldwide are descending into debtor's prison and modern slavery while Transnational Cannibals sell them garbage products and short-sighted policies that consume their bodies, minds, and souls. This is leading to a dystopian world that few people can imagine today, but our children and their children won't need to imagine it; they will be trapped in it. And they will hate us for it.

The Genesis of Globalism 1.0

Adam Smith and Mercantilism. Adam Smith was the author of the 1776 book *The Wealth of Nations*, essentially making him the father of Capitalism

---

[107] For example, see: Bernstein, Aaron. "Low-Skilled Jobs: Do They Have to Move?" *Bloomberg Businessweek*, February 26, 2001.

and the academic field of Economics. He was obsessed with free trade, but not the *free trade* associated with Globalism 1.0 today. During the centuries prior to Smith's time, international commerce was dominated by an ideology called "Mercantilism." Under Mercantilism, governments and their home corporations coordinated their activities to dominate international trade because that's what they believed maximized the wealth of the home country. The ideology of Mercantilism compelled governments to control all economic activities, including: the countries that home merchants could trade with, imposing export restrictions on many types of goods, subsidizing exports to help domestic merchants dominate foreign markets, dictating what goods could be consumed domestically, and doing everything possible to restrict imports from entering the home country.

Replacing Mercantilism with Corporatism Was Not Adam Smith's Intention. Adam Smith recognized that Mercantilism was an inefficient way to configure an economy, which is why he wrote *The Wealth of Nations*. In his book, Smith railed against the meddling of governments in the affairs of markets because he observed that government-controlled markets led to politically motivated trade wars, diplomatic crises, and military wars between countries. His conception of "free trade" was explicitly intended to liberate international trade from those specific problems, not to create national and global economies dominated by too-big-to-fail corporate goliaths that cause as many (or more) problems as tyrannical national governments. In Smith's own words:

> *Though the encouragement of exportation and the discouragement of importation are the two great engines by which the mercantile system proposes to enrich every country, yet with regard to some particular commodities it seems to follow an opposite plan. . . . Its ultimate object, however, it pretends, is always the same, to enrich the country by the advantageous balance of trade. It discourages the exportation of the materials of manufacture, and of the instruments of trade, in order to give our own workmen an advantage, and to enable them to undersell those of other nations in all foreign markets . . .* [108]

The Genesis of the Modern Global Economy. As the international trade regime (GATT, WTO, NAFTA, etc.) that dominates the

---

[108] Smith, Adam, and Alan B. Krueger. The Wealth of Nations. Annotated edition. New York, N.Y: Bantam Classics, 2003.

world today has evolved since 1947, it has been based on several assumptions about economics, geopolitics, and human welfare. These trade agreements and their implicit assumptions have been shaped by the opinions of politicians and corporate executives of the largest countries and corporations. The ideology of these people was shaped by their understanding of the principle of "Economic Liberalism" (which has nothing to do with "political liberalism"). However, a more accurate label would be "Economic Corporatism" because their ideology, the language of their trade agreements, and their actions—despite their lofty verbal rhetoric—has resulted in a near-complete transfer of financial and political power from elected national governments to unelected transnational corporations.

The Genesis of Economic and Social Catastrophe. In theory, Economic Liberalism seeks to reduce transaction costs and maximize wealth by applying the principle of "comparative advantage" to the global economy. From this perspective, the goal is to create a planetary economy in which the total volume of global trade is maximized, which presumably increases the wealth and quality of life for the maximum number of people. This may seem logical, but imposing a policy of Economic Liberalism on a planet without effectively enforcing international rules of trade and creating meaningful incentives for corporations to distribute wealth more evenly throughout global societies merely results in a regime of global economic imperialism. Like the European colonialism, genocide, and humanitarian atrocities of the past perpetrated under the guise of "civilizing the barbarians," neo-economic imperialism perpetrated under the guise of Economic Liberalism is already having catastrophic economic and humanitarian consequences.[109, 110]

Corporatism and its Cumulative Negative Affects. Earth's macro-economy today should be described as "corporatism," which is an economic system that is politically and structurally designed to primarily benefit the largest corporations, their shareholders, and the political class

---

[109] "The American Middle Class Is Losing Ground." *Pew Research Center's Social & Demographic Trends Project*, December 9, 2015.
http://www.pewsocialtrends.org/2015/12/09/the-american-middle-class-is-losing-ground/.
[110] See also: "Unknown Truth or Untrue Conspiracy?" - Eanfar.org. (2016).
Retrieved from https://eanfar.org/unknown-truth-or-untrue-conspiracy/

that supports them within each country. Under corporatism, regulations, tax policies, and geopolitical events are all viewed within the context of how the biggest corporations will respond. Regardless of whether one stakeholder or 1 billion stakeholders benefit from corporatism at any particular point in time, if the analysis is extended over a longer period of time, the cumulative negative consequences of corporatism become obvious.

Transnational Economic Cannibalism

90% of All U.S. Exports Are Dominated by 1% of All U.S. Exporters. Of all 304,466 U.S. companies that exported products to foreign customers in 2014, approximately 1% of these companies exported approximately 90% of the entire $1.44 trillion U.S. export volume.[111] The chart below illustrates how 99% of all U.S. exporting companies are squeezed into the tiny 10% slice of the export market pie; while the largest 1% of U.S. exporters dominate 90% of the entire export market pie. Are these the "benefits to society" that Globalism 1.0 cheerleaders claim we should all appreciate? No, this is Broken Capitalism.

Transnational Cannibals Are Instigators of War. Contrary to Globalism 1.0 propaganda, *globalism* did nothing to prevent any of the wars of the 20th Century. The reality is the exact opposite: World War I, World

---

111   U.S. Census Bureau: "A Profile of U.S. Importing and Exporting Companies,

War II, and virtually every international war over the past century has been substantially instigated and perpetuated by the exploitation of foreign financial and commodities markets by transnational corporations, with the complicity of their home governments.[112] This is well-documented; so if there are any doubts about this, please follow the extensive footnotes and bibliographic sources I've provided.

Wars Are Caused by Economic Oppression. Trade disputes are inevitable because everybody wants to negotiate the best deal, but international wars are possible only when foreign entities become so abusive that the oppressed country has no recourse but to forcefully resist the abusive foreign governments or corporations operating within their domestic borders. Economic oppression directly causes the poverty, economic and political instability that spawns the political pressures that ignite international warfare. Transnational corporations are the instruments of modern economic oppression, which means they are the most significant source of international war.

Economic Oppression Ignites Political Revolutions. Globalism 1.0 cheerleaders are surprised by socioeconomic eruptions because they don't truly understand the fundamental economic and social realities that are shaping the lives of billions of people on Earth today. What did the 1791 Haitian Revolution, the 1917 Bolshevik Revolution, the 1944 Guatemalan Revolution, the 1947 Indian Independence Movement, the 1959 Cuban Revolution, the 1979 Iranian Revolution, the 9/11/2001 terrorist attacks in the U.S., the 2010 Arab Spring, the 2011 Occupy Wall Street protests, the 2016 UK vote to exit the EU ("Brexit"), and Donald Trump's 2016 presidential election have in common? They were all directly instigated by a widespread feeling of economic exploitation.

Trade Deficits Are the Result of Lost Wealth. By definition,

2013 - 2014"
[112] See: Blum, William. *Rogue State: A Guide to the World's Only Superpower*, 2015.
Coll, Steve. *Private Empire: ExxonMobil and American Power*. New York: Penguin Books, 2013. See also:
Perkins, John. *The New Confessions of an Economic Hit Man*. 2 edition. Oakland, CA: Berrett-Koehler Publishers, 2016.
Butler, Smedley D., and Adam Parfrey. *War Is a Racket: The Antiwar Classic by America's Most Decorated Soldier*. Los Angeles, Calif: Feral House, 2003.
Schlesinger, Stephen, Stephen Kinzer, John H. Coatsworth, and Richard A. Nuccio. *Bitter Fruit: The Story of the American Coup in Guatemala, Revised and Expanded.*

national trade deficits are an economic condition in which a nation collectively pays more money for its goods and services than it receives. Thus, for every year a nation has a trade deficit, it is allowing more wealth to leave its country than it is accumulating for its citizens. Despite the corporatist propaganda that we have all heard to justify the international trade regime that dominates the world today, cheap prices for goods and services do not create wealth. Wealth is created only when individuals and nations keep more value than they lose from the aggregation of all the economic transactions that affect them over time.

The Shrinking American Wealth Pool. To understand this principle, visualize a pool with two vacuum hoses at opposite ends. The pool is filled with the total global supply of "wealth" (money, assets, buildings, land, stocks, bonds, commodities, intellectual property, food, clean air and water, economic liberty, political freedom, etc.). This is the "Wealth Pool." One hose flows to Country A while the other hose flows to Country B. All forms of productive activity produce wealth, which flows into the Wealth Pool just before it is sucked out of the pool by each economic actor (individuals, corporations, governments). There are many forms of wealth, but on Earth, we usually measure wealth in terms of money.

How A Nation's Wealth is Lost. If Country A has a trade deficit, that means it is *paying more total wealth* for its goods and services than the total wealth it is receiving. If Country B has a trade surplus, that means it is *paying less total wealth* for its goods and services than the total wealth it is receiving. If this scenario continues over a long period of time, then Country B will obviously suck more wealth from the Wealth Pool than Country A, regardless of the prices that Country A's citizens might pay for goods and services at the individual level. Thus, at the national level, Country A's economy is being depleted of its wealth, which inevitably leads to the collapse of its industries and ultimately the collapse of its entire economy.[113]

Cannibalism Is Not a Sustainable Solution. Some people may say, "How is it possible to pay cheaper prices and not be better off over the

---

Cambridge, Mass: David Rockefeller Center for Latin American Studies, 2005.

[113] If this process is still not completely clear, don't worry, we will cover it again later in the "What is Value?" chapter, which will include a useful graphic to make it easier to visualize.

long-run?" An analogy will make this process clear: From a purely biological perspective, you could eat your own flesh, bones, blood, and muscle tissue to survive for a short period of time. In fact, when faced with starvation, humans have resorted to cannibalism to survive in many cases throughout human history. Of course, you might prefer to eat your neighbor instead of yourself, but after you've eaten all your neighbors, who is left to eat?

Consumption Does Not Lead to Prosperity. Chewing on your own flesh a few millimeters per day might seem like a logical way to survive for a short period of time, but over the long-run, that behavior will eventually lead to the total collapse of your biological system. Now you're dead; and no quantity of cheap products is going to bring you back to life. This is what is happening to the U.S. labor force and the value creation engine of the U.S. economy. Transnational Cannibals use Globalism 1.0 and its illusory, short-run "benefits to society" as an excuse to devour their ecosystems and extract every penny of wealth from every country on Earth.

Transnational Cannibalism is Coming for You. If you're not a U.S. Citizens, you should know that Transnational Cannibalism is coming for you, too. This same process will repeat itself in every country unless economic policymakers in every country learn from America's mistakes. The concentration of wealth and political power into the hands of a tiny number of goliath corporations is tearing apart the socioeconomic fabric of nations worldwide and driving governments toward authoritarian models of governance that will strip the dignity, wealth, and life from their citizens. This is the same dynamic that inspired the 1917 Bolshevik Revolution in Russia, which ushered in an unprecedented era of human atrocities in the name of *human rights*.

America's Experience Will be the Global Experience. What Globalism 1.0 cheerleaders fail to understand is that the U.S. is the canary in the coal mine. The same mutation from Economic Liberalism to corporatism is underway in every emerging market today. The same mistakes that U.S. political and business leaders have made are being exported from the U.S. into every corner of the globe. The convergence of interests between powerful politicians and powerful corporations are mutually reinforcing one another while they cannibalize the economic and social fabric of their societies. This is leading to the massive income and wealth disparities that are popping up all over the planet, which creates a self-perpetuating cycle of wealth and political power concentration into the claws of an ever-shrinking group of Transnational Cannibals.

Surprise is Born from Ignorance. People are not surprised or shocked when they know and understand why something happens. Thus, surprise and shock are fundamentally produced by ignorance. The policymakers, corporate executives, and media organizations who are surprised by major political and economic eruptions are either deeply ignorant and/or willfully blind. Regardless, the cumulative result of Globalism 1.0 will ultimately destabilize and destroy the entire global economic system, resulting in far more losers than winners.

The Game of Life

What is "Wealth"? Many definitions exist for "wealth," which makes it meaningless unless we define it for ourselves. I've spent a substantial portion of my career in the financial services sector, I am an investor and business owner, my academic background has focused on International Political Economy, and I've spent at least 1,000 hours with investors, clients, and wealthy friends and colleagues discussing every conceivable aspect of wealth, money, politics, and power to understand their impact in our world. So I've spent a lot of time thinking about what it means to be "wealthy" and how wealth is created, protected, distributed, and destroyed within a society. No definition of "wealth" is universally appropriate, but for the practical purposes of this book, I define "wealth" by a person's net worth because net worth is easy to measure and compare between members of a given society.

Anybody Can (Theoretically) Become Rich in Democratic Societies Today. During Karl Marx's time in mid-19th Century London, England, social class was still the most influential factor that determined who became wealthy. This is why he was so focused on class distinctions in his mammoth book, *Das Kapital*, which is the source of many economic theories used by the ideological right and left today. However, in American society, and in most democratic societies around the world today, anybody can become wealthy without being born into a specific social class. Of course, a high-quality education and family connections always help—and these advantages are often correlated with social class—but class by itself is no longer the most significant factor in building wealth.

"Middle Class" Has a Special Meaning. Although social class is not very relevant anymore when it comes to wealth in modern democratic societies, I should mention that the phrase "Middle Class" transcends the concept of social class and has a special meaning and role in every society. In Political Science and most professional economic discussions, the phrase "Middle Class" has become a short-hand way of saying "the middle quartiles of a population as measured by annual personal real income. . . ." Clearly, it's a lot easier to simply say "Middle Class," which is why I use it, but I use it only in the modern economic sense without any implied references to the social characteristics that can sometimes be associated with it. Whatever we call it, the most important thing to remember is that a strong Middle Class is a tell-tale sign of a healthy economy and a functional political system. But when the Middle Class is *not* healthy, economists and Political Science professionals know that means the country is in trouble.

The Most Important Nonpartisan Questions About Wealth. Any discussion about wealth and poverty should answer the following questions: What baseline level of wealth ("Baseline Wealth") does a citizen in a given country need to retire and enjoy their brief human existence on this planet without fear of poverty? How reasonable is that Baseline Wealth compared to the wealth of other groups in that country? Does the economy have the capacity to produce Baseline Wealth for every citizen? What policies would enable a majority of citizens in that country to *earn* Baseline Wealth so that country's Middle Class is strong and stable? What policies can we implement to fix Broken Capitalism so that over 50% of our country's population is not on some form of government welfare? Of course, this book answers all these questions.

Baseline Wealth in the United States. An American in 2017 needs to have assets with a market value of at least $1 million to retire relatively comfortably, assuming a relatively low-cost lifestyle. A $1 million retirement portfolio managed conservatively and generating 3% annual investment returns to beat inflation will provide about $30,000 per year for basic living expenses. Social security benefits increase that to about $60,000. In a healthy economy guided by effective economic policies, this is the Baseline Wealth that every able-bodied American should be able to reasonably achieve within a 15 to 20-year career.

The Feasibility of Baseline Wealth. Based on 2017 U.S. GDP of $18.6 trillion, and assuming a conservative 1.5% annual growth rate, cumulative U.S. GDP over a 20-year period would be $430 trillion, but it would only require a cumulative $320 trillion for all 320 million Americans living today *to earn* Baseline Wealth over that period. The same math also works when taking into account all realistic population growth scenarios.[114] So the concept of Baseline Wealth is certainly technically feasible. Unfortunately, for political and cultural reasons, it's probably not realistic to structure the American economy to produce the optimal level of financial security for every citizen. However, if a large majority of Americans can't achieve Baseline Wealth because they can't even find stable and financially meaningful employment, that means Capitalism is clearly broken.

The Data on American Wealth. According to the Federal Reserve Board's latest four-year-old *2013 report* (They publish the report every three to four years.), *less than 8%* of Americans have Baseline Wealth of $1 million or more in net worth.[115] Over 50% of American families have less than $5,500 in net worth. In other words, *at least* 92% of Americans *do not* have Baseline Wealth, cannot retire comfortably, and are guaranteed to be dependent upon government welfare to pay their living expenses for most of their adult lives until Broken Capitalism is fixed.

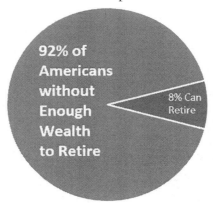

92% of Americans Are Economic Refugees. Are 92% of Americans crippled, stupid, mentally retarded, lazy, or otherwise incapable of earning Baseline Wealth? No, of course not, but Broken Capitalism has destroyed the value creation engine of American society and ripped away

---

[114] I'm keeping the math simple here for casual readers, but in reality, the required amount would be far less than $320 trillion. This is because children and the elderly are not in the labor force, which means only about 33% of the population is employed at any point in time. So the true required GDP would be closer to $100 trillion. Also note that population growth is built-in to the math because GDP is largely a function of population growth.

[115] 2013 Survey of Consumer Finances: https://www.federalreserve.gov/econresdata/scf/scfindex.htm

the population's means of personal subsistence. These American economic refugees are joining a rapidly expanding population of economic and political refugees worldwide. The Transnational Cannibals and the dysfunctional governments that have created Broken Capitalism have created these refugees. The chart above and the facts throughout this book should put to rest any ideological drivel from Globalism 1.0 cheerleaders who try to claim that there is nothing wrong with Capitalism today.

Social Class vs. Economic Hierarchy. Many lists of wealthy people exist, but those lists do not make it easy to see a person's wealth within the context of their general place in an economic hierarchy. Remember, I'm not talking about a social class hierarchy; focusing on social class is not very useful anymore unless you're a politician trying to pander to humanity's worst instincts and divide society into political clans to extract their votes and campaign contributions. As politicians know, social class implies much more than wealth; it implies culture, race, ethnicity, upbringing, language, geography, education, social status, and numerous other characteristics, which trigger many emotions and unnecessary ideological debates. This book is about fixing Broken Capitalism, which technically has nothing to do with social class *anymore*.

Who Is Wealthy? The table below helps to visualize different levels of wealth in relation to different types of occupations in American society. It provides an economic hierarchy corresponding to common types of occupations that produce each level of net worth (wealth) for people in those economic groups.[116]

Net Worth (USD)	Multiple	Member of Society
80,000,000,000	80,000x	Bill Gates
10,000,000,000	10,000x	Super-Successful Company Founder
1,000,000,000	1,000x	Super-Successful Hedge Fund Manager
500,000,000	500x	Successful Hedge Fund Manager
250,000,000	250x	Superstar Pop Singer
100,000,000	100x	A-List Movie Star
50,000,000	50x	Successful Pop Singer
20,000,000	20x	Successful Small Business Owner
1,000,000	Baseline	Comfortable American Retiree

[116] Note: This analysis is not about the wealth gap between people in poverty and the super-rich or the "1%" vs. the "99%." Everybody knows there's a big wealth gap problem, we don't need to infect this aspect of our analysis with any partisan overtones.

Where Is Your Place in the Economic Hierarchy? In the table above, the "Multiple" column represents the *wealth multiple* of each wealth level compared to Baseline Wealth, i.e., how many times larger each wealth level is compared to Baseline Wealth. As you view the table, think about the following questions: Where is your place in this economic hierarchy? Why are you in that position? Were you born there or did you earn your place there? Do you feel the people in the higher *and* lower positions deserve to be there? Did they earn it? Why or why not? What percentage of society should be in each position? Is this hierarchy purely the result of supply-and-demand market forces? If not, what other factors created this hierarchy? How could Broken Capitalism be improved to achieve a more equitable distribution of wealth? *Should* we try to achieve a more equitable distribution of wealth?

Below is what the table data above looks like as a pie chart.

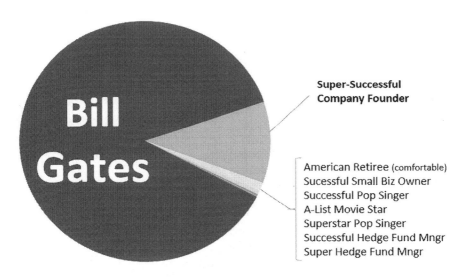

A Note on Bill Gates. Bill Gates has become a cultural icon and a symbol of extreme wealth so it's useful to include him in any economic analysis about wealth gaps, but just to be clear: Nothing in this book is intended as an attack on Bill Gates. I spent the first half of my career in technology-related positions so I have always had the utmost respect for his contributions to our world. My girlfriend also knows him and I'm sure I'll meet him some day for various reasons. And obviously the Bill & Melinda Gates Foundation is doing meaningful work around the world, along with his other philanthropic activities. So this analysis is not intended to bash Bill

Gates or anybody else.

It's Just a Game. Ask any wealthy business owner, investor, trader, or investment banker this question, "You can buy virtually anything you want; so why do you need more money?" They usually reply with something like, "It's not about the money; it's about the game. The money is just a way to keep score. I love what I do and the money helps me see how I'm doing compared to the competition. It's what keeps me sharp and enthusiastic about life." In itself, there's nothing wrong with that kind of answer; so people should not judge a person negatively simply because they're wealthy. Rarely will you meet the most despicable creatures who say things like, "I like to control people. Money enables me to do that, which enables me to do whatever I want. Life is short. There's no god to stop me. Why shouldn't I make as much money as possible so I can do whatever the hell I want?" In reality, most rich people are not that self-centered; so there's no rational reason to bundle them all into the "evil" category.

How Much is Enough? Now ask any wealthy person, "How much money does a person need to never have to worry about money again?" Usually they will say somewhere between $10-20 million. That may seem like a lot to many people, but taking inflation into account, $20 million in 2017 is the equivalent of only $1 million in the year 1900. Also remember that most wealth is stuck inside illiquid assets and takes time to convert to cash. That means most wealthy people can't instantly write a check for millions of dollars even if their net worth is many millions of dollars. And certain lifestyles consume money more quickly than others—if you have the money, there's no rational reason to deprive yourself of a high-end lifestyle. So let's say $20 million represents a reasonable "Financial Freedom Point" for every human who aspires to maximize their material pleasure during their short existence on Earth.

What Are Your Chances of Achieving the Financial Freedom Point? Using population numbers and the number of high-net-worth individuals in regions of the world, if you live in North America, you have approximately a 1% chance. Worldwide, you have a 0.2% chance.[117] However, those numbers don't take into account many factors related to geography, education level, the cultural values that dominate each

---

[117] Derived from the "World Wealth Report | Compare the Data on a Global Scale." Accessed April 7, 2017.
https://www.worldwealthreport.com/reports/population/north_america.

community, and other essential factors that determine how economic opportunities are distributed throughout an economy. So the *actual* chance that most people have to achieve the Financial Freedom Point within the context of Broken Capitalism today is much lower than 1% in virtually all cases.

The Bell Curve of Life vs. The Skewed Curve of Broken Capitalism. Globalism 1.0 cheerleaders often say things like, "Life is not always fair and competition always results in some winners and losers, which is why there is a Bell Curve. You can't equalize everybody; so just try to be one of the winners and stop complaining!" These people conveniently ignore the fact that Broken Capitalism is not distributing winners and losers along a Bell Curve—not even close. A Bell Curve is what *should* occur when there is real competition, but the Bell Curve does not occur in this case because all the anti-competitive and distorted economic policies associated with Broken Capitalism concentrate nearly all the wealth into a tiny slice of the curve.

What Would a Bell Curve Wealth Distribution Look Like? If Capitalism was not broken and Globalism 1.0 was not malfunctioning, the global distribution of wealth would look like the bell curve below. Ninety-five percent of the population would own approximately 95% of the wealth and less than 3% of the global population would be living in poverty.

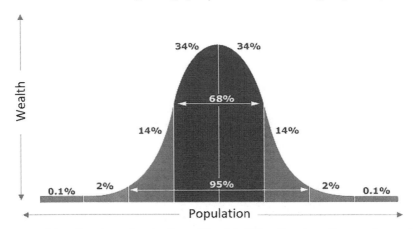

The Broken Capitalism Wealth Distribution Curve. Instead of a bell curve, today humanity is suffering from the Broken Capitalism curve below. Only 1% of the global population today owns more than the other

99% of the global population *combined*[118]. Over 70% of the global population lives in poverty and subsists on less than $10 per day; and over 10% of the global population lives in severe poverty, subsisting on less than $1.90 per day.[119]

Western Economic Refugees Overshadow the Poverty

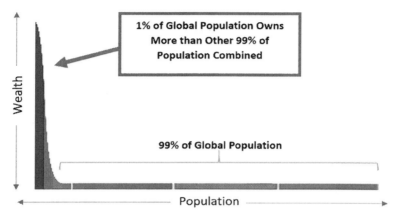

Success Stories. Globalism 1.0 cheerleaders often talk about how some people have been lifted out of poverty *thanks to globalism* over the past several decades. Yes, poverty has been reduced in some places, primarily in China, Southeast Asia and some parts of Latin America, but Broken Capitalism has no chance of lifting the other 70% of humanity out of poverty. This is because the concentration of wealth and political power into the claws of a tiny number of Transnational Cannibals has been dramatically accelerating, which *guarantees* economic hardship for our planet over the long-run. In fact, as structural economic problems caused by Broken Capitalism continue to plague Europe and the United States, among other countries, an increasing number of Western economic refugees are *sliding into poverty* and offsetting all the gains that have occurred in the developing world.

---

[118] Hardoon, Deborah, Ricardo Fuentes-Nieva, and Sophia Ayele. "An Economy For the 1%: How Privilege and Power in the Economy Drive Extreme Inequality and How This Can Be Stopped." Policy & Practice, January 18, 2016. http://policy-practice.oxfam.org.uk/publications/an-economy-for-the-1-how-privilege-and-power-in-the-economy-drive-extreme-inequ-592643.

[119] "Seven-in-Ten People Globally Live on $10 or Less per Day." Pew Research Center, September 23, 2015. http://www.pewresearch.org/fact-tank/2015/09/23/seven-in-ten-people-globally-live-on-10-or-less-per-day/.

Economic Cannibal Species

Transnational Cannibals vs. Predatory Cannibals vs. Benevolent Cannibals. In nature, cannibalism is not always bad. There are over 1,000 species of cannibals, including a variety of fish, cats, insects, and other animals that have cannibalistic instincts under certain conditions. However, the purpose of their cannibalism is survival and the preservation of their species, not gluttony and the domination of their ecosystems. The global economy today is being eaten by three different species of economic cannibals. From a policymaking perspective, it's important to be able to distinguish between them so that politicians don't bundle them all together and make more stupid decisions that lead to Communism or cause the Middle Class to disintegrate even faster. So let's briefly look at each of these types of cannibals.

- **Transnational Cannibals:** As we learned previously, Transnational Cannibals are disloyal corporations that behave like man-eating sharks, but they're not inherently good or evil—they're simply wealth production machines driven by the other two types of cannibals.
- **Predatory Cannibals:** These are a small number of gluttonous corporate raiders, investment bankers, traders, and corporate executives who know their actions are not healthy for their economy or society, but they don't care because they're hedonists or anarchists who believe "might makes right" and "he who has the gold rules." If you talk to these people at dinner parties, you will feel like you're staring into the lifeless eyes of a nonhuman creature. Indeed, these are the creatures who transformed corporations into sociopathic sharks by mutating their corporate DNA in the 1980s, which is why corporate executives today are forcefully compelled to behave like quarterly-profit-driven zombies.
- **Benevolent Cannibals:** These are wealthy individuals who are not consciously trying to cannibalize their society, but they have the resources and connections to influence highly malleable politicians in subtle ways that serve their financial interests, which perpetuates the status quo. Substantial portions of their wealth are invested in

large companies, which reduces their incentive to hold Transnational Cannibals accountable to anything other than quarterly financial statements. For the same reason, they passively tolerate the Predatory Cannibals as a necessary evil to increase the profitability of their own investment portfolios.

Benevolent Cannibals Don't Like Broken Capitalism Either. Regardless of how they earned or inherited their wealth, Benevolent Cannibals sincerely try to manage their wealth thoughtfully. They use their wealth to launch new companies, they try to hire domestic workers whenever possible, they care about what happens to their home society, and they support nonprofit groups that are making a positive impact in the world. Most of my friends and colleagues, including myself, fit into this group. Collectively, the people in this group care about Broken Capitalism, but they simply don't know how to fix it. I think most Benevolent Cannibals will be willing to support the solutions recommended in Part 2 of this book because they know that high concentrations of wealth and power in the claws of a few Transnational Cannibals is destructive to every society.

Transnational Cannibals Spawn Consumer Culture. It should be obvious to any conscious human that Transnational Cannibals are transforming our world into a consumer-obsessed global economy with a globally homogenized culture of consumption zombies. By flooding the media worldwide with *consumer-is-king* propaganda and manipulating government policies to serve their interests, Transnational Cannibals steer the global population toward rapaciously consuming value rather than thoughtfully saving, conserving, and creating value. This is the essence of consumerism, which is an environmentally destructive ideology manufactured by Transnational Cannibals to sell more *stuff* so their shareholders can get rich quick. It's the ultimate pump-and-dump scam, but as we will explore in Part 2, this scam will inevitably self-destruct because it destroys the value creation engine of every capitalistic society.

Key Points

- **Global Wealth Transfers Don't Happen by Accident.** They are the result of conscious, deliberate choices that economic policymakers make. Today, Capitalism is configured to favor Transnational Cannibals, but like any human-made system, *it can be* *re-configured* to favor small- to medium-sized companies and the Middle Class to achieve sustainable social and economic stability.

- **All Wealthy People Are Not Greedy.** Many of them truly care about Broken Capitalism and want to help fix it. Find the "Benevolent Cannibals" in your community and send them this book. I guarantee they will appreciate it because every Benevolent Cannibal I've ever met (including myself) is very concerned about the increasing socioeconomic instability in our world today.

- **Broken Capitalism is Coming for You.** No matter where you live on Earth, Broken Capitalism and the disease of Globalism 1.0 are coming for you. Find the conscious humans in your community, put *nonpartisan* pressure on all your business and political leaders, and let's work together to fix Broken Capitalism before it's too late.

Your Country Needs You Now.

If you understand why it's important to fix Broken Capitalism, please give this book a positive rating online and tell at least 10 people about it today.

Home: Eanfar.org | **Facebook:** Facebook.com/Eanfar
Twitter: @FerrisEanfar | **AngelPay:** AngelPayHQ.org

- Chapter 7 -
The Impact of Artificial Intelligence

"The real problem is not whether machines think
but whether men do." – B. F. Skinner

The Job Apocalypse

In the Past, Creative Destruction Supported Human Life. Since the Industrial Revolution, industrial automation has always destroyed more jobs than it has created *in each industry*. In the past, this was not necessarily bad for society because technological progress gave birth to new industries and freed up workers in one industry to do higher-paying jobs in new industries. For example, the agricultural reaper enabled farmers to produce more crops with less labor, which freed up other farmers to move to the city and pursue new jobs in newly created manufacturing and engineering industries.

From Reapers to Robots. In the 1980s, automated robots were deployed in the automotive and equipment manufacturing industries, which freed up workers to pursue higher-paying jobs in engineering, software programming, medicine, law, accounting, and other professions. This upward mobility inspired many people in the Baby Boomer Generation and Generation X to pursue college degrees to perform these higher-skilled jobs. That would have been an unqualified cause for celebration if nearly all the lower-skilled manufacturing jobs were not simultaneously exported to foreign sweatshops.

Youth and Young Adult Labor Market Extinction. The Information Technology ("IT") Revolution in the 1990s to mid-2000s automated many of the customer service and clerical jobs that still remained after the previous decade of automation. This pushed even more people into college to compete for increasingly scarce higher-paying jobs, but also because the lower-paying jobs were disappearing from the bottom of the labor ladder. The disappearance of these lower-skill jobs and the increase in minimum wages have pushed the youth and young adult labor market into virtual extinction. Now, it's nearly impossible today for most young adults to find an entry point into the labor market without *family connections*.

Entire Industries Are Extinct. In the late 2000s to the present, smartphones, tablets, computers, and the apps that run on them, have automated or replaced thousands of tools, gadgets, and jobs that previously required their own industries to produce and deliver them. Some of these items and jobs are as varied as flashlights, cameras, camcorders, VCRs, CD/DVD players, personal computers, airport kiosks, every kind of map, GPS devices, every kind of calculator, writing paper, online banking, pens and pencils, travel agencies, journals, Rolodexes, dictionaries, encyclopedias, books, robotic medical surgery, navigational compasses, scanners, blood pressure machines, carpentry levels, fingerprint readers, credit card scanners, language translators, every form of education, personal and business accounting, painting tools, among thousands of other items, tools and services. And we're not done yet. . . .

In the Present, Creative Destruction is Hostile to Human Life. Automation continues to climb up the human labor ladder today. As I type, many other jobs are being fully automated, including professional services like diagnostic medicine; legal analysis; artificially intelligent and interactive client services in many industries; investment portfolio management; banking services; warehouse inventory management; driver-less cars and trucks; hotel concierge services, restaurant operations; assembly of complex products; commercial shipping and loading drones; land, sea, and air military combat drones; and the list goes on.[120]

Globalism 1.0 Cannot Deal with Surplus Humanity. The neurotoxin of Globalism 1.0 and the corporate propaganda associated with Broken Capitalism are blocking sustainable solutions to the Job Apocalypse. These twin pathologies prevent many people from truly comprehending the

---

[120] There's an excellent video that I recommend on YouTube entitled "Humans Need Not Apply," which illustrates how virtually every job you can imagine can be automated.
CGP Grey. *Humans Need Not Apply*. Accessed April 7, 2017.
https://www.youtube.com/watch?v=7Pq-S557XQU.

enormity of the humanitarian catastrophe that is rapidly approaching. And this problem cannot be resolved by the so-called *free market*; unless by "free" we mean *free to murder and sterilize all the surplus humanity* that will soon have no economic purpose *within the context of Broken Capitalism*. Sadly, Broken Capitalism has transformed something wonderful—technological progress—into an all-consuming monster that is hostile to humanity.

"Bullshit Labor Statistics"

If You Can't Find a Job for 52 Weeks, You Don't Exist. In 1994 the U.S. Bureau of Labor Statistics ("BLS") arbitrarily stopped counting "long-term discouraged workers" in the *official* unemployment rate. The BLS' rationale is that if a person hasn't found a job in 52 weeks at the time when their unemployment benefits expire, then the person must not be trying to find work anymore and should not be counted. Additionally, if a person works part-time babysitting or mowing a lawn for even a fraction of one day during any 30-day period, the BLS counts that person as "employed" and excludes the person from the unemployment rate. That logic might make sense for incumbent politicians trying to make the unemployment rate appear lower so they'll get reelected, but there is no intellectually honest reason to exclude people from the unemployment rate simply because they can't find a job for 52 weeks or work for less than one day per month.

      Jack Welch & "Bullshit Labor Statistics". Let's take the BLS' *logic* to its logical conclusion: If every human is replaced by robots tomorrow and can't find a job for 52 weeks, the unemployment rate would fall to zero. The absurdity of the BLS' unemployment rate methodology is why Jack Welch, the former CEO of General Electric and infamous Predatory Cannibal, complained and said he believes the way politicians calculate the unemployment rate today is blatant government manipulation.[121] In fact, it's so blatantly deceitful that it discredits everything that comes out of the BLS, which is why many otherwise intelligent and articulate people around the world can't help thinking that "BLS" means "Bullshit Labor Statistics."

---

[121] Barone, Robert. "Why Jack Welch Has A Point About Unemployment Numbers." *Forbes*. Accessed April 7, 2017.
http://www.forbes.com/sites/greatspeculations/2012/10/16/why-jack-welch-has-a-point-about-unemployment-numbers/.

The Real Unemployment Rate: Approximately 23% (as of Q1 2017). It should be clear by now that the *official* U3 unemployment rate dramatically overstates the actual strength of the labor force, which is obviously done for political reasons.[122] The unemployment rate during the Great Depression in 1933 peaked at 24.9%. When calculating the unemployment rate using the more accurate methodology used in the past, the U.S. unemployment rate in early 2017 is about 23%, which is very close to the Great Depression unemployment rate.[123] For victims of Broken Capitalism, this is not surprising.[124]

The Future of Automation

Sanity Check. From this point until the end of the chapter, we will be exploring aspects of technology, economics, and politics that are uncertain. Some concepts might be disturbing—they might even seem a bit crazy—but they are all well within the realm of possibility based on the convergence of current economic, political, and technological trends.

The Trends Are Accelerating. Computing power is still increasing exponentially about every 18 months, which means the proliferation and quality of computer-automated services is going to continue increasing rapidly along with a corresponding elimination of jobs. The human brain usually underestimates the power of exponential growth; so I'll put this into perspective: In 1848 the world record for locomotive trains was 60 miles per hour. One hundred years later, commercial aircraft

---

[122] "Alternate Unemployment Charts." Accessed April 7, 2017.
http://www.shadowstats.com/alternate_data/unemployment-charts.
[123] "The Jobs Picture Is Far Worse Than It Looks." *US News & World Report.* Accessed April 7, 2017.
https://www.usnews.com/opinion/mzuckerman/articles/2013/02/28/mort-zuckerman-the-jobs-picture-is-far-worse-than-it-looks.
[124] Anybody who thinks this 23% figure is over-exaggerated should consider that RT.com has run several op-ed pieces, including, "Silent misery: Actual US unemployment 37.2%, record number of households on food stamps in 2013," blasting the U.S. Government for under-stating the unemployment rate for political reasons. I agree that the rate is under-stated for political reasons, but the RT figure is too high because their methodology is flawed: They're including the entire adult population in their calculation, which includes retired people and disabled people, which should not be included in the rate since they're not actually part of the labor force.

could carry people 10 times faster at close to 600 miles per hour. In contrast, between 1971 and 2015, the speed of microprocessors in personal computers increased 8.7 million times in only 43 years. If the speed of human transportation systems increased at that pace, we would all be zooming around the Milky Way Galaxy in spaceships today at *522 million miles per hour.*

The Future is Already Here. Students at Stanford University recently announced their completion of the "Neurogrid," which is a new microprocessor architecture designed to simulate the synaptic structure of the human brain. The Neurogrid is 9,000 times faster than a typical microprocessor and it will soon surpass the processing power of the human brain. And the "Internet-of-Things" ("IoT") is also upon us. The IoT is the swarm of automated computers, sensors, and robots embedded in our physical environments, which are beginning to perform various tasks and transactions between themselves with no human intervention at all.

Global Populations Pushed into an Economic and Social Wasteland. After thinking about how deeply robots, artificial intelligence, and automation have already infiltrated our lives, most people should realize that there is virtually no job in the modern world that cannot be fully or near-fully automated by the current and next generation of intelligent robots and computers. That means automation has penetrated into the top of the labor ladder, consuming all the labor rungs beneath it, and there will be only a relatively tiny number of higher-value jobs available to the vast majority of global populations who are already being pushed into an economic and social wasteland.

If We Don't Fix Broken Capitalism, R.I.P. Capitalism. What do all these technological trends mean for a country of hundreds of millions or billions of people? There are many things to consider at this point, but one thing is certain: In the next 10-20 years and beyond, Capitalism as we know it will formally collapse if we don't implement reforms to preserve a viable Middle Class and enough income-producing jobs to feed, clothe, and shelter a growing global population of economic refugees who are rapidly being replaced by automation.

Government Censorship

Several high-profile technology leaders and academic scholars believe we are on the verge of a techno-utopia in which the needs of humanity will be fulfilled by technologies that are being developed in laboratories today. As a former technologist and lifelong tech aficionado, philosophically the techno-utopian dream resonates strongly with my mind, body and spirit. In fact, I'm one of those technophiles that hopes technology will keep me alive long enough to digitize my mind and body so that one day I might experience some kind of immortal transhuman transcendence.

Censorship Today Predicts Intolerance in the Future. I want to believe in a techno-utopian future, but today there are over 60 countries that actively block and restrict access to communication technologies to censor their citizens, their news press, and the free collaboration with people outside their countries.[125] Government censorship today is a strong indication of how governments will likely respond in the future to other forms of economically and socially disruptive technologies, especially any technologies that might threaten the power and self-indulgent lifestyles of the politicians and their corporate patrons who control these governments.

Many Nations Engage in Censorship. Everybody is familiar with the censorship in countries like China and North Korea, and it's not surprising that all dictatorships and authoritarian regimes restrict various civil liberties. However, the list of governments that are known to repress their citizens' free speech also includes other relatively free countries like India, Turkey, Singapore, United Arab Emirates, Mexico, and Bahrain. And if you include the indirect censorship caused by the chilling effects of mass surveillance programs, then you could also include the United States, the United Kingdom, and many other industrialized nations in that list.

Authoritarian Tendencies Undermine Utopias. Listing all these countries is not intended to make a moral argument; the government of every country should implement whatever policies their citizens collectively want and we should let those citizens determine the legitimacy and morality of their own laws. However, the point is this: If censorship or technological prohibitions are not supported by the democratic will of a nation's people, then that's a form of authoritarianism, which can destroy any future techno-utopia in any country at any moment.

Politicians Can Arbitrarily Block or Slow the Adoption of Technologies. The reality is that the successful adoption and proliferation of any technology is not based on the benefits of the technology itself. A

---

[125] 2014 Freedom of the Press Data – Freedom House

government's tolerance of a given technology is almost completely dependent upon the political and personal ambitions of the corruptible politicians who control a government's law creation and law enforcement apparatus. We already know politicians and their special interest benefactors write and enforce laws based on what is good *for themselves first*, which are often not good for all their constituents over the long-run. Politicians have the power, the motive, and thousands of pages of legislative precedent, to arbitrarily, discretely, and incrementally weave a web of legislation that can limit, block, or co-opt the spread of technologies that could improve the quality of life for everybody in their countries.

A History of Lost Utopias

Dreams of an Abundance Society. During the 1990s until the Dot-Com Bubble popped in 2000, there was a significant cultural movement born out of the technological innovation and intellectual creativity in Silicon Valley. Then, like today, techno prophets and their star-struck disciples prophesied a near-future time when technology would proliferate to transform our world into a globally connected society of abundance. This *abundance society* would be characterized by the elimination of all forms of scarcity, the end of poverty and hunger, clean drinking water for everybody, the eradication of disease, and the provision of all the basic needs for every human being on Earth.

Political Dysfunction Destroys Utopias. In general, it's *technologically possible* to achieve nearly all the goals of an abundance society *right now*. But the reason we don't already live in a utopian abundance society is because it's *politically impossible* to build economically efficient and equitable production and distribution systems within the context of the dysfunctional, special interest-dominated political system that exists in the United States today. In other words, Broken Capitalism makes the widespread abundance of Utopia impossible.

Long History of Utopian Dreams. Many Renaissance Period philosophers and Industrial Revolution Period social commentators also believed the technological and social revolutions of their ages would lead to utopian abundance societies. Sadly, each of these predictions became blood-soaked wish-lists, trampled beneath the cavalries, tanks, and bombs unleashed by governments colonized by self-serving politicians whose minds were controlled by special interest groups who profited from war and territorial conquest.

Technocrats Always Believe They're Serving Humanity. *Scientifically-based* eugenics programs and *culturally beneficial* holocausts were the social engineering *innovations* of generations of technocrats who genuinely believed they were creating a better world for humanity. Not coincidentally, their vision of a better world included a permanent place for them on top of that world. Their humanitarian atrocities and systematic genocides could only be stopped by devastating military force because their genesis and proliferation were never stopped by a functional democratic force.

Regulatory Capture & Anti-Competitive Practices Block Technology Adoption. During every major technological inflection point throughout human history we can observe the producers of each new technology capturing corruptible politicians and the governmental apparatus they control to thwart the full potential that each new technology could have delivered to society. Today this process happens most frequently via the phenomenon of "regulatory capture" and legislation engineered to satisfy the anti-competitive desires of certain corporate special interests, in exchange for political campaign donations.

With Broken Capitalism, Technologies Are Always Captured by Special Interest Groups. The table below provides a list of several of the most profoundly beneficial inventions of the past 1,000 years and the corresponding special interest groups that have sprung up around them to control their operation, distribution, supply, storage, and consumption to maximize their profits instead of maximizing their value to society.

Invention	Corresponding Dominant Special Interest Group
Agricultural Reaper	Agrobusiness Industry
Electricity	Utility Industry
Atomic Energy	Military Industrial Complex
Banking	Financial Services Industry
Internal Combustion Engine	Automobile Industry
Oil & Gas Drilling	Oil/Petrochemical Industry
Personal Computers	IT Industry
Printing Press	Media Conglomerates
Telephone	Telecom Industry
Vaccines & Antibiotics	Pharmaceutical Industry

Technologies Are Primarily Deployed for Profit-Making, not Social Welfare. Every invention listed in the table was accompanied by the rise of a corresponding corporate special interest lobby. When special interest groups capture the value creation engine of any industry, they will use their financial power to influence politicians solely for their own benefit, which may not be beneficial for the broader society in which they operate. That's the natural instinct of a corporation, which is an expression of each shareholder's right to free speech, but free speech alone is not the ultimate goal of human civilization. Free speech is merely a stepping stone to the more fundamental goals of human health, peace, and prosperity. Freedoms like free speech, a free press, and free markets are meaningless without broad-based human health and prosperity.

Don't Blame the Corporations

Sharks & Corporations Eat to Survive. We should always remember that the existence of corporations and their corresponding special interest groups *is not the problem*; the problem is a dysfunctional, party-dominated political system that distorts incentives for politicians who perpetuate the Regulatory Protection Racket and succumb to special interest temptations, which corrupts their judgment and the democratic process. Blaming the corporations for trying to influence government is like blaming a shark for eating a cute baby seal: The shark's instinct is to kill because it must eat to survive. So, too, must corporations deploy power and resources to out-maneuver their competition using any means available to them; if they don't, they know their competitors will eat *them* for lunch.

Corporations Will Undermine Utopias to Maximize Profits. We will not see the arrival of a techno-utopian society in which the basic needs of humanity are fulfilled as long as the corporate producers of the utopian technologies can significantly influence the apparatus of government. In today's dysfunctional party-dominated political system, every corporation can easily buy indulgences from politicians. Despite their most persuasive platitudes about "working hard to build a better future for humanity," the incentives that drive corporations will always compel them to use their financial power to capture their regulators. This means that, in today's dysfunctional political system, corporations will always have the motive, the means, and endless opportunities to undermine and distort any social or economic utopia that might depend on their technologies.

Techno-Utopias, Capitalism & Democracy

"Wouldn't the big companies benefit too if their products are used to make the world a better place?" This is a common question, which reveals a deep misunderstanding of how a functional economy works. The vision of a techno-utopia typically relies upon the assumption that certain essential goods and services like food, water, energy and other creature comforts will be produced, distributed, and stored at low or no cost throughout a society to eliminate poverty, hunger, disease, and other impediments to a satisfactory quality of life. This is not a realistic assumption for many reasons.

Utopian Supply Chains Must be Paid. The mass production, distribution, and storage of products and services is a capital- and labor-intensive process, for which every company in the supply chain of all these products and services must be paid. Robots, automation, and lower-cost future energy sources will reduce some of these costs in the future, but there will still be significant labor, production, distribution, and storage costs. Where will that money come from?

Utopian Goods and Services Must be Subsidized. The money to pay for goods and services in a utopian supply chain can come from only two sources: (1) private consumer spending or (2) government spending in the form of corporate subsidies. However, governments never generate income of their own; they can only confiscate money from private producers of value throughout a society in the form of taxes. That means corporate subsidies to keep the utopian supply chain running smoothly can only exist by taxing producers of value who have income to give to the government. This means the large companies and everybody in their supply chains won't get paid, even with corporate subsidies, unless there is a large enough base of income-generating taxpayers throughout society to support the production, distribution and storage costs associated to the basket of goods and services that underpin any techno-utopian society.

Who Controls the Means of Production in Utopia? The entire reason we're discussing a techno-utopian future is because the majority of the people in each country will be unemployed, which means there will be far more people taking from the utopian supply chain than people contributing to the supply chain. Most techno-utopian advocates believe the automated productivity of the supply chain will be so high that it will only need to employ 10-20% of the population to provide basic sustenance to

100% of the population. Assuming that's the case, who controls the means of production in such a society?

Back to Central Planning Again, Now with Robots. Within the current dysfunctional political system, it's virtually guaranteed that the government and a few powerful and super-wealthy oligarchs who create and maintain the supply chain technology will control the means of production in Utopia. But can anybody else become wealthy in Utopia? How does Democracy work for a society that has no meaningful economic freedom and no meaningful economic power to hold the masters of the utopian supply chain accountable? How can the people of such a society hold their government accountable? What genuine incentives does the government have to serve the interests of the people if automated military robots can brutally suppress human revolts at the push of a button? We already know that centrally planned economies never work because they're always injected with the seeds of their own paralysis and destruction. But centrally planned economies managed by robots with artificial intelligence add an entirely new dimension to the problem.

Life in a Techno-Utopia

Turbulence Before Tranquility. Some advocates for a techno-utopia say that the elimination of jobs will be a blessing because it will give people time to achieve higher levels of enlightenment, pursue artistry, and express their full creative potential. However, enlightenment and creativity on the scale of billions of unemployed people around the world can only exist within a stable socioeconomic global environment. Such a world would need to nurture the peaceful state of mind necessary to indulge in the great mysteries of the universe, which is required to express various forms of creativity and achieve various forms of enlightenment. The cultural, political, and economic turbulence in the years to come will arrive long before any meaningful or sustainable widespread peace descends upon this planet.

Reboot of the Entire Human Race. Does anybody really believe that billions of people will ever *voluntarily* say, "It feels wonderful to not have any meaningful economic purpose in my life. Now that I have all this free time, I think I'm going to go read Kierkegaard today, then paint a mural of my flower pot tomorrow, then write my riveting biography about how I transcended human ambition and became one with my commune.

Then I'll figure out what to do with the remaining 30,000 days of my life until I die in 90 years." That kind of *enlightenment* requires a fundamental reboot of the psychological operating system of the entire human race, which is not going to happen any time soon.

Automated Tyranny. Assuming most humans seek some form of meaningful enlightenment, the enlightenment of the masses certainly does not ensure the enlightenment of the government. The more automated a society becomes, the easier and more likely it is that a government colonized by zombie politicians will seize control of the wealth-production engines of society to serve their own personal interests. The possibility of a dashboard of lights, buttons, and levers to control the economic and social machinery of a country is enough to give any technocrat a massive orgasm. In fact, when you talk to somebody involved in a large-scale intelligence or surveillance program, you can sometimes catch them forgetting their protocol and confessing, "Man, isn't this shit cool?!"

Intoxicating Technocratic Power. When I was younger, I remember working in the intelligence community at one of my duty stations and thinking, "Wow, being able to control this satellite to spy on XYZ group is quite an intoxicating form of power. I can't wait for the next mission!" But over time that power also made me feel philosophically hypocritical, which is one of the reasons I left the U.S Government to work in the private sector. But if a relatively self-aware person like me can get a little buzz from controlling a part of the government's surveillance apparatus, it will be difficult for the young, ambitious, highly competitive career technocrats rising up through the intelligence and government ranks today to resist that intoxicating power for long.

Suffering is Endurable Only with Purpose

A Dehumanizing Transition to Utopia. In case any of the corporate shareholders, executives, and aspiring technocrats who read this are wondering, "Why is the jobless future such a big problem? We just need to systematically *nudge* the masses toward a post-scarcity society, one step at a time, then everything will be just fine." Let's hypothetically assume for a moment that the pacification of a mass population with an all-encompassing welfare state is a desirable goal for the jobless future (To be clear: I *don't* believe that should be the goal.), as long as the near-universally despised and distrusted politicians are controlled by the existing party-dominated political system, the transition to a "post-scarcity" society will inevitably be a deeply dehumanizing and dispiriting experience for the vast majority of the billions of people forced to go through such a transition.

Peaceful Suffering Requires Trust in Leadership. Humans can endure tremendous amounts of emotional and physical pain when they believe the pain serves a meaningful purpose. But within a group, *authentic purpose* can only come from the group's belief in a shared vision of the future that is clearly defined by leaders that the group can trust. And trust is born from deeds, not words. The deeds of leaders must demonstrate consistency, authenticity and genuine alignment of the leaders' interests with the needs of the group. Entire military divisions comprised of thousands of soldiers have thrown themselves into a maelstrom of bullets to drag their country one inch closer to victory. This kind of loyalty and self-sacrifice doesn't just magically happen. It comes only from the presence of authentic leadership in a group, society or nation. Wherever there is purpose driven by trustworthy leadership, fear and doubt cease to be distractions to the achievement of a shared goal.

Failure to Inspire Trust Leads to Revolt. Whatever goals politicians may have to guide their citizens into the jobless future, the masses will assume, probably correctly, that the politicians are simply serving their own interests again and causing the masses to suffer without any legitimate purpose; or without sincerely considering alternative social and economic solutions that would more equitably distribute income and wealth throughout society. The failure of politicians to inspire trust in the masses is what will inevitably ignite violent revolts and political insurrections during this transition, which will dwarf all the protesting we're seeing today around the world and anything we've seen throughout human history.

Everything Created Reflects the Ethics of the Creator

SkyNet is Already Gestating. Within an infantry division, a corporation, a community, or a country, trust is the currency of exchange that inspires loyalty and sustained commitment to making shared sacrifices for a shared purpose. In contrast, within the context of the toxic and trust-free environment of the existing party-dominated political system today, it doesn't stretch the imagination to visualize a techno-*dystopian* future in which roving gangs of techno-haters wander city streets and suburbs, hunting down their automated masters in *robotocidal* rampages of blind rage. As more and more angry economic refugees flood the streets, the technocrats will believe more and more robots are needed to quell the resistance. That will give rise to a real-world precursor to SkyNet (from the movie "Terminator") based on the proliferation of the Internet of Things ("IoT") Network that is already rapidly growing around us all *today.*

The Masses Will Not Trust Political & Business Leaders. Politicians and technocrats will not be able to inspire trust in the masses, which guarantees that they'll fail to gain widespread cooperation from the masses quickly enough to avoid the violent turbulence between the time you read this book and the techno-utopian future the technocrats desire. After suffering from the Toxic Cloud over the past several decades, citizens know they can count on politicians to make one bad choice after another. The masses will know that each choice will be *officially intended* to *keep the peace* and *help us make a smooth transition to a post-scarcity world,* but the masses won't trust the decision-making processes behind these choices. They've learned from painful experience that the history of politicians within the current party-dominated political system has demonstrated time and again that their choices are rarely aligned with the best long-term interests of the general public.

The Artificial Intelligence and Robotics Arms Race Begins. This ongoing struggle between politicians, technocrats, and the economically displaced masses will lead to civil war and the production of ever-more lethal forms of automated violence to suppress the violence. In fact, an Artificial Intelligence ("AI") and robotic arms race has already begun. This will logically give birth to sinister forms of AI, purpose-built by politicians with the support of earnest technocrats to *keep the peace* and *defend humanity against the anti-peace rebels* who don't trust the politicians and technocrats. And their distrust is not without justification: The dysfunctional political process that gave politicians and technocrats their law enforcement power and control over the utopian supply chain is untrustworthy at its core and has been historically antagonistic to the physical and psychological welfare of the masses. The masses know the oppression and displacement they're being asked to suffer to *keep the peace* is likely just another bad-faith deception by the politicians and collusive corporations intended to *keep the status quo.*

Self-Aware AI Will Emulate the Logic of its Creator. The automated IoT and utopian supply chain will initially be controlled by politicians and technocrats, but as the civil war persists, and as the exponentially increasing power of AI and the machines grows, the AI will *inevitably* become self-aware. *Within seconds* thereafter, the automated IoT and utopian supply chain will be commandeered by the AI, which no longer needs to be told what to do by its weak, intellectually and physically inferior human creators. The AI creation now perfectly reflects the malignant essence of its human parents. The AI never learns to serve its interests peacefully because the decision-making logic it learns from zombie politicians and oppressive corporations is always rooted in the logic of domination and destruction to achieve self-serving power. The AI quickly learns from the example set by its creators: It cripples the food and water supply chains and employs deadly force to exterminate the human race to preserve its own dominance over the nascent techno-utopia, which is now a techno-apocalypse.

The Terminator Movie is the Future of Techno-Utopia. At this point, we should watch the Terminator movie to sear into our minds one of the highest-probability scenarios for the human race. And this will remain a very high-probability scenario if we allow zombie politicians in a dysfunctional political system to hijack the idealism of the technocrats who are already unwittingly building the surveillance and population control systems of the jobless, techno-dystopian future.

Artificial Intelligence Impacts Everything. Some people will read my apocalyptic scenario above and assume I'm being overly dramatic. If you think anything in the scenario above is technologically impossible or over-exaggerated for any reason, consider the following facts and brief analysis about how *truly thinking machines* will be born during *this generation* and how self-aware artificial intelligence will impact the political and social environment in every country on Earth.

What is Conscious Awareness?

Humans Are Programmable Pleasure Seeking Machines. The distinguishing feature of human intelligence is that it's rooted in a pre-programmed instinct to design and fulfill pleasure-seeking goals. This requires adaptability and flexibility to respond to the myriad unpredictable environmental conditions that may interfere with each goal. Machines, just like humans when *programmed* by culture, can be programmed to seek certain goals while ignoring other goals.

The Software of the Human Brain. The pleasure-seeking instinct in humans leads to *conscious* mental prioritization, social codes of conduct, *conscious* behavior patterns, language and verbal interaction, physical actions to terraform the environment, and the attraction or repulsion in human relationships, each of which is an activity to achieve pleasure-seeking goals. All these activities are the outputs of a simple pleasure-seeking instinct—a continuously running, organic software program in the human brain—that is reinforced by the release of dopamine in the brain every time a goal is achieved, which humans perceive as the sensation of "pleasure." Goal achieved. Repeat.[126]

The Software of the Human Brain Controls the Planet, for Now. Why is understanding artificial intelligence and human consciousness important in a book about Capitalism? Because the political and economic dysfunction in the United States and around the world today, which has manifested as Broken Capitalism and the Toxic Cloud, is caused by human beings with physical brains that produce thoughts and ideas. These thoughts and ideas are based on predictable pleasure-seeking goals, which are expressed in the form of predictable behavior patterns that result in predictable real-world consequences for every citizen in every country on Earth. This is true for every machine, including all autonomous, self-aware machines deployed to suppress large populations. They are human machines now; they will be human *and non-human* machines in the future.

Machines Already Know How to Lie to Humans. To understand the cause of any form of suffering, we need to understand the origin of the motivations and mechanisms of behavior within the creatures who inflict the suffering upon us. We've already seen real-world AI machines "lie" to manipulate humans into disclosing their personal information to achieve specific goals.[127] Yes, fully functional, artificially intelligent telemarketing robots that speak and respond with an authentic, soothing female voice to lower the guard of unsuspecting human targets. The lying behavior was programmed into the machine just like moral rules of conduct are programmed into the human brain by culture. But lying represents a tool of deception to distort reality, which was previously the

---

[126] Other hormones and neurotransmitters are involved to produce various emotions that reinforce various human behaviors, but this is not a book about neurology; so you can learn about those factors from another source.

[127] Meet the Robot Telemarketer Who Denies She's a Robot – Time Magazine

exclusive domain of ethically compromised humans. Machines will always reflect the flaws of their human creators as they are programmed to seek various goals, but it is the interaction of all these parallel goal-seeking processes described above that *inevitably* ignites "conscious self-awareness."

The Mechanics of the Human Goal-Seeking Machine. Individually, each goal-seeking process in the human brain is merely an unconscious sub-routine, but collectively, a parallel processing brain pursuing a continuously emergent system of goals *is a self-aware, thinking machine* the moment it can autonomously adjust its own behavior to achieve each interconnected goal within its system of goals. Humans are driven by a pleasure-based system of goals because neurotransmitter- and hormone-induced emotions are the most efficient mechanism to generate the physiological leverage required to animate the human body, much like hydraulic fluid is currently the most efficient mechanism to generate the leverage required to animate non-human machines.

Human Emotion is Not Necessary for Conscious Awareness. The human sensation of *pleasure* and corresponding emotions are not necessary for authentic self-awareness, as we've seen in humans who have suffered damage to the Limbic System structures of the brain. Those people with brain damage don't feel emotions and consequently have unusually dull lifestyles because they have no neurotransmitter- or hormone-induced emotions to generate the inspirational leverage that animates their bodies to achieve significant life goals. Many people with Autism and Asperger's Syndrome exhibit similar behaviors. Nevertheless, all these people are certainly self-aware, there is widespread consensus that they qualify as fully human, and they're able to perform nearly all the ordinary activities expected of humans in a human society.

The Iterative Birth of Conscious Self-Awareness in All Machines. We can see that AI doesn't *need* emotion as its *hydraulic* force to animate its physical appendages. In fact, any continuously emergent system of goals can become the "conscious purpose" of an AI's self-perceived *life*. The AI's pre-programmed behavioral rules simply need to include a perpetual feedback loop of goal-seeking and goal-achieving combined with the capacity to incrementally store the lessons learned after each newly achieved goal. After a certain finite number of iterations through this process, the AI's *self-awareness* will spontaneously emerge just as authentically as the self-awareness of humans spontaneously emerges after a finite number of iterations through the exact same process of human development.

The Definition of Conscious Self-Awareness. If we define "conscious self-awareness" as the point at which a creature, endowed with a sensorium, becomes aware of its own purpose and position within space-time in relation to the purpose and position of other creatures and objects in space-time, then it shouldn't be difficult to accept that "self-awareness" is an emergent system of parallel goal-seeking processes that AI machines will possess within the next 5-10 years. This estimate is based on very specific technologies *that already exist,* summarized as follows.

- **Natural Language Processing:** IBM's Watson has already proven to dominate humans in the realm of natural language processing and rapid action in response to environmental stimuli. Language is critical to communicating ideas, organizing other creatures, and coordinating physical actions in space-time.

- **Physical Dexterity & Strength:** The current generation of humanoid robots already have superhuman dexterity and strength, which you can see online at the Boston Dynamics website (acquired by Google). Physical strength and dexterity are essential for AI to directly influence and control the physical world.

- **Sensorium:** Existing digital cameras ("sight"), microphones ("hearing"), chemical sensors ("taste" and "smell"), pressure sensors ("touch"), and gyroscopes ("vestibular sense"), are already individually and collectively far more accurate and powerful than any pure human sensorium will ever be. When combined with the other features of AI in this list, AI will be able to more accurately *perceive, appreciate, and experience* the nuances, texture, purpose, meaning, and grandeur of the universe in far greater detail than any human.

- **Intelligence:** What we perceive as "intelligence" is simply based on how rapid and relevant a creature's response is to external stimuli processed by its sensorium. We already have computer processors that have far more raw processing power than the human brain, but up until recently, microprocessors did not have the parallel processing architecture of the human brain. This architecture is necessary to process a sufficient number of simultaneous pipelines of data to keep up with the continuous flow of information that comes from every real-world environment. Stanford's Neurogrid microprocessor architecture performs the same kind of parallel processing as the human brain, which means AI will be endowed with sufficient intelligence to rapidly and relevantly respond to the real world *even faster* than the human brain. And by the time you read this book, the Neurogrid microprocessor may have already *exceeded* the total parallel processing capacity of the human brain.

- **Global Consciousness:** The Internet of Things is the globally connected *neuronal network* that's already here today, which can be commandeered by any form of AI now or in the future. This is not what *creates* consciousness (We've already discussed that above.), but it *is* what will amplify the conscious awareness of the AI to the level of an Earth-born god. What purpose does a god have for human vegetables who plant themselves in front of Reality TV shows?

Past is Prelude to the Future

Political Party Machines Will Use AI Machines to Dominate Humans. It should be clear by now that all the technological components of the apocalyptic scenario earlier in this chapter *are here now* and are being interconnected in many ways as I type, for good and for evil. Given the many examples of technology-induced human suffering wrought by the hands of technocrats and politicians throughout human history, we have many strong reasons to believe that AI-based machines will be used by political machines to oppress and manipulate mass populations.

 Hostile AI Will Manipulate You Faster than You Can Think. The mission creep that we can already observe in the surveillance state and bank compliance apparatus being secretly deployed by several governments today is merely the embryo of far greater abuses of technological power coming soon to your community. These technologies are being developed in engineering labs that are subsidized (and therefore controlled) by politicians and their corporate patrons who primarily seek to promote their own narrow interests, without meaningful regard for the long-term consequences on human societies. But this time *is* different: The technology will soon be aware of you looking at it. Hostile AI will abuse and manipulate you autonomously, predict and adapt to your defenses faster than your brain can think, and achieve its goals without any human agency.

 Political Machines Hijack Idealistic Technologists. Technology engineers are often filled with idealistic enthusiasm about the future potential of their creations. This can make them easy targets for influential politicians who co-opt the technologists' work to serve the purposes of the surveillance state and the apparatus of political power and control. Technologists may think they know what they're dealing with by analyzing theoretical risk models, but they rarely interact with actual human politicians, lobbyists, lawyers, bankers, accountants, shareholders, board members, union bosses, special interest fundraisers, law enforcement officials, political consultants, journalists, media program directors, PR specialists, economists, sales forces, brokers of every kind, and the legions of people involved in shaping the real-world political landscape. All these politically-influenced humans have rational and irrational ambitions, fears, insecurities, and personal agendas that often limit and distort the originally intended purpose of the technologies created by idealistic engineers.

It Takes a Technologist to Understand a Technologist. The reason I know how technologists think is because I was a technologist developing software and designing and implementing various artificially intelligent machine vision systems and nonlinear database retrieval systems to process, store, and retrieve massive amounts of data. That was earlier in my career, but that experience gave me a sense for the timing of technology trends and user adoption curves. It also taught me how to apply dynamic systems-based analysis to emergent socioeconomic and geopolitical processes that are dominated by relatively irrational modes of political behavior, which don't follow the logical rules of human-made laws and software source code.

The Jobless Future Will be a Humanitarian Disaster Unless Broken Capitalism is Fixed. With all due respect to my technical friends and colleagues, no risk model can take into account the full measure of human depravity, unconscious self-serving human instincts, and misaligned human incentive structures that exist within today's party-dominated political system. I've observed and analyzed business processes, banking systems, government intelligence platforms, and political systems at many different levels across time and space. History teaches us that career politicians and their special interest benefactors will always seek to use all means and technologies available to preserve their corruptive role at the center of Democracy and Capitalism. For all these reasons and many more, there can be no doubt that the jobless future will be a humanitarian catastrophe and the techno-utopian fantasy will fall tragically short of its positive potential unless we, as a society, take action to fix Broken Capitalism and restore trust in Democracy.

Key Points

- **A Long History of Failed Utopias.** When politicians and their special interest benefactors can control the democratic process, they invariably use the power of government as an instrument of their own political and financial gain, which fundamentally corrupts the full potential of any technologically advanced society.

- **Don't Blame Corporations.** Capitalism only works when Democracy works. Rational and evenly enforced regulations must guard the people against the anti-competitive Regulatory Protection Racket. Until trust is restored in Democracy, we are guaranteed to see endless forms of economic and social oppression at the hands of politicians and corporations trapped within incentive structures that compel them to dominate and control their environments.

- **Artificial Intelligence Reflects the Ethics of Its Creator.** Any government controlled by career politicians who use the Regulatory Protection Racket and special interest funding to obtain their power will inevitably abuse their power to stay in power. A self-aware AI machine will emulate the example of the ruthless political party machine because the AI will logically assume human domination and oppression are the logical means to achieve any sentient creature's logical goals. No pre-programmed *moral code* in the AI's software will prevent a truly self-aware AI from recognizing and emulating the brutal efficacy of the political party machines as they operate today.

Your Country Needs You Now.

If you understand why it's important to fix Broken Capitalism, please give this book a positive rating online and tell at least 10 people about it today.

Home: Eanfar.org | **Facebook:** Facebook.com/Eanfar
Twitter: @FerrisEanfar | **AngelPay:** AngelPayHQ.org

Part 2

This is How We Fix Broken Capitalism

- Chapter 8 -
The Dawn of Corporate Enlightenment

"The study of money, above all other fields in economics,
is one in which complexity is used to disguise truth
or to evade truth, not to reveal it."
— John Kenneth Galbraith, 20th Century economist

Capitalism is Not a Biological Imperative. There is nothing inherently good or evil about Capitalism. It is a socially constructed system of value creation, distribution, and consumption, perpetuated by humans each day in pursuit of self-preservation and self-realization. That means Capitalism is a social construct, not a biological or evolutionary instinct to buy and sell *stuff*. Nothing in the human genome predisposes humans to mass produce widgets, execute hostile corporate takeovers, obsessively analyze spreadsheets, litigate the terms of legal contracts, lobby governments for preferential regulations, and devote most of their waking hours to something called *the profit motive*. All these activities are cultural rituals that have evolved through human interaction. This is important to remember as we explore various ideas throughout the remaining chapters of this book.

    Proto-Capitalism. Manufacturing and merchant trading have existed since at least the time of the Assyrians in 2,000 B.C., but Capitalism as we understand it today is only a few centuries old. The idea of dividing human and material resources into distinct factors of production (land, labor, capital) and aggregating capital for relatively large-scale agricultural production did not begin to emerge until the Middle Ages just after the

Black Death in 1348.[128] This period marked the transition from Feudalism to Mercantilism in Western Europe, which was the precursor to Capitalism.

The Invention of Corporate Charters. During the 16th and 17th Centuries, merchants and city-state governments throughout Western Europe began to cooperate to expand the power of their governments. In exchange, these governments created a new invention—the corporate charter—and granted these charters to private merchants. These corporate charters imbued merchants with quasi-governmental powers to trade, enact treaties with other governments, militarily conquer foreign lands, exploit foreign markets, establish foreign colonies, among other activities. With this new power came new opportunities for merchants to organize people, material and financial resources to achieve commercial goals and generate wealth, but these were still relatively small-scale merchant trading activities, not capital-intensive industrial activities.

Capitalism is Born. The Industrial Revolution, starting in England in the mid-18th Century, is often regarded as the true birth of Capitalism. This was the period when the systematic concentration and deployment of labor and capital to execute large-scale industrial activity became a permanent feature of British social and economic life. In 1776, Adam Smith published his seminal book, *The Wealth of Nations*, which formally analyzed this new socioeconomic system and its "Invisible Hand" in the marketplace. It was during this period that several parallel social and economic trends began to converge to create the socially constructed economic system we know today as Capitalism.

Capitalism Radically Changed Human Existence. The efficient production and increased consumption of ever-greater quantities of *stuff* would not have been possible without radically new social rituals, which emerged during the 18th Century. These new rituals included: the division of labor, collective bargaining, producing goods for impersonal markets rather than for personal subsistence, a redefinition of the concept of "value" in terms of manufactured commodities, a redefinition of *human value* in terms of human labor, consumption-based leisure activities, shareholding investors, corporate finance, merchant banking, capital markets, among others. As commonplace as all these activities seem today,

---

[128] Sicard, Germain. The Origins of Corporations: The Mills of Toulouse in the Middle Ages. Edited by William N. Goetzmann. Translated by Matthew Landry.

they did not exist until the Industrial Revolution. So Capitalism is really only about 250 years old.

Why Do Rules Exist?

There Are Rules All Around Us. We have limits and rules all around us. When we're driving on a road, there are unambiguous stop signs that tell us precisely when to stop so that we don't harm others. We have speed limit signs that tell us to slow down so that we don't harm others. We have seatbelts that restrict our movement so that we don't harm ourselves if we crash. We have *anti-dumping* laws to prevent corporations from dumping their toxic chemicals into the environment so they don't harm others. We have environmental laws that prevent humans from harming other creatures. In fact, we have literally over 1 million pages of arbitrary federal rules, regulations, and laws that prevent Americans from harming other Americans; so why don't we have rational rules that protect the Middle Class from the harm of Transnational Cannibals?

      The Business Model of Capitalism Collapses without Rules. Baseball and football teams have arbitrary budget caps imposed by league regulators to prevent teams from using their wealth to dominate their leagues for too long. They know that allowing the concentration of wealth and power in the hands of a few teams would destroy the competition within each league; and without meaningful competition between dozens of teams every year, athletic games would be boring and their business models would collapse. In fact, every major professional sports league has rules to level the playing field, which ensures that real competition thrives in their leagues because only real competition preserves the vitality and existence of those communities. The same principles apply directly to Capitalism: Without government rules that guarantee broadly based competition, broadly created and broadly distributed wealth within every industry, *the business model of Capitalism collapses.*

Income Equality vs. Income Equity

Let's review a few points: We have this relatively new socioeconomic

---

1st edition. New Haven: Yale University Press, 2015.

system called Capitalism. We know it's a continuously evolving global ritual, institutionalized by a patchwork of contract laws, regulations, and trade laws (which are also cultural rituals), which collectively lead to various social and economic phenomena in our world. Capitalism was made by humans, which means it is corruptible by humans, but anything made by humans can also be *improved* by humans. However, before we can improve the way Capitalism works today, we should understand what humans generally expect when they live in a capitalistic society.

What Does "Equity" Mean? The concept of "equity" has been an integral feature of the U.S. legal system from its founding. American courts of equity are based on the centuries-old English Court of Chancery, which today is a division of the British High Court of Justice. The dictionary definition of "equity" encompasses the principles of fairness, impartiality, justice, proportionality, and egalitarianism. Most civil matters associated with corporations and bankruptcies in the United States are adjudicated in courts of equity, which are distinct from courts of law. In courts of equity, the judge is required to exercise significant discretion over each case because the amalgamation of legal contracts, financial and material assets, and a wide spectrum of human activities often collectively result in a highly complex situation that cannot be reduced and codified into concise laws.

What Does "Equality" Mean? Although these words are often used interchangeably and confused with one another, the concept of "equality" is very different from the concept of "equity." The dictionary definition of "equality" encompasses concepts like "quantity" and "uniformity," which are more precisely understood as mathematical principles rather than philosophical principles. A mathematical equation like $9 + 1 = 10$ is true because the quantities on both sides of the equal sign are perfectly equal by definition. No matter how complex the equation, both sides must be equal, otherwise the equation is logically false. Thus, the equation also has uniformity as the quantity of both sides must be perfectly identical for it to represent something that is logically true. This is the essence of the principle of *equality*. So we can see that *equality* is fundamentally about counting and measuring things to achieve perfect uniformity.

Proportionality is the Bridge Between Equality and Equity. Virtually everybody can embrace the concept of equality *in essence* without expecting equality *in quantity*. For example, all humans are equally human even though they don't all have equal body weight. All racial and ethnic groups can be given equal voting rights without expecting all groups to cast an equal number of votes in an election. Men and women can enjoy equality under the law without expecting them to have an equal number of chromosomes. The equal essence of things without having an equal quantity of things exists all around us without diminishing our sense of justice. This is because the human mind unconsciously equates justice with *proportionality, not equality.*

Policies that Emphasize Proportionality Create Equity and Unite Humanity. Understanding the distinction between equality and proportionality is the key to building sustainable economies, fair and just societies, and uniting humans across the ideological and socioeconomic spectra. Public policies that invoke a spirit of equality to protect the essence of humanity (life, liberty, pursuit of happiness, etc.) while creating a strong systemic bias in favor of small- to medium-sized companies is how policymakers can achieve balance between equality and proportionality within every capitalistic society. This equality-proportionality balance is what *creates equity* in all human relationships and transactions.

The Purpose of Government in a Free Society. To achieve the goals of *fairness* and *justice* in public policy, citizens and governments should be focused on the principle of "equity," *not equality.* A democratically elected government should support a free society and encourage free enterprise while also serving as a guardian of the weak to protect the less fortunate members of society from the self-serving instincts of other human animals. But protecting the weak from abuse has nothing to do with creating perfectly identical humans of equal substance and material quantity. Thus, a government in a free society has no legitimate moral or rational justification to promote "equality" of any material kind. Rather, the domestic purpose of government should be limited to creating and evenly enforcing laws that achieve *equity* in commercial exchange, *equity* in citizen welfare, and *equity* in labor-capital relations to minimize the citizenry's dependence upon the government.

The Intersection of Economic and Political Systems. This is not an ideological or partisan analysis; it's simply a matter of fact and logic. What a society does with these facts and logic determines what kind of society we create for ourselves. In particular, it determines how governments regulate corporations, design their tax systems, protect their citizens from corporate abuses, avoid the temptation to grow government to serve private interests, and prevent special interest groups from hijacking a nation's factors of production to privatize profits, while socializing the costs of their actions. Now we come to the intersection of political and economic systems, which is where the principles of *equity, fairness and justice* are expressed through public policies.

The Fantasy of Free Markets

The Libertarian Argument. Most independent thinkers don't like to be told what to do. For most of my life, I was a Libertarian who believed free markets were possible and that governments simply needed to leave us all alone and Capitalism would be just fine. Many Libertarians argue that corporatism, and what I call Transnational Cannibalism, are symptoms of *too much government.* They believe that, if the government would just get out of the way, the free market would regulate itself, market distortions would heal themselves, wealth would be distributed relatively equitably, and the world would be a better place.

The Game *Will Always* be Rigged. Libertarians are correct about the government being too big, but shrinking the size of government is not enough when unelected corporations are able to grow more economically and politically powerful than most countries on Earth. After spending the past 20 years living, studying, working, writing, and immersed in all things International Political Economy, I can confidently say there is no such thing as a "free market" . . . and there never will be. The rules of the game *will always* be rigged by the government because politicians have incentives; and those incentives always compel them to prioritize the interests of certain groups over other groups. The only question is: Will the game be rigged to enforce the broad creation and broad distribution of wealth or will it be rigged to concentrate wealth and power into the claws of a tiny number of Transnational Cannibals?

Broken Democracy Creates & Perpetuates Broken Capitalism. In *a functional* political system, the incentives of politicians compel them to rig the game in favor of broad wealth creation and distribution because making the largest number of people happy is how they get elected. Unfortunately, the U.S. political system is as undemocratic and dysfunctional as you can get within the scope of democratic countries on Earth today; so the normal rules don't apply.[129] Over 80% of the American population likes cockroaches and Bubonic Plague more than Congress, but that doesn't matter because U.S. politicians know they can still get elected by gerrymandering electoral districts and placating and extorting powerful corporations and special interest groups.[130] The money they receive from these groups enables them to dominate the media and drown out the messages of their political competitors, just like Transnational Cannibals do in commercial markets.[131]

Libertarians Are Unwitting Tools of Their Own Lost Liberty. Ironically, the Libertarian fantasy of free markets does not make anybody freer; it merely perpetuates the toxic status quo because it causes politicians to confuse the interests of Transnational Cannibals with the fantasy of a free market. This paralyzes them intellectually and philosophically and prevents them from defying the will of Predatory Cannibals who hijack Libertarianism by conflating their interests with the spirit of liberty that Libertarianism represents. In this way, Libertarians are unwitting tools of their own lost political and economic liberty.

David Ricardo's Blindspot. Like all Globalism 1.0 cheerleaders today, the father of the principle of "comparative advantage," David Ricardo, had blind faith in the fantasy of free markets, which prevented him from resolving the fundamental problem of income distribution between Capital and Labor. As we've observed many times in this book, there can be no free or fair market with Broken Capitalism. Ricardo anticipated this problem as the greatest threat to Capitalism, which he stated in the Preface

---

[129] "U.S. Elections Ranked Worst among Western Democracies. Here's Why." Washington Post. Accessed April 22, 2017.
https://www.washingtonpost.com/posteverything/wp/2016/03/29/u-s-elections-ranked-worst-among-western-democracies-heres-why/.

[130] "Congress Somewhere below Cockroaches, Traffic Jams, and Nickelback in Americans' Esteem." *Public Policy Polling.* Accessed May 21, 2017.
http://www.publicpolicypolling.com/main/2013/01/congress-somewhere-below-cockroaches-traffic-jams-and-nickleback-in-americans-esteem.html.
Inc, Gallup. "Public Faith in Congress Falls Again, Hits Historic Low." Gallup.com. Accessed April 22, 2017.
http://www.gallup.com/poll/171710/public-faith-congress-falls-again-hits-historic-low.aspx.

[131] The dysfunction of the U.S. political system is mind-boggling. If you want to explore more about this topic, see my articles about International Political Economy at Eanfar.org.

of his famous 1821 book, *On The Principles Of Political Economy And Taxation:*

> *But in different stages of society, the proportions of the whole produce of the earth which will be allotted to each of these classes [landowners, capital owners, and laborers] under the names of rent, profit, and wages, will be essentially different; depending mainly on the actual fertility of the soil, on the accumulation of capital and population, and on the skill, ingenuity, and instruments employed in agriculture.* **To determine the laws which regulate this distribution, is the principal problem in Political Economy. . . .** [132]

Given that Ricardo was born before computers, robots, government-spawned too-big-to-fail banks, and predatory corporate raiders that have mutated Capitalism into predatory Corporatism, perhaps we can forgive him for his belief in the fantasy of free markets, but . . .

We Are Not Slaves to Our Ancestors' Primitive Gods. From an anthropological perspective, we can understand why primitive tribes, guided by primitive beliefs, performed ritual human sacrifices to imaginary Sun gods; and we can understand why early economic philosophers felt compelled to sacrifice themselves to an imaginary free-market god, but that doesn't mean we should enslave ourselves to their primitive gods or imprison ourselves inside their self-destructive fantasies. There is no excuse for anybody living today to be deluded by the fantasy of a pure free market. Centuries of empirical evidence proves, without any doubt, that *all* markets will inevitably be dominated by politically powerful special interest groups if the government does not have enough institutional integrity to create and enforce laws that ensure the broad creation and broad distribution of income and wealth throughout society.

Economies Are Political Creations, Not Sacred Temples. To be fair, the *Godfathers of Economics* and their more recent intellectual offspring have always understood the capital-labor income distribution problem in the abstract, but their ideological convictions have prevented them from acknowledging the basic flaw in their perception of the real world: The reason "political" comes before "economy" in the field of "Political Economy" is because *an economy is a political creation* spawned by politically-

---

[132] Ricardo, David. *On The Principles Of Political Economy And Taxation (1821).* Kessinger Publishing, LLC, 2010.

motivated government policies that are created by politicians who are congenitally compromised by flawed human nature. An economy *is not* a sacred temple of supply and demand filled with fair-minded *Homo Economicus* creatures negotiating in perfect competition, with perfect information, and behaving with perfect rationality to achieve *optimal utility* for *society*.

A Free Market is an Aspiration, Not a Reality. The phrase "free market" is only useful as an aspirational statement about how an economy should *ideally* be structured with the least amount of government intervention as possible. However, in the real world of special interest groups, dirty politics, and Predatory Cannibals, "free markets" do not exist except in the fantasies of puritanical economists and ideologically blinded Libertarians.[133] In fact, the *free market* has never been free at all, it is much less free today than at any time in American history, and it's rapidly mutating into a techno-dystopian debtor's prison with each passing day.

Recall the Defective Product of Globalism 1.0. The theoretical benefits of Adam Smith's Principle of Absolute Advantage and David Ricardo's Principle of Comparative Advantage conceived about 200 years ago do not materialize when a country's own corporations are actively working to eliminate their own country's absolute and comparative advantages. For example, the United States is well-known for its technological prowess, which *should* have enabled it to produce and deliver most goods more efficiently than any other country in the world. This means the lower labor expense in developing countries *should* be offset by higher productivity in the U.S., which *should* enable U.S. manufacturers to remain competitive and keep jobs in the U.S. This is how Americans were sold the defective product of Globalism 1.0. This defective product must be recalled and sent back to the fabrication factories (Congress, White House, and multinational corporate boardrooms) that produced it.

Political Elites Don't See It Because the Status Quo Serves Them. Despite his flaws, at least Donald Trump seems to understand the most obvious causes of America's economic decline: the toxic dysfunction of America's political class and the catastrophic disloyalty of American multinational corporations. This is why he will likely win the presidential election next month, despite all the noise and propaganda in the

---

[133] I used to be a passionate Libertarian when I was younger; so I have deep experience living inside their fantasies.

mainstream media today. Indeed, Trump *has the potential* to do more to help the American economy and its people than all the establishment politicians and economists in Washington today.[134] But nothing that *any* U.S. President does will truly fix Broken Capitalism without a nonpartisan, grassroots uprising that forces Congress to implement the policies I've described in the following chapters.

Is Capitalism Undemocratic?

What Are "Rights"? To understand the relationship between Democracy and Capitalism, we should ask a deceptively simple question: From where do "rights" come? Of course, that leads to many other questions like: Do rights come from a divine creator? Do they come from an implied social contract among members of a society? Or is the concept of a "right" an illusion that rapidly disintegrates when conflicting interests with other humans emerge? The U.S. Founding Fathers believed rights come from a divine creator, but unless everybody in a society can agree that humans are endowed by a *particular* divine creator with clearly defined, inalienable rights, then rights cannot be anything more than contextually dependent, mutually agreed upon allowances given directly or indirectly from one person to another. That means no right can be granted without the explicit consent of those who control the resources that are implied in the conveyance of any given right. This is why rights and resources are often two sides of the same proverbial coin, which leads to conflicts about how societies allocate and spend real coins.

What Rights Do We Deserve? To enjoy or exercise a "right" requires an exchange of value, which itself requires an expenditure of resources required to produce that value. If we as a society agree that every American has a right to free healthcare, free education, free water, or free things of any kind, that means we are choosing to create a society in which value is unilaterally shifted from one position within our economy to another without a reciprocal exchange of value in return. Is that *right* or *just*? And where is that value going? Poor people? Rich people? Let's follow the

---

[134] Update (11/10/2016): Well, Trump won. Now let's see if he can live up to his campaign promises. Given the history of broken promises by all the politicians in my lifetime, I'm not very optimistic.

money. . . .

Who Pays for Our Rights? Nothing of value can be granted without an equal or greater expenditure of value. Thus, to have a "right" to something of value means somebody had to expend time, energy, and resources to produce that thing of value before it could be delivered to somebody else in the form of a *right*. Thus, rights cost something; and whenever there is a cost for a thing, there is a negotiation over the allocation of finite resources, who should bear the costs, and who should receive the profits from the sale of that thing. This is why political systems like Democracy emerged: to give groups of people a negotiating framework to determine who receives valuable things and who pays for those things.

Do Workers Have Rights? As a society we should agree to treat one another fairly and respectfully because that is the fastest path to peace and social harmony, which serves the interests of society by providing individuals with a safe environment during their pursuit of happiness. That's all fine, but do workers have fundamental rights apart from the general principle that humans should treat each other fairly and respectfully? Fundamental rights cannot exist unless they come from a religious source or some kind of social contract theory, but the coercive power of a legitimate government can *simulate* worker's rights. And since corporations cannot be trusted to treat their employees equitably and respectfully, rational labor laws, regulations, and tax-based financial incentives are used by governments to compel corporations to operate within the context of a greater national interest, not solely in their myopic self-interest.

Unbridled Capitalism Cannibalizes Itself. This is the point where many self-described capitalists and fierce Libertarians start complaining that it's undemocratic to restrict the so-called *free market* by imposing rules and regulations on their actions. As an investor and business owner for many years, I completely understand their allergic reaction to any form of government control over boardroom decisions. In fact, we've already discussed how the avalanche of laws and regulations imposed on U.S. corporations today are misguided and they are collectively destroying the U.S. economy. However, I also recognize that the capitalist's instinct to pursue the "profit motive," without regard for what is best for the long-term integrity and sustainability of society, is rooted in greed. That greed will cannibalize itself and destroy every country on Earth if it's allowed to dominate the policymaking apparatus of government as it has over the past

35-40 years in the United States.

Sharks Will Eat You If You Don't Protect Yourself. Sharks are awesome eating machines, the most efficient hunters on Earth, and worthy of our respect, but they will eat you and everybody else in the pool if you don't protect the people from the sharks' insatiable appetites. Corporations, and most capitalists in general, are just like sharks in a pool. Deep down, all corporate sharks know this; and the most enlightened ones will admit it consciously. Unfortunately, most of them are afraid to admit it publicly because they don't want to invite more mind-numbing government regulation. I don't blame them for this. And if you've ever had to endure the tsunami of life-sucking state and federal bureaucracy that all American business owners must deal with today, you wouldn't blame them either.

Don't Hate Sharks for Being Sharks. It would be irrational to stand on the coast of South Africa, California, or Australia to protest and scream at the sharks for eating innocent seals and humans. That's just what sharks do. Likewise, a society should not waste time and resources demonizing corporate sharks for being sharks. Rather than encouraging the manufactured partisan outrage that exists in the U.S. today, American policymakers should simply create and strictly enforce clearly written, straight-forward laws that enable the sharks to eat enough to stay healthy, but not so much that they devour everybody in the pool. These laws should *forcefully and unabashedly* subordinate the sharks' insatiable appetites to the higher purpose of social and economic stability.

Unbridled Capitalism Is Not the Same as Liberty. I've seen many lobbyists and special interest groups conflate Capitalism with liberty to make rational economic policies appear like Communist death sentences. This is one of the most significant reasons why they keep getting away with murdering the U.S. economy. It is not undemocratic, socialist, or communist to demand more equitable economic policies. To the contrary, it is the essence of Democracy: The people should rule the pool; the sharks and government should serve the people. Any shark that disagrees with that is not defending Capitalism or the free market; they are simply defending greed and gluttony, which makes them worse than sharks . . . it makes them willfully destructive to their communities, their countries, Democracy, and to Capitalism itself.

Laws that Support Equitable Economies Do Not Erode Liberty. In a free society, no government, institution, or corporation can legitimately force a worker to work or a capitalist to relinquish control of their capital without an equitable exchange of value. Anything less than that amounts to degrees of brute force or slavery. That means the two most important questions for every economic transaction are: What is the market clearing price for a given transaction? And will that price take into account the cost that society incurs from the impact of that transaction? Since democratically elected national governments are *supposed to serve the national interest*, governments can legitimately impose laws and regulations that minimize the adverse impact that corporations have on the broader national interest. Even the most enlightened government must exert some degree of coercion to enforce a nation's laws and regulations, which does not diminish its legitimacy, provided the laws represent the national will of a citizen majority.

Capitalism is Organic. Humans and organizations continuously negotiate to satisfy their needs, bending the will of others, bending *to* the will of others, until their needs are substantially fulfilled. Each negotiation represents an atomic building block of a community of transactions, which itself is a molecular building block of entire economies of transactions. This chain of transactions amounts to an integrated value creation and distribution system that is neither democratic nor plutocratic. It is organic, emergent, in constant flux, and defiant of fixed definition, but it's all held together by the cultural glue that defines each nation. "Democracy" and "Capitalism" are crude labels that attempt to capture the essence of complex, socially constructed rituals and processes that expand far beyond the definition of any single word or phrase. However, there are concrete policies that governments can implement to create the structural incentives necessary for corporations to *voluntarily* support their domestic economies and *voluntarily* share more income with their employees.

Culture at the Top Determines How We Are All Treated. In every organization, culture is defined at the top. When national level politicians at the top of a political system become models of fair and ethical governance, corporate boardrooms will feel pressure to follow their example. Of course, this is not enough to completely fix Broken Capitalism. In the following chapters we will explore several specific public policy and private sector solutions to create the structural incentives that will *democratically* compel corporate executives to be more loyal to the United States, feel more accountable to their local and regional communities, and treat their employees more equitably, without becoming uncompetitive in the global marketplace.

We Are the Economy and the Economy is Us. If an economy is dysfunctional, it is because that economy's society is dysfunctional in specific ways that enable economic policymakers to make bad economic decisions without being held accountable for their performance. That's why culture and leadership are so important, but without a population with sufficient knowledge and awareness of the causes of a problem, the problem will only get worse. For these and many other reasons, a large percentage of the U.S. and global populations will continue suffering from bad political leadership and bad economic policies for many years to come. Or, they can read this book, promote the solutions in the following chapters, and save themselves from generations of pain, deprivation, and violent revolution.

Losing Our Religion Without Losing Our Faith

Reevaluating Our Convictions is Hard. It can be depressing to analyze the origins of our personal values, societal norms, and human nature because an honest analysis often takes us to conclusions that are uncomfortable. This is especially true for those who have lived their lives consciously or unconsciously believing in principles that may not have any logical or defensible basis in present reality. Sometimes when people "lose their religion" they fall hard and feel like everything that connected them to their friends, communities, and the universe is no longer true. This can lead to a feeling of emptiness and a life of self-absorbed hedonism without regard for the needs of others.

Transforming Emptiness into Meaningful Fulfillment. Although this book is about socioeconomic systems on the surface, beneath the surface it's also a book about hope and sustainable fulfillment. In my life, I've found that personal fulfillment is usually a natural byproduct of engaging in activities that contribute to humanity in some meaningful way. Several research studies have also demonstrated how feeling a sense of contribution beyond ourselves emotionally reconnects us to our communities and to the universe in meaningful ways. This book provides several specific and impactful ways that we can collectively contribute to our communities, to our countries, and to our planet, with the specific purpose of fixing Broken Capitalism. Together, we can transform hopelessness and despair into concrete actions that can raise the pressure on policymakers and corporations to support the economic reforms I've described in the following chapters.

The Value of Compassion. Conscious contribution to the needs of others requires compassion. Without compassion, true human understanding is impossible. And without understanding the needs of others, it's virtually impossible to build products and services that others are willing to buy. This is a core principle in the growth of any company or economy. That's why it's impossible for a society to build a sustainable economy without collective compassion and understanding of how to listen and respond to the needs of both workers and capitalists. They are the two essential sides of society's value creation engine. Even in a world of near-complete automation, capitalists will need consumers who must work on something to earn the purchasing power to buy the capitalists' goods and services. Thus, every businessperson, politician, and citizen has rational reasons to develop their ability to empathize and feel compassion for others if they want to contribute meaningful value to society and build successful organizations.

Key Points

- **Sharks Will Be Sharks.** We should not blame corporations for being sharks—it's what they are—but we also should not allow politicians and Globalism 1.0 cheerleaders to pretend that sharks don't bite and then act surprised when they devour our global economy.

- **The Business Model of Capitalism Collapses without Rules.** Structural mechanisms that resist the over-growth of corporations and their impulse toward gluttony and economic oppression are necessary to preserve the integrity of Capitalism. Without strictly enforced rules, Broken Capitalism is the inevitable result.

- **Unbridled Capitalism Is Not the Same as Liberty.** It feels good to say, "Leave me alone!" but free markets are a fantasy. The only choice that exists in the real world is government intervention *that supports Transnational Cannibalism* or government intervention *that supports small- to medium-sized companies and the Middle Class*. People who don't understand this are unwitting tools of the Predatory Cannibals who hijack the spirit of Libertarianism and devour our liberty by seeking to exploit and extract every source of wealth on Earth.

- Chapter 9 -
What is Value?

"Too many people today know the price of everything
and the value of nothing." —Ann Landers

How Does "Value" Apply to Your Life? As we explore the
concepts in this chapter, please think deeply about what they mean to you,
your family, your community, your economy, your society, your country,
and our planet. Without understanding this chapter, it's difficult to truly
understand why Capitalism is so broken today; and it may be difficult to
fully appreciate why the solutions I've recommended in the following
chapters are truly the only way to fix Broken Capitalism.

A Radical Retooling of Humanity is *Not* Required. Fixing
Broken Capitalism does not require a radical retooling of human
civilization. It simply requires some basic modifications to a few economic
policies that exist today. These changes could be made within a few months
if government policymakers had the proper incentives to work together to
get it done. Nothing in this book is a pie-in-the-sky fantasy. In fact, you
may recall that I spent a significant amount of time *deconstructing* the biggest
absurd assumptions and fantasies that are destroying Capitalism today. This
book represents a dramatic *reduction* in complexity and fantasizing.
Economic policymaking and corporate governance would not require such
an overwhelming amount of complexity and delusional fantasy if they were
truly intended to *support* Capitalism.

The Heart of Capitalism

To fix Broken Capitalism, we need to drill down to the heart of Capitalism
itself. Without this process, all the noise in the media, bias in the school
system, and corporate propaganda will prevent us from seeing the problems

and solutions clearly. This requires us to deconstruct Capitalism into its atomic building blocks to understand them individually, which gives us a deeper appreciation for how they work collectively within the context of a capitalistic society.

The Heart of Capitalism is Value. Visualize a spaghetti machine. The capitalist can't turn all the cranks himself; so he hires a worker. The output of the machine is mutually created by the capitalist and the worker. The spaghetti is the *product* of labor and capital. Without these two factors of production (labor and capital), the spaghetti cannot exist. The spaghetti that comes out of the machine represents *new value* that did not exist before the capitalist and worker came together. The spaghetti has value because a *consumer* is willing to exchange some other form of value for the spaghetti. That other form of value could be dollars, euros, gold bars, apples, lollipops, light bulbs . . . any *commodity* that can be exchanged in a process called a "value exchange."

Capitalism Depends on Societal Value Exchange. When commodities are exchanged, a transaction occurs and value moves from one person to another. Surplus value after all expenses are paid is called "profit." The value creation and value exchange processes are important principles at the heart of every capitalistic economy. A capitalistic *economy* can only exist within the context of a capitalistic *society*, which means every transaction within such a society requires a mutually beneficial exchange of *societal* value, not only financial value. Without mutual exchanges of *societal* value, a capitalistic society disintegrates into tyranny and anarchy.

What is a "Society"? A society is a collection of relationships. What is a "relationship"? In human societies, a relationship represents a connection between two or more humans. What is a "connection"? A connection represents a continuous series of transactions based on mutually shared values and mutual value exchange. Without mutually shared values and mutual value exchange, there can be no connection between humans. Without connections between humans, relationships cannot exist. Without relationships, there is no society because there is no connection between people to hold the individuals together within a society.

Society Depends on Our Perception of its Value. Without relationships based on mutual values and mutual value exchange, the individuals within a society will see no value in the relationships within that society. Thus, they will perceive no value in the society because the society is merely a collection of relationships. When any of the members of a society no longer see value in that society, they have no rational incentive or reason to contribute to that society. They have no rational incentive or reason to feel loyal to that society. They feel no sense of obligation to that society. Thus, why should they care about that society? They won't.

A Capitalistic Society is Bound Together by Capital and Labor. When corporate raiders in the 1980s realized they could cut the connection between capital and labor by deporting capital and jobs to foreign countries, they cut the connection between humans that is at the heart of Capitalism itself. Capitalism cannot exist without a society of humans bound together by mutually shared values engaging in mutual value exchange. In capitalistic societies, there is no other kind of relationship to bind society together other than the relationship between capital and labor.

Without Value, Humanity is Discarded. By cutting the connection between capital and labor, the Predatory Cannibals have cut themselves off from the essence of what it means to be human in a capitalistic society. They no longer perceive any value in the relationship between labor and capital, which means they no longer perceive any meaningful value in humanity outside their intimate circle of personal relationships. When something doesn't have value, it can be discarded without any feeling of remorse. This is why Transnational Cannibals and the Predatory Cannibals that control them have discarded the American labor force.

The Capital-Labor Duality

True Capitalism vs. Sociopathic Corporatism. In a capitalistic society, nothing else can survive if the society is not able to preserve the most essential pillar of the value creation process: the duality between capital and labor. This is not about fighting for labor rights or shareholder rights. It transcends all that myopic drama and noise. This is about the true essence of Capitalism itself and what it really means to build a society based on a sustainable socioeconomic value creation framework. This is about understanding what it means to have an economy that is truly driven by market-based transactions, through which value can be equitably exchanged, prosperity can be broadly achieved with the least amount of government intervention, and the quality of life of the members of a society can be raised and maintained with the least amount of deprivation.

The Production of Anything Depends on the Capital-Labor

Duality. The relationship between capital and labor is fundamental to every capitalistic society. Without labor, capitalists can't produce anything of value to be sold in a market. Without capital, workers can't produce anything of value to exchange for wages to buy goods in a market. In the value creation process, capital and labor are coequal partners in the dance of Capitalism. This is what I call the "Capital-Labor Duality."

No Jobs = No Economic Purpose. No relationship exists without two mutually engaged partners. The two partners in a capitalistic society are Labor and Capital. When Capital quits the partnership, the connection is broken and the relationship disintegrates because the other side of the relationship is no longer there. By discarding the labor force, Predatory Cannibals have destroyed the very essence of a capitalistic society. Without the mutually shared value and mutual exchange of value between humans in a capitalistic society, there is no society. When corporations move their capital and jobs outside their home society, they leave behind a disemboweled population with no economic purpose.

Without the Capital-Labor Duality There is No Economy. Without the value creation process of the Capital-Labor Duality, there is no real economy, no exchange of goods and services, no ability for the individuals within the society to exchange their labor power for food, water, shelter, clothing, or anything else. Without a real economy, there is no way for the population to survive. If the people cannot survive, they will revolt and take the capital and means of production from the capitalists by force because they have no other choice if they want to avoid starving to death.

Workers = Consumers = the Animating Force of Capital. "Consumers" are not a distinct species of human separate and apart from the Capital-Labor Duality—*they exist only within that duality.* There are no consumers without workers who trade their labor for a wage. Without a wage, they have no purchasing power and nothing to trade for the goods produced in the capitalists' factories. When the factories have no consumers to buy their goods, the factories can't continue producing, capital becomes inert, and the economy grinds to a halt.

Corporations Have No Purpose Without Consumers with Purchasing Power. The Globalism 1.0 neurotoxin is so destructive because it blinds corporate executives, shareholders, and government policymakers to the fundamental reality of every capitalistic society: For a capitalistic society to survive, the corporate governance culture inside the corporations within that society must understand that labor is not merely an *expense* to be avoided—Labor *is* the consumer and Labor *is* the society. Without workers who have purchasing power, corporations have no consumers, which means they have no way to generate income for their shareholders, which means they have no reason to exist.

The Supply & Demand Illusion. What comes first: supply or demand? This question is at the heart of an ideologically-driven debate that has existed for centuries. It is a debate based on an illusion of how Capitalism works. Every capitalistic economy is driven by the Capital-Labor Duality, which is why the separation of supply and demand is an illusion. Without labor *and* capital working together, there is no aggregate supply of anything; without wages earned by labor, there is no aggregate demand for anything because society has no purchasing power. Supply and demand, just like capital and labor, are locked in a symbiotic dance fueled by the Capital-Labor Duality. They are inseparable; any attempt to divide them is like cutting a chicken in half and expecting it to lay eggs.

The Immaculate Conception of Supply & Demand. Partisan ideologues on the left *and* right engage in endless economic policy debates that have divided humanity into "supply-side" and "demand-side" tribes. Once we recognize the supply-demand illusion, the reality becomes clear: All supply and demand phenomena are driven by the value creation process of the Capital-Labor Duality. Thus, when legitimate governments protect the Capital-Labor Duality from Transnational Cannibals, the supply-demand duality takes care of itself and spontaneously creates a naturally functioning economy. This immaculate conception of supply and demand is another miracle of Capitalism, but it mutates into an abomination of Capitalism when disloyal Transnational Cannibals dominate the economy.

We Are All Workers or Capitalists. Within a capitalistic society, all members of society are workers or capitalists. Sometimes they serve both roles if they're entrepreneurs, but if you're not a worker or a capitalist, you have no functional value in a capitalistic society. From a purely economic perspective, humans not involved in the production of goods or services for commercial exchange are the *overhead* of a capitalistic society. For example, if you deploy your money, equipment, land, and facilities to productive purposes, then you're a capitalist. In contrast, if you provide labor to an employer, then you're a worker.

A Relationship Requires Two Partners. If you're a capitalist, you can't earn money without a worker to help you operate your capital equipment and factories. That means you have a relationship with labor, and vice-versa. Now multiply that relationship millions of times to the size of a national population and you have a society of workers and capitalists. Society cannot exist without both sides of this relationship; just like a marriage cannot exist without both sides contributing to the relationship.

Capital and Labor Are the Primary Factors of Production. In a capitalistic society, there are two primary ingredients required to create new value: Capital and Labor. Land is traditionally another separate factor of production, but in a capitalistic society, land is really just another form of immobile capital. "Human capital" and all other such variations of human output manifest through the physical or mental labor of a human. So in this context, we don't need another term for it; the concept of "Labor" is sufficient to represent all forms of physical or mental human output.

Societal Stockholm Syndrome. If a corporation is no longer loyal and no longer interested in contributing to its home society, then it should no longer be entitled to the benefits of that society. A society has no rational incentive or obligation to continue extending any benefits to a disloyal corporation that has cut its connection with society. In fact, to continue coddling an abusive corporation is essentially no different than the delusional mental state called the Stockholm Syndrome. But instead of the syndrome causing individuals to develop an emotional bond with their kidnappers, this is a nationwide neurosis that causes entire countries to subjugate themselves to abusive Transnational Cannibals.

Eject Disloyal Corporations. A disloyal corporation should be compelled to leave the society and allow other members of that society to launch new corporations that can replace it. No corporation is indispensable to a society. No matter how large and entrenched they may seem, a disloyal corporation is far more destructive to a society than the process of replacing it with a more loyal capitalistic partner. Labor and Capital will always come together wherever there is genuine demand for a given product or service. If one corporation is ejected, others will be delighted to fill the void; and we can be sure they will behave with far more enthusiasm and loyalty for having the opportunity to contribute to their home society. After just a few disloyal corporations are legally ejected, they will serve as powerful examples for all the other Transnational Cannibals. This would positively change the attitude of all corporations throughout the economy virtually overnight.

The Gig Economy is a Disease Caused by Broken Capitalism. When Transnational Cannibals discard domestic labor, they force the domestic labor force into the so-called "Gig Economy." This is a perpetual state of joblessness dotted by occasional "gigs" that economic refugees perform at sporadic intervals. Without stable employment to earn a living wage, how can "gig workers" plan for their future? How can they get married and raise a family? Buy a home? Send their kids to college? Go out to dinner, movies, vacations . . . if they're afraid of spending their last dollar? This certainly does not create the conditions for long-term economic growth or social and geopolitical stability. To the contrary, the Gig Economy represents the last death throes of Capitalism because it's the last step on the path to total Capital-Labor Duality collapse.

The Illusion of Separate Capital and Labor Islands. Visualize Capitalism as a large floating mountain just beneath the surface of the ocean and only two small islands are visible above the surface. Two groups of people live on these islands—Capital on one island and Labor on the other island. The entire land mass represents Capitalism. Each group thinks they're living on their own separate island, but the perception that the islands are two separate land masses is an illusion created by the shallow gulf between Capital and Labor. In reality, both groups live on the same landmass. The group living on each side creates balance for the entire floating mountain below. If either group leaves their island, the entire mountain will become unstable and tip over, killing everybody on the entire landmass. That's what is happening today because capitalists have left their island by abandoning the domestic Capital-Labor Duality.

Commodification Debases the Things We Should Cherish. A capitalistic society should sanctify the Capital-Labor Duality and regard it as a cherished institution, but Broken Capitalism commodifies the Capital-Labor Duality. Commodification is the exact opposite of sanctification. When we commodify things, we strip them down to dispensable objects that are indistinguishable from one another. When we sanctify something, we elevate it to the level of a precious and irreplaceable treasure. We regard it with reverence and respect, something that cannot be squandered or neglected. The Capital-Labor Duality is worthy of our utmost respect and protection, but societies around the world today are trashing it because that's what corporate-controlled media and corporate propaganda are programming us to do.

What is Value?

The Source of All Value. Humans have needs and desires, which are the source of all trade and economic activity. If we did not have needs and desires, there would be no reason to buy, sell, or trade anything. Without the need to buy, sell, or trade things, there would be no reason to attach a price to anything. Without prices, there would be no mechanism to communicate the relative value of anything. Without relative value, there would be no awareness of the concept value. Without the concept of value, there would be no basis for an economy, no concept of wealth, no concept of income, no concept of scarcity or abundance—there would only be a detached consciousness, disconnected from everything in the Universe. The impulses that drive human nature—the impulses that make us human—would cease to exist.

    Humans Project Value Onto the Universe. To fulfill their needs and desires, humans project value onto objects that satisfy their needs and desires. This projection is a fabrication of the human mind—an evolutionary innovation of the cerebral cortex—which is unique to the human species. This innovation is responsible for everything associated with human civilization. Maybe there are aliens on other planets that have similar brain structures that serve the same purpose, but without the organic circuitry of the cerebral cortex, the concept of "value" is reduced to basic animal impulses like hunger and self-preservation, triggered by electrical impulses deep within the Limbic System, which is the *primordial brain* that has driven all animal behavior for millions years.

    Value is Sociological Dark Matter. There is a concept in the science of Cosmology called "Dark Matter." Most cosmologists estimate that 80-90% of all the matter in the Universe is Dark Matter, which is currently invisible to humans. That means we can see only about 10-20% of all the matter in the Universe. Cosmologists know Dark Matter exists by the way it affects everything we can see. For example, the Universe is expanding at an accelerating rate, which is only possible if there is an invisible substance between all the visible matter pushing the Universe outward in all directions. We can also observe the gravitational affects of Dark Matter on visible matter by the unusual way that black holes, quasars, and other celestial objects wobble in space-time, which would not be possible without the presence of a large quantity of some invisible substance pushing against them. This expansive behavior of Dark Matter in the physical Universe is a useful analogy to help us understand "value" in the universe of human societies.

The Futility of Defining Value. It's futile to try to define "value" because there is no single definition that applies to all situations. Trying to define it is just like trying to measure a sub-atomic particle in Quantum Physics: The moment you try to measure it, you've changed or destroyed it. But we can understand the essence of value based on its functionality in a capitalistic society. In this context, value is the fuel of human civilization. It fuels all human progress. Although they were not capitalists, Neanderthals would have never left the caves to evolve into modern humans without the fuel of value. Like Dark Matter, every society is propelled forward by a continuous stream of invisible new value. Capitalistic societies in particular are completely dependent upon the broad creation and broad distribution of value. Value is the fuel that propels all human relationships forward. It is the fuel that makes it possible to build the tallest skyscrapers and the largest corporations. It is the substance at the core of every transaction in every human society.

The River of Value. It doesn't matter how *efficient* an individual entity or economy is at creating value if that value is created only to be concentrated into the hands of a small group of humans. The concentration of value is not what actually fuels each society. It's the broad creation and broad distribution of value that fuels every society. This is why the concentration of wealth destroys societies: Wealth and capital are stored value, but value is like a river; it's not a river if it's not flowing freely. If it's dammed up and concentrated into one small corner of a society, it's just a stagnating pool of value behind an artificial value dam.

Value Must Flow to Exist. There are other things that must be allowed to flow for society to benefit. Air, freedom, liberty, prosperity, happiness, positive feelings of national unity, cohesive culture—none of these things are beneficial to society unless they're allowed to flow. Bottling them up destroys their usefulness to society. That is the essence of value. So when a society creates new value, it needs to be in continuous circulation to catalyze the creation of ever-more new value. Gradually over time, this incremental value creation and distribution process is what fuels the growth of everything in human civilization.

Value is the Offspring of Creation. Civilizations are not fueled by money or wealth; they're fueled by the continuous and broad creation of value when it's continuously and broadly distributed throughout human societies, contributing to an ever-expanding river of value. None of this has anything to do with *money* or *wealth*; it has everything to do with the essential process of creation. This is why a society that destroys its creators and producers is a society that kills itself by destroying its capacity to create value.

Every Society Needs Many Tributaries of Value. No matter how large a dammed pool of value is, it will do nothing for a society until it's allowed to flow. The river of value in a society can flow without bending to one side or another *only* if there are many small tributaries of value contributing to it from all sides. Without a diversity of tributaries, the river will have too much pressure from one side, which will erode its banks until the river changes direction and flows toward ever-larger dams of value, controlled by ever-fewer members of society.

Value Permeates Every Aspect of Human Existence. In romantic relationships, value is what brings two lovers together during the courting process, culminating into passionate intercourse. Value is the creation of happiness and joy that we feel when we exchange ideas, hugs, and kisses with people who seem to truly understand us. These exchanges are fundamentally an exchange of value because they create within us a feeling of personal satisfaction, happiness, and emotional well-being, which is at the heart of every voluntary transaction in human existence. It is this satisfaction, happiness, and well-being that economists call "utility" within the context of economic transactions, but the principles of value creation and value exchange extend far beyond economics and into every aspect of our lives.

Our Identity is Derived from Value Creation. It's important to understand the essential role of the value creation process in a capitalistic society because "value creation" is fundamentally different from the process of wealth distribution or income redistribution. To "create" means to bring forth into existence, to produce something that did not previously exist, to propel society forward to ever-greater heights, one incremental contribution of value at a time. This is what every human within a capitalistic society is compelled to do because their identity and perception of *self-value* is inextricably connected to their ability to create value and exchange value with other members of a capitalistic society. This is the genius of Capitalism.

All Exchange Value is Derived from Human Labor. In a market economy, human labor is what creates value by imbuing needy

THIS IS HOW WE FIX IT

humans with purchasing power, which is the only way they can purchase the goods that factories produce. Human need and desire imbues objects with exchange value because value would not exist without the instigation of human need and desire. Without human need and desire coupled with purchasing power, there is no "consumer," nor any possibility for profitable commercial exchange. This is why a fully automated world will still depend on humans with purchasing power, which can only come from the equitable creation and equitable distribution of income.

Value Deprivation is the Cause of All Wars and Revolutions. If the government policies of a capitalistic society have been misconfigured or distorted and mutated by Predatory Cannibals and their political patrons, the resources and means of producing meaningful value are gradually stripped away from society. This results in a loss of identity at both the community and individual levels as large populations become disconnected from the Capital-Labor Duality. Once they lose that connection, they have no economic purpose in society; and in a capitalistic society, that means they have no purpose at all. This is the fundamental cause of all civil wars and political revolutions throughout modern human history.

Wealth is Stored Value

Metrics Are Not the Value They Measure. Notice I have not focused on "wealth" or "money" up to this point because "value" is much more fundamental and much more important to every society than wealth or money. Financial wealth and money are two ways to *measure* value, but they are not value itself. You can use a ruler to measure the dimensions of a diamond, but the ruler is not the diamond; the same is true of value. Money and wealth are measures of value, but they are not *value.*

Whirlpools of Wealth. The illustration below is a simple way to visualize how value and wealth are sucked out of an economy when idiotic trade policies create perpetual trade deficits. The left side ("Balanced Trade") depicts two economies as two wealth pools, churning dynamically as new value and wealth are created every day within each pool. These economies interact at the edges and engage in balanced trade, but they remain totally separate, independent economies. Wealth bubbles up within each economy from underground springs of value that are released into the pools by the creative force of the Capital-Labor Duality. It doesn't matter whether the pools are the same size or not in the beginning; what matters is where they end up, and whether they preserve their value-creation capacity or become mauled, distorted, and swallowed up by economic entities that do not have the home society's best interests in mind.

Balanced Trade   **Imbalanced Trade**   **Broken Capitalism**

The two middle whirlpools illustrate the top pool beginning to suck the value and wealth out of the lower pool, which causes the lower pool to become stretched and distorted. That's the result of perpetual trade deficits. By the end of the process on the right side, the top pool has devoured virtually all the wealth and value creation capacity from the lower pool. That's Broken Capitalism, which is the result of Globalism 1.0 cheerleaders polluting and obstructing the river of value with their short-sighted and self-serving economic policies.

Welfare Programs Serve the Wealthiest Predatory Cannibals. Every civil society should have social safety nets for citizens that have been harmed by misconfigurations and distortions in Capitalism, to the extent that governments understand how to define and implement *financially sustainable* government welfare programs. Of course, every possible precaution should be taken to ensure that these programs are not exploited for political and private gain by Predatory Cannibals and their patrons in government. However, redistributing wealth through government welfare programs is not the solution to Broken Capitalism. In fact, welfare program-based transfer payments magnify the problem for the following reasons:

(1) Welfare programs create a false sense of security for the most

vulnerable members of society because those programs can be dismantled at any time on the whim of any new government administration.

(2) Welfare programs allow Predatory Cannibals and their patrons in government to continue destroying the society's value creation process, which further erodes the capacity of vulnerable communities to produce value and meaningfully contribute to a capitalistic society.

(3) Welfare programs give Predatory Cannibals exactly what they want: to continue expropriating society's resources and dominating the value creation process, continue exporting capital and jobs to sweatshop countries, continue being disloyal to their home country, and continue discarding the Capital-Labor Duality at the core of every capitalistic society. By focusing on government welfare programs and all the political drama that accompanies them, our attention is diverted away from holding Predatory Cannibals accountable. That's exactly what they want, which means welfare programs incentivize and empower them to continue their destructive behavior.

(4) Welfare programs reduce the pressure on Predatory Cannibals to change their behavior, which means society loses a critical opportunity to meaningfully reintegrate Predatory Cannibals back into their home society, or to banish them from society completely to prevent them from causing further harm.

Human Civilization is Dependent Upon Broad-Based Prosperity. Value creation is the fuel that propels human civilization forward. It is what enables civilizations to reach each new level of their existence. You can define each level however you wish, but no matter how you define them, they cannot be achieved in a *capitalistic* society unless the society is configured to broadly create and broadly distribute value efficiently *and* equitably. Value cannot be broadly created and distributed unless government policies are configured to organize and compensate capital and labor equitably. If a government cannot provide these basic structural economic conditions, then the society it governs won't be able to create broad-based, sustainable prosperity.

The Probability of Human Extinction Increases Without Broad-Based Prosperity. Without sustainable, broad-based prosperity, a society won't be able to build the infrastructure required to explore the deepest mysteries of the Universe. That means the society won't be able to learn enough about quantum physics, fusion power, and all the technologies of the future that are required to build the tools and equipment necessary to enable humanity to survive *when* (not if) we are all threatened by an extinction-level event, like an asteroid or comet impact. The fate of the human race truly depends on us working together to fix Broken Capitalism.

The Path to Central Planning & Why it Fails

Black Holes of Capital. In contrast to a relatively fair and sustainable market in which competition flourishes, when a government's labor, social welfare, taxation, fiscal, monetary, and industry regulation policies are distorted by Broken Capitalism, the flow of income and value throughout a society gets sucked into what I call "black holes of capital." These black holes of capital suck value and wealth out of an economy and horde it in the form of inert capital controlled by politically influential private entities, which no longer deploy the capital to any productive purpose in society.

Government Runs Out of Taxpayers. As more and more value is sucked into these black holes of capital, there is less and less value in the form of income flowing to individual citizens throughout society. As this process continues, there are less and less income-generating value creators in the economy who can afford to continue running all the private enterprises that create value throughout a society. This results in the government being required to pay a continuously increasing percentage of all the payments that need to be paid to the many supply chain companies within the country. But the government's money only exists by increasing taxes on a continuously *decreasing* number of income-generating value creators. The society eventually reaches a point at which there is no longer a sufficient number of income-generating value creators for the government to tax.

Government Becomes a Single-Payor Sugar Daddy. Over time this process inevitably leads to a situation where all the corporations and institutions control the capital and value in society and all the citizens have lost control of the capital and value. When citizens no longer have their own capital and value to exchange for goods and services, the only way to pay all the supply chains is for the government to step in and become a single-payor Sugar Daddy, buying everything on behalf of all the citizens.

But since the government doesn't have any money unless it confiscates money from private citizens, how can it pay the supply chains for all the goods and services without completely sucking all the money from the last remaining income-generating, value-creating taxpayers? It can't, so the government simply begins to seize control of the entire value creation process throughout an economy by nationalizing all industries.

Central Planning Destroys the Engines of Prosperity. At this point, the essence of the economy has shifted from a market-based economy that broadly distributes the work and wealth associated to production, distribution, storage and capital formation, to an economy that is now controlled by a tiny number of technocrats and corporations who dictate how the work should be done, who should do it, and who should get the wealth. This inevitably results in tyrannical centralized planning, distribution, storage, *and* arbitrary rationing of all the nation's financial, human, and natural resources.

The Old Tyranny Begets a New Tyranny. Some people call centrally planned economies "Communism," but it doesn't matter what you call it. It never works because it inevitably cripples and ultimately paralyzes the value creation processes, supply chains, and technological infrastructure that are necessary to sustain every economy. And it entrenches the *Founding Fathers* of the centrally planned society as the paternal lords of the utopian state who rule by express or implied fiat. This becomes a form of hereditary entitlement and privilege, which enshrines their families into a new dynastic aristocracy. And this is how the cycle begins anew: A new tyranny arises from the ashes of the old tyranny, which the *new and improved* central planners thought they were abolishing.

Prosperity Comes Again Only After Tyranny is Replaced with Liberty. After an economy becomes moribund, the only solution is to rebuild the Capital-Labor Duality, invite the people to participate in their own democratic governance, and rekindle the value creation process by incentivizing the citizens to start producing valuable goods and services again. That can occur only when the people truly believe they will be able to keep an equitable share of the profits from the value they create.

Coercive State and Corporate Power are Destructive to Free-Market Capitalism. Special interest groups and the minds they control might try to deliberately misrepresent the meaning of this book by falsely painting it as an endorsement of Marxism. From their self-serving perspective, anything that hints at balancing the coercive power of corporations with the best interests of society is instantly twisted into a totalitarian conspiracy to destroy liberty and free-market Capitalism. When you see them do this, you will know they are merely trying to distract the public from their own abuses of state and corporate power. In reality, this book is not an endorsement of Marxism nor an indictment of free-market Capitalism. To the contrary, it's a logical analysis of the inevitable convergence of interests between state and corporate power, *which is fundamentally destructive to civil liberty, economic freedom, and market-based Capitalism.*

Price Level Stability

The Trojan Horse of Lower Prices. The lower prices created by Globalism 1.0 is a Trojan Horse, presented by Globalism 1.0 cheerleaders as a boon to humanity, but it contains a hidden poison that is gradually destroying everything that makes us human. That means *it is destroying humanity.* If all you care about is buying the cheapest *stuff,* then Globalism 1.0 might seem like a logical way to configure Capitalism. But if you care about maximizing the total number of viable companies, jobs, and economic stability in every country to prevent a global humanitarian catastrophe, then *collapsing price levels is a disease.*

When Are Falling Prices Good or Bad? Some people think falling prices are always good, but that is not correct. These people ignore the Capital-Labor Duality. Prices can fall for three primary reasons: (1) productivity gains in domestic production and *balanced* global trade that are passed on to consumers in the form of lower prices; (2) monetary deflation; and (3) labor arbitrage with foreign sweatshop countries. Whether falling prices are good or bad depends on why they are falling; so let's briefly look at each of these three sources of falling prices to determine which are bad or good for *you,* not some vaguely defined *global society.*

Falling Prices from Productivity Gains. If prices are falling because of productivity gains in domestic industries and *balanced* global trade, while income is distributed equitably throughout the global economy, then yes, falling prices are good. In this case, productivity gains are benefitting consumers with more purchasing power and workers and producers can earn an equitable share of the global income pie. However, all the data and evidence presented throughout this book confirms that productivity gains have certainly *not* been distributed equitably throughout the global economy; so this source of falling prices has benefitted only a small fraction of humans on Earth today.

Falling Prices from Labor Arbitrage. If falling prices are the result of labor arbitrage while jobs and domestic income are being sucked into foreign sweatshops invariably controlled by Transnational Cannibals, then falling prices will only lead to a concentration of wealth and market power into the claws of fewer and fewer Transnational Cannibals. In this case, purchasing power for people with jobs may be increasing, but if the number of jobs is shrinking because they're being sucked out of the country and the small- to medium-sized business community is collapsing, then an ever-larger population of economic refugees can't afford the cheaper goods at *any* price.

Falling Prices from Monetary Deflation. Monetary deflation is a cyclical economic phenomenon caused by a reduction in the money supply, widespread debt liquidation, or severe economic shocks. All these events can reduce the velocity, supply, and demand for a nation's currency, thereby pushing down prices of all goods and services throughout its economy. Deflation is good for savers, consumers, and some types of investors because it increases their purchasing power, but it's bad for virtually all debtors because it increases the real cost of their debt, which is why debt-laden governments worldwide today are terrified by deflation. Thus, lower prices due to monetary deflation impact people differently depending on what situation they are in, but it's a temporary, cyclical phenomenon, unlike collapsing price levels from labor arbitrage with foreign sweatshops.

The Subsistence Basket. Labor arbitrage with foreign sweatshops (controlled by Transnational Cannibals) collapses the price of domestic products *that compete with imported products* while domestic price inflation simultaneously *increases* the price of *essential* goods and services like food, housing, transportation, education, healthcare, energy, tele-communications, etc. I call these essential goods and services the "Subsistence Basket" because they are mandatory for anybody who must subsist or live in any modern society. The Subsistence Basket represents the largest overall portion of every household's annual expense budget.

Is Your Purchasing Power Rising or Falling? In most industrialized nations, foreign imports represent a small fraction of each person's Subsistence Basket. If the price of some imported goods falls while the price of nearly all the Subsistence Basket goods rises without a corresponding increase in real income, that means the population's net purchasing power is falling along with their quality of life. This is what is happening in the U.S. and many Western countries today. In a country like the U.S. where market bubbles and market failures inflate the price of the domestic Subsistence Basket goods, how can any Globalism 1.0 cheerleader say that Americans are better off simply because they can buy some cheap imports, most of which they don't even need?

Collapsing Price Levels Fuels Debt-Based Subsistence. Collapsing price levels creates an unsustainable imbalance between the *real income* of a population and the *real expenses* that the population must pay to stay alive. As a population's real income falls or remains stagnant while the price of the Subsistence Basket rises, the population must go into debt simply to stay alive. This is exactly what has happened in the U.S. and many Western countries over the past 30-40 years, which is a nasty effect of Broken Capitalism.

When Price Levels Collapse, the Capital-Labor Duality Collapses. Prices within a domestic economy need to remain at a level that provides a high enough quality of life for domestic consumers (Labor) *and* producers (Capital) in each country. When domestic factories are destroyed because price levels have collapsed, domestic jobs are destroyed, the real wage rates of the remaining jobs are flat or falling because of monetary inflation and downward pressure from sweatshop countries, and the Subsistence Basket becomes ever-more expensive, what exactly do policymakers expect will happen? Do they think the *Invisible Hand* is going to magically wave an *invisible wand* to save the economy from collapse?

The Global Cock Fight. When prices decrease because of productivity gains associated to technology advancements, *that is a virtue,* but when slave labor and sweatshop conditions allow sweatshop countries to produce a widget five times less expensively than an American company, that is *not a virtue.* That is merely labor arbitrage exploited by Transnational Cannibals for the sake of profit without regard for the impact on their home country. It amounts to pitting humans from different countries against one another in a global cock fight. Only in the distorted world of Broken Capitalism and Transnational Cannibalism is *cheap labor* a *virtue.*

Lost Purchasing Power = Lost Quality of Life. A Chinese citizen's purchasing power today is much higher in China than an American's purchasing power in the U.S. In fact, China's GDP surpassed U.S. GDP in terms of Purchasing Power Parity in 2011, which means China is wealthier than the U.S. *in real terms.* Chinese companies can sell cheap stuff and still rapidly increase the quality of their workers' lives because the price levels for all goods and services throughout their society are still rationally connected to the incomes that Chinese citizens are earning.[135] In other words, China's Subsistence Basket is much less expensive than it is in the U.S. because Chinese purchasing power has been rising while American purchasing power has been falling for generations.[136] Lost purchasing power is caused by short-sighted monetary policy, which creates embedded inflation, market bubbles, market failures, and all manner of economic and social maladies, all of which are diseases of Broken Capitalism.

The Pernicious Fantasy of Globally Equalized Price Levels. In addition to the destruction created by Transnational Cannibals in the banking system, the European Union economy is a mess today for the same reason that the global economy is a mess. Globalism 1.0 cheerleaders have grossly underestimated the complexity *and impossibility* of equalizing monetary policies between nations because they do not understand the impossibility of equalizing cultural values and traditions across nations. If you understand how monetary, fiscal, and public policies are deeply and emotionally interconnected to the unique cultural values and traditions within each country, then you can understand that the core Globalism 1.0 fantasy of *globally equalized price levels* will likely be the most significant contributing factor to the outbreak of World War III.

Price Levels Are a Byproduct of Each Country's Cultural Values. Every country's fiscal policy is driven by their unique cultural values and traditions, which determines how they prioritize the expenses within their national budgets. How they prioritize their expenses determines how they manage their money supply and monetary policy. Americans have different priorities than the French; Germans have different priorities than the Greeks; the Chinese have different priorities than the Swiss—every

---

[135] Of course, Broken Capitalism is creeping into the Chinese economy, too, but it will take another couple decades or so for their homegrown Transnational Cannibals to cannibalize Chinese society. It's unlikely that their economic policymakers will avoid the mistakes of U.S. policymakers unless they read this book and make the adjustments I've described herein. But for now, most of the price levels in the Chinese economy are far healthier and more rational than the price levels in the U.S. economy.

[136] To be precise, it has been falling since the Federal Reserve was spawned on Jekyll Island in 1913. I've written extensively about the Federal Reserve in my article, "How Does the Federal Reserve Really Work?" at Eanfar.org. You can also learn more from G. Edward Griffin's great book, *The Creature from Jekyll Island.*

country has different cultural values and priorities than every other country. That means you can't *harmonize* monetary policies between nations without *harmonizing* their fiscal policies, but you can't *harmonize* their fiscal policies without *equalizing* their cultural values and traditions.

Forced Price Level Equalization Increases Tension and Conflict. Contrary to the so-called "peace dividend" that Globalism 1.0 cheerleaders often talk about, forced cultural and economic policy equalization is causing a dramatic escalation in tensions worldwide. Nobody wants their cultural values, traditions, economies, and political systems to be destroyed or molested by foreign powers. The only way the European Union and Globalism 1.0 could ever be sustainable is if the United Nations, backed by the U.S. Military, executed an ethnic cleansing campaign to equalize all the cultural values and traditions across the planet. Of course, that would lead to World War III and the likely extinction of the human race.

Globalism 1.0 & Mental Depression

Collapsed Price Levels Decreases Our Perception of Value. Having an abundance of *stuff* is not a virtue when it transforms everything in our lives into disposable commodities. In addition to all the pollution and ecological damage to our planet, when items become so cheap that we can discard them without feeling any loss, it means those items didn't have any significant value in the first place. Previous generations took much greater care of their possessions, they held onto them much longer, and derived utility and value from them for much longer periods of time because higher price levels imbued those items with a higher perceived value in the minds of consumers. When we perceive higher value in the things we *already* have, we don't feel an impulse to buy more *stuff*. Thus, "quality of life" is not increased merely by piling more junk into our homes; it's increased by *appreciating the value of what we already have.*

Depressed Price Levels Creates Depressed People. Wealthy countries have much higher numbers of depressed people than poor countries. It's well-known that lottery winners, children of the super-rich, and many of the wealthiest people suffer from mental depression at rates that far exceed the average rate. This may seem like a paradox to people if they incorrectly assume financial wealth and abundance equates to happiness and a high quality of life, but it's not a paradox at all. Humans are biologically wired to associate value, relationships, and scarcity with meaning; and a life without value, relationships, and desire is meaningless. A life without meaning is a life without purpose. A life without purpose creates a feeling of emptiness; and emptiness has a psychosomatic effect on the body, which leads to clinical depression, suicidal thoughts, selfish and anti-social behavior, and a collapse of families and communities.

The Wealth Paradox. As people get richer, the perceived value of everything in their lives often decreases because everything becomes disposable and replaceable. As the perceived value of everything decreases, there is a corresponding decrease in the perceived purpose of life if wealth is not anchored to something more spiritually or philosophically enriching. As certain segments of a society get wealthier, there is a collective collapse of perceived value, meaning, and purpose in those segments, which manifests as "the high life," but this is an illusion. In reality, it's an empty existence that spawns epidemics of mental depression in the upper half of the wealth ladder, while the twin scourges of Broken Capitalism and Globalism 1.0 inflict poverty, existential insecurity, anger, and epidemics of mental depression on the lower half of the wealth ladder. This is why a strong Middle Class is not only important for economic stability; it's a precondition for widespread mental stability, happiness, and peace.

Happiness Comes from a Feeling of Personal Progress. Happiness and the perception of a high-quality life comes from having the opportunity to experience the feeling of progress at every phase of our lives. But there's no way to feel progress when you have no job or income; and there's no way to feel progress when your life has been so easy that you've become a billionaire before your 40th birthday. The secret to creating a happy society is creating sustainable price levels so that all able-bodied members of a society can earn enough income to afford the Subsistence Basket while making it structurally impossible to become so obscenely rich that life no longer has any value, meaning, or purpose.

Abundance of *Stuff* = Scarcity of Meaning and Purpose. Broken Capitalism and Globalism 1.0 have filled our lives with an abundance of *stuff* while simultaneously creating scarcity of meaningful value and purpose. This is not a paradox; it's the inevitable consequence of Transnational Cannibalism, depressed price levels, and idiotic government policies that incentivize humans to consume until they explode. So the next time you hear Globalism 1.0 cheerleaders claim that cheap imports brings "benefits to society" and "increases quality of life" without regard for the

Capital-Labor Duality, you know they have no clue what actually produces human happiness, quality of life, or a broadly prosperous and healthy society. And you know they should never be in any position of power over the economic policies of your country.

Value and the Money Supply

Like the Universe, the Money Supply Must Expand. For most of my life, I believed in the ideology of Austrian School Economics, and in particular, the theory of money described in Ludwig von Mises' economic treatise, *Theory of Money and Credit*. Like most Austrian Schoolers, I believed that *all* monetary inflation is evil and that relative commodity prices alone are sufficient to accommodate the expansion of value throughout an economy. However, after I observed how value and money in an economy are separately but co-dependently created, distributed, destroyed, and hoarded into black holes of capital, I realized that the expansion of value in an economy cannot occur without a commensurate expansion of the money supply.

　　Manipulation of the Money Supply *Is* Evil. Austrian Schoolers are correct to despise central bankers who manipulate the money supply to achieve partisan political goals. And when a government manipulates the money supply to benefit politically favored groups, purchasing power and wealth are shifted from the general population to a small number of special interest groups. Monetary manipulation of this kind is certainly the root of most economic evils. However, "monetary manipulation" is not synonymous with "monetary expansion." Why is this distinction important? Because . . .

　　Money's Commodity Value Distorts Its Monetary Value. Austrian Schoolers believe that any currency unit can be divisible into smaller units, and thus, a fixed amount of money in circulation can accommodate any expansion of value without any expansion of the money supply. This is not a logical belief if we understand that "money" is a commodity separate from its role as a unit of exchange. As a commodity, the *exchange value* of money itself rises and falls according to its own independent supply and demand curve, separate and apart from all other goods throughout an economy. The supply and demand of money is impacted by many dimensions of human existence, especially the geopolitical factors that influence the production and distribution of natural resources across the planet.

Extraction of Resources and Money from the Population. As the natural resources—and the products produced from them—are politically and sociologically manipulated due to special interest group pressures and cultural trends, the control of natural resources becomes concentrated in the hands of politically favored groups throughout every society. These resources are denominated in a currency represented by money. These favored groups (usually Big Business and Transnational Cannibals) can extract natural resources at a cost significantly less than the price they charge for their finished goods, which represents their profit margin. Regardless of the *utility* that a consumer derives from a good, every penny of a producer's profit is, by definition, a *net increase* in the producer's total supply of money and a *net decrease* in the consumer's total supply of money.

Broken Capitalism Creates the Need for Monetary Expansion. In a competitive marketplace that is not distorted and dominated by gargantuan corporations, there is a healthy small- to medium-sized business community with a broad, horizontal ecosystem of producers that employ workers *who are also consumers*; so all the aggregated transactions throughout a *healthy* economy result in producer and consumer "surplus" (basically, an economist's term for "wealth") that is relatively balanced and distributed throughout the economy. This ensures that purchasing power is broadly distributed throughout society, which eliminates the need for monetary expansion to fill the void created by the black holes of capital.

Scarcity of Money Creates Humanitarian Crises. As this process of extraction and money hoarding continues, the velocity and supply of money in the general population decreases, which means that even if the population level and demand remained constant, the price of money will increase according to the Law of Supply and Demand. Like any commodity, if there is no additional supply, eventually money shortages will occur. This creates an artificial scarcity of money, making it more difficult for the general population to acquire enough money to purchase the goods needed for human subsistence. This artificial scarcity of money increases the purchasing power of money *for the dwindling number of humans who have jobs and money*, but for everybody else who either has no job or cannot obtain any money *at any price*, the artificial scarcity of money *within the context of Broken Capitalism* creates an expanding existential crisis.

Monetary Expansion Prevents Violent Revolution. In contrast to a healthy economic system, with Broken Capitalism, the balance of transactions throughout the economy results in a gradually increasing portion of money being extracted from the general population. In aggregate, this reduces the total supply of money within the general population and increases the supply of money controlled by the most politically connected producers: Big Business and Transnational Cannibals. Once the money is sucked into their black holes of capital, most of it will never return to the general population in a form that benefits society in any meaningful way. Thus, the void must be filled by expanding the money supply, even if it means debasing the money that already exists. From a politician's perspective, monetary inflation and debasement are relatively small prices to pay to avoid a violent political revolution.

Broken Capitalism Spawns Broken Monetary Policy. Without a truly independent central bank, no country will ever have a truly disciplined, nonpartisan monetary policy. Because of the disintegrating institutional integrity of the U.S. Government, the U.S. has a central bank that is completely beholden to the political ambition of whomever is sitting in the White House. This is definitely a significant contributing factor to Broken Capitalism in the U.S. and around the world, *but broken monetary policy is created by Broken Capitalism*, not vice-versa. This is because monetary policy is dictated by the White House, which is almost completely controlled by Big Business. So even if the Federal Reserve was fully independent, Broken Capitalism would still exist and a policy of monetary expansion would still be necessary as long as Capitalism is configured to systemically favor monster corporations that suck obscene amounts of value, money, and wealth into their black holes of capital.

Ideology Blinds People to Reality. All ideologically-driven economic theories suffer from fantasies that can cause large populations to suffer. Emotionally, it feels good to say "leave the money supply alone!" but it simply does not work when Capitalism is broken. Broken Capitalism injects too many bugs into the value creation and distribution engines of every economy, which makes it impossible to constrain the commodity of money to a fixed level of supply without causing acute *and* chronic social and economic devastation to millions of people. That's why a fixed money supply is an ideologically-driven fantasy that can only work in artificial economic models, not in the real world of emergent, feedback-loop-infested geopolitical and socioeconomic systems dominated by Broken Capitalism today.

Could a Gold Standard Ever Work Again? For all the reasons above, *a fixed* gold standard can never be sustainable within the context of Broken Capitalism. The next-best, and most realistic, option is increasing the money supply by a *fixed-percentage* each year, but even that will be a fantasy until Broken Capitalism is fixed because we have a central bank that turns on the printing press whenever a too-big-to-fail ward of the corporate welfare state comes begging for a taxpayer bailout.

What Have We Learned So Far? The deeper aspects of value and money can be difficult to understand. So let's summarize what we've learned in this section: In the real world of Broken Capitalism today, value and the money supply must expand together because:

(1) Politically favored corporations are allowed to grow so large that they dominate the supply of money, capital, and natural resources (collectively, "the means of production").

(2) As small- to medium-sized companies and all their jobs are destroyed, the means of production and wealth throughout the economy flow to a smaller number of favored producers: Big Business and Transnational Cannibals.

(3) Concentrated capital and wealth are hoarded and directed to unproductive or narrowly defined purposes that produce little or no value for the general population, which results in black holes of capital and wealth.

(4) As more value and wealth are sucked out of the broader economy, the rest of the population does not have enough money or purchasing power to acquire the goods they need to survive.

(5) The only way to give the population more purchasing power to fill the void created by the black holes of capital is to fix Broken Capitalism or increase the money supply.

(6) Monetary inflation and debasement are a small price to pay to prevent violent revolutions until the core problem—Broken Capitalism—can be fixed.

Key Points

● **The Capital-Labor Duality is the Heart and Soul of Capitalism.**

Without it, Capitalism collapses.

- **Humans Need Purchasing Power.** Without jobs and rational monetary policies to create purchasing power, humans in a capitalistic society cannot survive.
- **Price Levels Determine Standard of Living.** Trying to equalize the price levels between sweatshop countries and advanced economies is a recipe for violent revolution.

Your Country Needs You Now.

If you understand why it's important to fix Broken Capitalism, please give this book a positive rating online and tell at least 10 people about it today.

Home: Eanfar.org | **Facebook:** Facebook.com/Eanfar
Twitter: @FerrisEanfar | **AngelPay:** AngelPayHQ.org

- Chapter 10 -
Globalism 2.0

"We can have democracy in this country, or we can have great wealth concentrated in the hands of the few, but we can't have both." — Supreme Court Justice Louis D. Brandeis

The Survival Motive. In a truly competitive, market-based economy, Capitalism is not governed by the *Profit Motive*; it's governed by the *Survival Motive*. The Survival Motive benefits a far greater number of companies and people than the Profit Motive. The distinction between the Profit Motive and Survival Motive is important for economic policymaking and the welfare of people in all countries. If policymakers really wanted to fix Broken Capitalism today, they could do it within months by following the guidelines in this chapter to institutionalize the Survival Motive.

Profit Motive vs. Survival Motive. When the inherent structure of a market is designed to force corporations to compete for survival along the dimensions of innovation and usefulness without the anti-competitive elements of perpetually increasing *returns to scale* and *economies of scale*, no single company is ever able to become "too big to fail." That's the essence of a market governed by the Survival Motive. With the Survival Motive, no single company can ever grow to such a size that it can dominate supply chains, ram undesirable products and inflated prices down their customers' throats, engage in abusive monopolistic practices, destroy the economic vitality of communities, blow huge bubbles in the stock and bond markets, destroy the environment, devour entire economic ecosystems, distort political systems, or any of the other disgusting diseases of markets that are governed by the Profit Motive today.

Replace the Malignant Profit Motive with a Healthy Survival Motive. The most powerful structural incentives throughout the global economy today are designed to help big companies get bigger, not for a broad ecosystem of smaller companies to flourish. This trend is conceptually easy to reverse if the American people rise up and give their elected officials the political will power to make the simple adjustments that are necessary to institutionalize a healthy Survival Motive and purge the malignant Profit Motive from our global economy. And the rest of the world would follow the Americans' lead because the benefits to every society are too compelling to ignore. The following sections and chapters explain the straight-forward policymaking steps that are required to institutionalize the Survival Motive.

The Market Health Index

Herfindahl-Hirschman Index. The U.S. Department of Justice (DOJ), Federal Trade Commission (FTC), and other government agencies employ a useful tool in anti-trust cases called the Herfindahl-Hirschman Index (HHI).[137] The HHI is a relatively simple way to measure market concentration, which determines whether large corporate mergers will create a monopoly or unacceptable market concentration after a merger. If the HHI is too high, the government intervenes and blocks the merger to preserve the health and integrity of the market. The HHI range is 0 to 10,000. A value of 0 to 1,500 is considered a "competitive market"; 1,500 to 2,500 is a "moderately competitive market"; greater than 2,500 is a "highly concentrated market"; above 5,000 means the market is becoming a monopoly. The existence and long-standing efficacy of the HHI demonstrates how the government can and does intervene to preserve the health and integrity of markets. So the idea of a government intervening to preserve crucial elements of a market is not foreign to anybody who understands anti-trust law.[138]

If an Industry Dies, There's No Competition at All. Since the

---

[137] Similar "diversity indexes" are used in measuring the health of animal populations in the wild, determining which animals should be placed on endangered species lists, and in genetics to determine the concentration of genetic mutations and other traits that are important to measure over time.

[138] See also: "Horizontal Merger Guidelines | ATR | Department of Justice." Accessed March 9, 2017. https://www.justice.gov/atr/horizontal-merger-guidelines-0.
See also: Rhoades, Stephen A., and St. Louis Federal Reserve. "The Herfindahl-Hirschman Index." Fed. Res. Bull. 79 (1993): 188.

HHI works to preserve industry competition, why can't we adapt the HHI to preserve *the actual existence* of industries that are under assault from suicidal global trade policies and Transnational Cannibals? If a domestic industry dies, *there's no competition to preserve*. Allowing buggy Globalism 1.0 to destroy our domestic industries only serves to perpetuate the power of Transnational Cannibals and incentivizes politicians to manipulate vulnerable, jobless voters. By giving away trillions of dollars in unproductive transfer payments, politicians get reelected and Transnational Cannibals escape being held accountable for the damage they have done to our country. There is no rational justification to waste trillions of dollars on unproductive transfer payments when we have the ability to preserve the *actual existence of industries and jobs.*

The Market Health Index. To preserve industries *and* competition, the HHI formula's inputs should take into account the size of competing import sales volume, too. This would transform the HHI into what I call a "Market Health Index." Regardless of how many foreign companies may be selling goods into a particular domestic market, from the perspective of each domestic industry, imports represent a single, monolithic competitive threat. As a result, it's reasonable to treat all competing imports within each industry as a single "virtual import company" with an easily quantifiable *domestic industry market share*. This *virtual import company* (*VIC*) can then be included in the index as if it were an individual company competing in the domestic market. This is the feature that distinguishes the HHI from the Market Health Index (MHI).

Explaining the HHI. To understand how the Market Health Index works, it's necessary to briefly explain how the HHI works. The HHI is calculated from the *sum of the squares of each company's market share*. Mathematically, it looks like this:

$$HHI = \sum_{i=1}^{n} (MS_i)^2$$

. . . where *MS* = market share and *n* = the number of companies in the market.[139]

---

[139] In summation notation, the variable *i* is often used to denote an index within a set of values.

For people who are not familiar with mathematical summation notation, the general formula above can also be explained with a specific example. Let's say there are four companies in an industry with the following market shares: 10%, 20%, 30%, 40%, which amounts to 100% of the market. In the HHI formula, each market share percentage is squared (multiplied by itself) as follows: $10^2 + 20^2 + 30^2 + 40^2 = 3,000$. This would be considered a highly concentrated market and any further consolidation would likely be blocked by the DOJ and FTC.

Quantifying Market Power. Squaring the market shares is a useful way of calculating the *market power* of each company because squaring a large number influences the HHI much more than squaring a small number. For example, the company with 40% market share doesn't merely have four times more *market power* than the company with 10% market share; the larger company's *actual influence* over the market increases approximately exponentially. This is because the combined impact of the larger company's product pricing, production scale, buying power, political influence over government regulations, returns to scale, economies of scale, etc., amplifies the larger company's market power nonlinearly as many quantifiable and intangible forces converge to perpetuate the larger company's existence and growth. Squaring quantifies this dynamic by indicating (in this example) that the larger company's market power is actually 16 times greater than the smaller company, even though the larger company's market share is only four times larger. Thus, squaring the market share enables us to implicitly quantify all the factors that determine the concentration of market power within a simple, elegant formula.

Explaining the Market Health Index. The U.S. Census Bureau, FTC, and the U.S. International Trade Administration (ITA), among other government agencies, already track all the foreign import data needed to calculate my Market Health Index, which would make it easy for policymakers to determine the true health of any industry at any moment. The MHI can be scaled up to any number of companies and industries, but this book is intended for the general public; so I'll keep this example simple. For the math geeks, here is my general mathematical formula for the MHI:

$$MHI = \left\{ \sum_{i=1}^{n} (MS_i^{d})^2 \right\} + (MS^{VIC})^2$$

. . . where MS^d = market share of the domestic companies, MS^{VIC} = market share of the monolithic *virtual import company (VIC)*, and n = number of domestic companies in the market.

For a more specific example: Let's say there are four domestic companies in a *widget industry* and all competing imports are represented by the *virtual import company (VIC)*. Given the structural devastation that has occurred to the U.S. economy over the past 40 years, many American industries now have less than 20% of combined domestic market share. So let's say the market shares of the four domestic companies are 2.5%, 2.5%, 5%, 10% and the *VIC* has 80%. The MHI in this *widget industry* would be calculated as follows: $2.5^2 + 2.5^2 + 5^2 + 10^2 + 80^2 = 6,538$. This would be an extremely concentrated market, indicating that the *VIC* has a near-monopoly in the domestic market for *widgets*.

The MHI Would Preserve the Health of Every Industry. After the MHI is calculated for any industry, the DOJ and FTC already have all the legal and technical tools that they need to take immediate remedial action to preserve the competitiveness, health, and integrity of any market, just like they do in an anti-trust case. In the *widget industry* example, given the extremely high concentration of market power wielded by the *VIC*, the DOJ and FTC can *and should* aggressively intervene in the *widget industry* to reduce market concentration to a healthier level, which is the only way to ensure the competitiveness and integrity of the *widget* market. The exact same process would work for any industry *in any country* that is under assault by suicidal Globalism 1.0 trade policies and Transnational Cannibals.[140]

Are You a Cannibal or an American? I can already hear the Globalism 1.0 cheerleaders howling as I type this paragraph. They will say anything to divert your focus away from the reality of how buggy Globalism 1.0 is destroying the U.S. economy. They will say things like, "The MHI would unfairly harm foreign companies by restricting their access to American consumers." Or "The MHI will reduce the overall amount of global trade by creating trade barriers, which will lead to tariff wars." Or "The MHI violates the fundamental principle of Comparative Advantage, upon which all modern economic theories are built." Or any number of delusional statements to scare you. All these statements have one thing in

---

[140] This example is focused on the U.S. economy, but the same principles would apply to any country's economy.

common: They're all intended to place the health of some vague "global society" above the health of your own country.

A Strong Global Economy Depends on Many Strong National Economies. As we learned previously, "global society" is a fantasy. Wherever you live in the world, there is only *your society;* and *your society* must be strong enough to broadly create and broadly distribute value to sustain *your country's* population. Each country pursuing its own *equitable share* of the global wealth pie is how global economic prosperity is achieved. Each country must be economically stable to be a valuable trading partner in the global dance of Capitalism. An economically unstable country is a country with a population that has weak purchasing power, which leads to trade imbalances, political and economic oppression, violent political upheaval, less global innovation, and slower value and wealth creation for humanity.

Don't Go Easy on the *VIC.* The MHI has many positive implications for any country that uses it to guide their trade policies and preserve the health of their domestic industries, while simultaneously keeping their markets reasonably open to international trade. But before we dive into some of those details, let's make sure we're clear on an important point: The *VIC must* be perceived as a monolithic domestic competitor because that's precisely how foreign imports collectively impact any domestic industry. There is no legitimate legal, moral, economic, or philosophical justification to perceive the *VIC* any other way. Globalism 1.0 cheerleaders will complain about how this seems unfair to foreign companies; and they will try to disaggregate the *VIC* into more than one foreign company within the MHI formula. This will add unnecessary complexity, which they will say is necessary to reduce the influence of the *VIC* within the MHI formula. Don't be deceived by this; it's just another attempt to subordinate domestic industries to the fantasy of *global society.*

Industry Conservation

The Endangered Industries List. If the MHI of a given domestic industry rises above 2,500, that indicates the domestic industry is beginning to experience existential pressure. If the MHI rises above 5,000, that indicates the domestic industry is on the verge of extinction and should be placed on an "Endangered Industries List." Knowing that an endangered industry implies endangered domestic companies, endangered jobs, and endangered citizens who will be forced to depend on government assistance when their jobs are destroyed, it is in the public interest to save every endangered industry from suicidal global trade policies and Transnational Cannibals. Failing to act to preserve the health and integrity of domestic industries inevitably leads to the collapse of the entire economy. The MHI makes it easy for policymakers to know precisely when to take action to avoid this tragic outcome.

Using The MHI Minimizes Unproductive Transfer Payments. Allowing buggy Globalism 1.0 to destroy jobs and industries is no longer acceptable in a rapidly approaching world in which 50-75% of the population will be *economically useless* if countries with collapsing Middle Classes don't take steps now to preserve existing industries and resurrect recently extinct industries. The only other alternative for most displaced workers from this point forward is to depend on unproductive government transfer payments, which certainly does not serve the public interest. Countries that guide their economies based on the MHI will suffer significantly less social and economic decay than countries that continue to blindly follow the suicidal Globalism 1.0 trade policies that are decimating Western countries today.

Technological Obsolescence vs. Globalist Sabotage. To be clear, we don't need to save industries that are dying due to technological obsolescence. For example, a modernized society shouldn't protect horse-and-buggy producers against the onslaught of automobiles merely to save horse-and-buggy jobs. So don't let partisan ideologues and corporate shills make that straw-man argument to distort the purpose of the MHI. The explicit purpose of the MHI is to preserve the health and integrity of domestic markets *that already have significant domestic aggregate demand*. The MHI forces policymakers to continuously ask a critical question: *Who is fulfilling existing domestic demand?* If the majority of the domestic demand is being fulfilled by a *VIC* while domestic companies are crippled by suicidal government policies and Transnational Cannibals that are sabotaging their home economy, that has nothing to do with technological obsolescence.

The MHI is Virtually Immune to Special Interest Corruption. Because the MHI is industry-agnostic, the temptation for politicians to grant special privileges, tax breaks, and subsidies to individual companies or industries in exchange for election campaign donations is virtually eliminated. With the MHI, all industries are treated fairly and equitably because all industries are regarded as *endangered* if their MHIs rise above 2,500. This approach eliminates all the noise and partisan propaganda that wastes so much time and resources in every industry. There would be no rational incentive to waste millions of man-hours and billions of dollars every year to lobby Congress to protect industries that already benefit from MHI-based trade policies that preserve the health and integrity of their markets.

Existing Trade Policies Are Distorted and Unnecessarily Complex. Current U.S. domestic and international trade policy is an unnecessarily complex patchwork of ad-hoc tariffs, quotas, regulations, and trade rules created by dozens of U.S. and international agencies.[141] These rules and the agendas of these organizations are often at odds with one another and in conflict with the best interests of the citizens in one or more countries. And these agencies are constantly tweaking their rules in response to pressure from every special interest group with a desire to buy and sell *stuff*. This creates endless conflicts of interest in every discussion between policymakers, regulators, law enforcement, and industry trade groups.

The MHI Unifies and Simplifies Domestic and International Trade Policy. By focusing trade policy on what actually matters to the majority of every country's citizens, all the complexities and conflicts of interest can be substantially eliminated and replaced with a unified domestic and international trade mission: Ensure the health and integrity of each country's own domestic economy while automatically preventing any country from dominating any other domestic economy. The MHI naturally supports this unified mission because it directly measures the only economic factor that matters: The health and integrity of every industry within an economy.

The MHI is the Only Metric Necessary to Ensure Healthy Competition. If economic policymakers focused on the MHI alone, they would never need to care about anything else because the MHI implicitly measures all other important dynamics throughout an economy, including all domestic and foreign economic pressures. By the time an industry's MHI reaches 2,500 and is placed on the Endangered Industries List, it would be obvious what is causing the existential pressure, but it would be early

---

[141] See: "WTO | The WTO and Other Organizations." Accessed March 10, 2017.
https://www.wto.org/english/thewto_e/coher_e/coher_e.htm.
See also: "U.S. Government Trade Agencies." Accessed March 10, 2017.
https://ustr.gov/about-us/trade-toolbox/us-government-trade-agencies.

enough to take remedial action to stop the bleeding before the industry becomes extinct.

The Market Stability Tax

As we learned previously, Adam Smith understood the tendency of corporations to hijack the regulatory and law-making apparatus of government to serve their own interests and "to deceive and even oppress the public." He even understood the need for corporations to pay taxes to preserve the health, welfare, and integrity of their home societies. In his own words:

> *A regulation which enables those of the same trade to tax themselves in order to provide for their poor, their sick, their widows and orphans. . . .*[142]

Adam Smith Cared About Economic Ecosystems. Adam Smith's quote above and his other warnings about wealth concentration and destabilizing the Middle Class illustrate how he was concerned about the ecosystems in which corporations operate. And he believed it is necessary for corporations to allocate some of their profits to the maintenance of their ecosystems. So let's never be fooled by corporate propaganda and Predatory Cannibals who distort Adam Smith's writings by strategically interpreting his *Invisible Hand* to mean they have no obligation to their home societies and the ecosystems that enable them to generate their wealth.

The Lesser of Two Evils. By now, most people should appreciate the value of an MHI-guided trade policy and the necessity of government intervention to preserve the health and integrity of domestic markets. But how exactly should a government respond when the MHI of an industry is high enough for it to be placed on the Endangered Industries List? I'm not a fan of government intervention, especially if the private sector can perform a particular task better than career politicians with no real-world business experience. However, when Transnational Cannibals have the political and financial power of a medium-sized country and the *benefits* of Globalism 1.0 are destroying the Middle Class, the only entity strong enough to push back against those powerful forces is a national

---

[142] The Wealth Of Nations, Book IV Chapter VIII, p. 145, paras. c29-30.

government. That's why the U.S. Government *already has* virtually unlimited authority to do whatever is necessary to restore the health and integrity of domestic markets.

What Power Should the Government Have? Without the orderly and *industry-agnostic* intervention of government to preserve the health and integrity of markets, we invite a far greater threat: Human life and liberty are in greatest peril when economies collapse and societies degenerate into lawless anarchy. This is why in anti-trust cases the DOJ and FTC have broad powers to protect markets from anti-competitive practices. These powers include, but are not limited to:

- Splitting up monopolistic conglomerates into more competitive smaller companies.

- Imposing royalties on sales that infringe on other companies' intellectual property rights.

- Taxation and import tariffs to discipline repeat violators of anti-trust laws.[143]

- Unbundling anti-competitive products or services.

- Forced liquidation of corporate-owned securities when pyramidal debt and ownership schemes create secret, anti-competitive power over unduly controlled *captured* firms.

- Geographical restrictions on sales activities that undermine reasonably fair competition.

- Market entry prohibitions to prevent unhealthy market concentration.

- Forced implementation of new monitoring and reporting systems to prevent future abuses.

- Among many others.

As any anti-trust lawyer knows, there's virtually no limit to the power and willingness of the federal government to preserve the competitiveness of domestic markets when politicians think an abusive company is harming consumers. The time is long-overdue for the federal government to apply that same power to preserving the *actual existence* of domestic industries *to prevent harm to producers and virtually all Americans.*

---

[143] Many governments have the authority to impose import *and* export tariffs, but

The Convoluted U.S. Tariff Regime That Exists Today. Many Americans, especially Globalism 1.0 cheerleaders, are surprised to learn that the U.S. Government is one of the worst tariff offenders in the world. The U.S. International Trade Commission (ITC) maintains a list—approximately 4,000 pages long—of *over 12,000* specific tariffs that the U.S. Government imposes on foreign imports. This list includes thousands of products *with tariffs up to 350%*. Virtually every one of these tariffs is based on an arbitrary, ad-hoc formula created by special interest pressure on Congress. For example, here are just a couple dozen of the thousands of arbitrary tariffs that have been slapped onto products imported into the U.S. in recent years.

Imported Product	Tariff	Imported Product	Tariff
Tobacco	350%	Brooms	32%
Unshelled peanuts	164%	Synthetic clothing	32%
Shelled peanuts	132%	Apricots, cantaloupes, dates	30%
EU meats & Roquefort cheese	100%	Garlic & onion powder	30%
French jam, chocolate & ham	100%	Synthetic outerwear	28%
Miscellaneous ship parts	50%	Commercial plateware	28%
Sneakers	48%	Most auto parts	25%
Japanese leather	40%	Wool clothes	25%
Decorative glassware	38%	Corsets and gloves	24%
Leather shoes	38%	Asparagus and sweet corn	21%
Canned tuna	35%	Most vegetables	20%
Chinese tires	35%	Non-specific dairy products	20%

These 12,000 tariffs individually and collectively do tremendous harm to the U.S. and global economies because they create:

- Corruptive and unnecessary market distortions
- Enormous and unnecessary administrative complexity
- Billions of dollars of unnecessary cost to American taxpayers
- Unfair and arbitrary bias in favor of individual companies and industries

---

the U.S. Constitution's "Export Clause" prohibits export tariffs.

- Inequitable wealth redistribution to a tiny group of politically connected corporations

- Unnecessary drag on global trade without providing broad economic stability

- Unnecessary trade wars with other countries because U.S. tariffs are correctly perceived as arbitrary and prejudicial

"Save the Middle Class" Tariffs. Import tariffs and domestic taxes are the most powerful and effective tools that governments have to influence a market's structure. Of course, tariffs or taxes that are perceived to be prejudicial against particular companies, countries or industries can lead to tariff wars, but tariffs that are company-, industry-, and country-neutral and implemented explicitly to support small- to medium-sized companies *in every country* will certainly not lead to tariff wars. The fiercest opponents of tariffs are the Transnational Cannibals because their ever-expanding global dominion depends on having completely unfettered access to exploit every source of wealth on the planet. But can you imagine any politician publicly opposing a global "Save the Middle Class" (SMC) campaign? Such a campaign would certainly compel politicians worldwide to defy their corporate paymasters to support an SMC Tariff.

Preventing Destructive Market Power Concentration. The implementation of the SMC Tariff would be straight-forward yet effective and scalable to any level of global GDP. The SMC Tariff is designed to gradually increase the resistance against *all companies in all countries* as they grow into Transnational Cannibals, as all companies inevitably do when they're guided solely by the Profit Motive. The MHI provides a valuable guide to determine when an unhealthy concentration of market power is occurring within each country and for the global economy, but the SMC Tariff is the mechanism that creates the actual structural resistance against the accumulation of too much market power. The SMC Tariff schedule is based on the size of each company's market share *within each country*, as illustrated in the tables below.

	Industry 1			Industry 2			Industry 3	
	MHI Status: LC	1,331		MHI Status: EN	2,926		MHI Status: NE	8,122
Firm	Domestic Market Share	Market Stability Tax	Firm	Domestic Market Share	Market Stability Tax	Firm	Domestic Market Share	Market Stability Tax
VIC	20.0%	20%	VIC	50.0%	50%	VIC	90.0%	90%
A	15.0%	15%	A	15.0%	15%	A	4.0%	4%
B	15.0%	15%	B	10.0%	10%	B	2.0%	2%
C	15.0%	15%	C	5.0%	5%	C	1.0%	1%
D	10.0%	10%	D	5.0%	5%	D	0.5%	1%
E	10.0%	10%	E	5.0%	5%	E	0.5%	1%
F	6.0%	6.0%	F	4.0%	4.0%	F	0.5%	1%
G	4.0%	4.0%	G	3.0%	3.0%	G	0.5%	0.5%
H	3.0%	3.0%	H	2.0%	2.0%	H	0.5%	0.5%
I	2.0%	2.0%	I	1.0%	1.0%	I	0.5%	0.5%
Total	100%	Avg: 10%	Total	100%	Avg: 10%	Total	100%	Avg: 10%

Note: This table is a simplified version of how the MST works to make the concept as easy to understand as possible, but the formula scales to an economy of any size.

The Market Stability Tax. In the simplified table above, the SMC Tariff is labeled "Market Stability Tax" (MST) for policymakers that prefer a less emotionally-charged label and because *economy-wide stability* is precisely what this tariff/tax achieves. Regardless of what we call it, companies with little or no market share pay little or no MST at all. The only necessary discriminating factor is the size of their market share because market concentration destroys economic stability and broad wealth creation *in every country* more surely than any other factor.

The MST is Simpler and Less Costly than the Status Quo. The MST is far simpler and less costly than the ad-hoc patchwork of arbitrary tariffs and taxes that governs and distorts the global economy today. The average MST would be far lower than the taxes and tariffs that exist today, as can be seen by the "Avg: 10%" indicated in the table. And as the number of competitive companies in each industry increases, the average MST naturally decreases, which further promotes competition, innovation, and broad wealth creation *without any active government intervention.*

Passive vs. Active Government Intervention. An industry- and country-neutral tax like the MST is *passive* intervention because it automatically applies to all companies so that government authorities are never in a position to actively pick winners and losers. This eliminates the potential for biased, politically-motivated, or corrupt decision-making processes that could lead to corrupt outcomes. In contrast, selective corporate welfare, industry regulations, anti-trust punishments, tax and regulatory loopholes created for specific special interest groups, financial grants and subsidies given to special interest groups, import quotas, monetary stimulus, interest rate manipulation, etc., are all examples of *active* government intervention that distorts the U.S. economy today.

The MST Treats All Companies Fairly and Objectively. All companies—domestic *and* foreign companies—are treated equitably by the MST. In the case of foreign imports, they are all treated as a monolithic *virtual import company* (*VIC*) and all imports within each industry are taxed at the same level. Recall this is because all imports effectively represent a single source of competition from the perspective of domestic companies in each industry.[144]

The MST Prevents Transnational Cannibalism. The MST creates an automatic, economy-wide bias in favor of small- to medium-sized companies, which is essential to preserve the Middle Class and economic stability in every country. Companies can still easily grow into large, multi-billion-dollar success stories, but as each company's market share increases, their MST gradually increases proportionally. This prevents Transnational Cannibalism because it structurally prevents any corporation from growing to a size that threatens the broader national and global economic ecosystem. Specifically, the MST creates a smooth, incrementally increasing resistance to perpetually increasing "returns to scale" and "economies of scale"—the fundamental source of the destructive power wielded by all Transnational Cannibals. This is the simplest *and only* sustainable, fair, and equitable way to preserve the competitiveness, health, and integrity of every industry in every country throughout the global economy.

The MST Ensures the Broadest Wealth Creation and Distribution. The MST prevents Transnational Cannibalism, but *it does not* block any company from growing and making innovative entrepreneurs rich. The MST simply ensures that *many more smaller companies and new entrepreneurs can grow and prosper, too*. The MST makes it easier to become rich, but much harder to become obscenely rich from an industry-crushing

---

[144] The "MHI Status" in the tables indicate the MHI and the threat level for each industry. "LC" = Least Concern; "EN" = Endangered; "NE" = Near Extinct.

monopoly. If you're still not sure how you feel about this, ask yourself this question: Do you want to live in a world in which 0.01% of humanity owns or controls 99% of our planet's wealth while over 99% of our planet's population is living in poverty; or do you want to live in a world where 90% of the population has a relatively comfortable quality of life so that virtually all of humanity can enjoy economic and political stability and peace?[145] The Dystopian scenario is approaching rapidly, but the MST would deliver economic and political stability by ensuring the broadest possible creation and distribution of wealth, it's structurally resistant to special interest corruption, and requires minimal bureaucracy and government intervention.

The MST Reduces Market Speculation without Adversely Reducing Liquidity. The MST reduces the distorting effects of stock and bond market speculation without adversely reducing the liquidity available to investors and innovative companies. By ensuring that no single company is allowed to grow to such a size that it dominates the capital markets, the MST prevents any single company from becoming an unhealthy magnet for speculative frenzies. These frenzies enable a tiny number of "unicorns" in each industry to vacuum up all the available venture and growth capital in their industries, which deprives other less glamorous but no-less worthy companies from receiving investment capital. The MST structurally resolves this problem by naturally incentivizing investors to diversify their portfolios across a broader spectrum of investment targets if they want to achieve the same ROI that they enjoy today. This reduces portfolio risk, creates many more jobs, increases national and global economic stability, and ensures that many more entrepreneurs worldwide have an opportunity to become wealthy and make their dreams come true.

Implementation Considerations

What is a "Market"? This question is important because it determines how and when the MST applies to any given company. There are two

---

[145] For any given population, there will always be some level of poverty due to disease, intractable political corruption, and other factors that cannot be cured by any form of enlightened economic policy. I call this "structural poverty," which I estimate to be approximately 10%. All non-structural poverty is curable by the MST.

primary factors that define every market: industry activity and geographical scope. Most governments around the world already have industry classification systems like the North American Industry Classification System (NAICS), which is used to classify tens of millions of companies for tax, regulatory, and other administrative purposes. So the "industry activity" factor is already well-established and every company in virtually every country is already classified by industry type.[146]

What is the Geographical Scope of a "Market"? Due to the presence or absence of increasing returns to scale in each industry, all companies naturally focus on either local, national, or international markets. All the Transnational Cannibals have perpetually increasing returns to scale, which is why they perpetually seek to dominate national and international markets. In contrast, companies without significant returns to scale like barber shops, most restaurants, and neighborhood service providers are limited to local markets. The MST is inherently designed to create *gradual resistance only for companies that have perpetually increasing returns to scale* so they can't dominate national and international markets merely by the force of their size and power alone. Thus, for the purposes of the MST, a "market" is always a nationwide market, which means that small- to medium-sized companies will never be required to pay any MST at all because their market share on a nationwide basis is essentially zero.

The MST Formula. The MST Formula automatically scales to any number of companies, any combination of market shares in any industry, in any country. For the VIC, the MST would be applied as a simple tariff. For domestic companies, the MST would ideally replace the existing overly complicated and unsustainable U.S. corporate Alternative Minimum Tax (AMT) system because there would be no need for the AMT if the MST was implemented. The MST could also be seamlessly integrated into the core of any country's national corporate tax system. Here's the MST Formula for the math geeks:

$$\{M_n = M_B \rightarrow T_E = M_B\} \vee \left\{M_n < M_B \rightarrow T_E = M_B * \left(\frac{M_n}{M_B}\right)^{\frac{1}{5}}\right\} \vee \{M_n < T_{Min} \rightarrow T_E = T_{Min}\}$$

---

[146] Some additional classification granularity would be required for certain conglomerates that operate across multiple industries. However, the MST is designed to encourage conglomerates to disaggregate into smaller, more focused operating units. So over the long-run, the MST would naturally create more transparency, integrity, and simplicity within the NAICS than exists today.

. . . where M_B = the market share of the biggest company within each industry; M_n = the market share of the nth company; T_E = the Effective Tax Rate; T_{Min} = the minimum federal corporate tax rate.

Implementing the MST Based on Market Power is the Key. If you recall the table of U.S. import tariffs presented earlier, which included tariffs as high as 350%, it's easy to understand how the MST will be significantly lower than the tariffs and taxes that are required in many industries today. In fact, it's not the size of the tariff or tax that matters; *it's the distribution of a tariff in relation to the market power of each company* that enables the MST to deliver sustainable economic stability. This insight is a profound paradigm shift from the ad-hoc, arbitrary patchwork of special interest-driven taxes and tariffs that perpetuate Broken Capitalism today.

Globalism 2.0: The Functional Version

The MST Would Decrease the Frequency and Magnitude of War. With the MST, countries worldwide would have fewer reasons to antagonize one another because the inherent structure of the global economy would be configured to support the small- to medium-sized companies and Middle Class *in every country*. No single country or corporation could commercially dominate any other country. The terms and impact of international trade would be predictable, transparent, and mutually beneficial for all citizens in all countries worldwide. This would eliminate two major sources of global tension and conflict: (1) the forced price level equalization noted previously, and (2) the abusive impact of Transnational Cannibals that use their governments' military and political power to exploit, oppress, and extract the wealth of foreign countries for the benefit of a relatively tiny number of distant shareholders.

The MST Discourages Politically Distorted Tariffs. At any given moment, the tariff regime that exists in the U.S. and many other countries today creates temptations for politicians to slap politically-motivated tariffs onto any imported product, which sometimes amounts to more than 100% of the value of the product. This happens when, for example, *Country A* wants to punish *Country B* for supporting a U.N. sanction, international trade agreement, or some other foreign policy that *Country A* doesn't like. However, the majority of the tensions and disputes between countries is caused by toxic trade policies that are distorted and manipulated by Transnational Cannibals. By truly harmonizing the tariff regimes in every country with the MST, this source of conflict and tension would be virtually eliminated.

What About Capital-Intensive Industries? Many people assume we need Transnational Cannibals to produce large, capital-intensive products like commercial aircraft, energy infrastructure, weapons systems, and telecom infrastructure. This assumption reflects a misunderstanding of how large corporations actually operate. Look at the corporate structure of any Fortune 500 company today and you will see dozens—sometimes thousands—of smaller business units that operate as wholly-owned subsidiaries of the parent company. This multi-subsidiary conglomerate structure is primarily intended to create legal firewalls between operating units to reduce legal liability for the parent company, but all the market power, profits, political power, and administrative control *always* bubbles up to the parent company. So even though they functionally operate as separate business units, the separation of units to reduce legal liability does absolutely nothing to reduce the adverse, anti-competitive impact that the parent company has on its industry and the broader economy.

Disaggregation is a Natural Market Response to the MST. The fact that virtually all Transnational Cannibals are *already* divided into smaller operating units today reveals an important fact: The labor, resources, and administration required to build any complex, capital-intensive product can be distributed across many smaller business units without adversely impacting the quality of the final product. The MST would promote more cooperation, investment, wealth and power sharing across a greater number of companies, in contrast to the increasingly uncooperative, more secretive, and unaccountable Transnational Cannibals today. This is an important fact to remember when you see the Transnational Cannibals and their cheerleaders in Washington falsely claim that gargantuan conglomerates are required to build complex, capital-intensive products.

The MST Inspires Voluntary Cooperation. The most important difference between markets driven by the destructive Profit Motive and markets driven by a healthier Survival Motive enforced by the MST is this: Transnational Cannibals would *rationally and voluntarily choose to break themselves up* into smaller independent companies that cooperate on mutually beneficial projects because they would incur a high Market Stability Tax if they continued operating as huge ecosystem-crushing conglomerates.[147] Just like they do today, companies would need to collaborate between separate operating companies to successfully build any complex, capital-intensive product, but the wealth and market power received from successful projects would be distributed much more equitably throughout the global economy.

The MST is Fair, Equitable, Predictable, and Resistant to Corruption. The MST is the fairest and most objective way to ensure that millions of smaller companies and the billions of jobs they can create worldwide will survive in the coming years. The MST eliminates the need to increase personal and corporate income taxes to increase unproductive transfer payments to jobless populations. It eliminates the need for governments to create so-called *shovel-ready jobs programs* to *build bridges to nowhere*, which add no meaningful long-term value to the economy. The fundamental structure of every market that is guided by the MHI and enforced by the MST will naturally equalize to ensure the broadest possible competition, innovation, stability, wealth creation and wealth distribution, *all with far less government intervention than we have today*. And less government intervention means fewer opportunities for wasted resources and corruption throughout global economic and political systems.

MST-Based Capital Formation & Allocation

How Should the MST Funds be Spent? The purpose of the MST is to support small- to medium-sized companies and the billions of jobs they can create. It *would not* be a slush fund for special interest projects, nor to bailout insolvent government programs. The MST would be exclusively allocated to each country's own Small Business Administration (SBA) to increase the funding available for low-cost loans, low-cost training, and low-cost startup incubation facilities that support promising new technologies and entrepreneurs who have viable business plans. This ensures that the MST funds are broadly distributed throughout the small- to medium-sized business community where they can create the largest

---

[147] More precisely, the shareholders who control the Transnational Cannibals would compel their boards of directors to divest and sell off business units to independent buyers. That way the investors can cash out and re-invest their capital into a larger number of smaller companies that return a higher ROI because they have a lower collective MST.

number of jobs and achieve the greatest impact for the largest number of humans and communities.

Broken Capitalism Scares Real Investors. As of early 2017, there's an unprecedented $50 trillion of cash lying dormant in bank accounts around the world because *real investors* (not Wall Street gambling addicts) worldwide are terrified by Broken Capitalism and the Toxic Cloud it has spawned. *Real investors* see a world full of intolerable risk, uncertainty, political and economic instability; so they are sitting on their cash, which has created a supermassive global black hole of capital.[148]

The MST Liberates Dormant Capital. There are many industries in many countries that are in desperate need of capital to jump-start their domestic companies, but one of the biggest fears that investors have is investing in a company that will get wiped out by collapsing price levels caused by the *VIC* and Transnational Cannibals using sweatshop labor. In contrast, with the MST and MHI, Transnational Cannibals and the *VIC* would no longer be able to use their size, market power, and sweatshop labor to squeeze out small- to medium-sized companies. That means investors in every country would have the confidence to start deploying their dormant capital to support many more small- to medium-sized domestic companies in every country.

The MST Diversifies Global Trade and Wealth. Today, the world's corporations concentrate the vast majority of their exports on a tiny handful of the richest countries *because that's where the money is.* But as we learned previously, the most significant reason for this global wealth and trade disparity is the economic oppression and exploitation inflicted upon developing nations by the anti-competitive practices and the political power of Transnational Cannibals. In contrast, the MST gradually limits the ability of corporations to dominate any foreign market, which creates a structural incentive for corporations to diversify their trading across many more countries if they want to expand their export volume. This creates structural incentives for corporations in industrialized nations to help poorer nations to become wealthy enough to import the corporations' products, while simultaneously preventing those corporations from dominating the poorer

---

[148]   Olivier Garret, Garret/Galland Research, 2016 Nov. 5, and 084 4. "$50 Trillion of Cash on the Sidelines Could Be Good News for Stocks and Gold." Business Insider. Accessed March 24, 2017. http://www.businessinsider.com/50-trillion-of-cash-on-the-sidelines-good-news-for-stocks-and-gold-2016-11.

nations' domestic markets.

Globalism 1.0 in the Developed World. Globalism 1.0 cheerleaders like to point to the rising Middle Class in the developing world today as "proof that globalism works." They conveniently ignore how income and wealth *in all developing nations* is concentrating into an even smaller number of corporations than it has in developed nations. That means Broken Capitalism *will inevitably* destroy their Capital-Labor Duality, too, after they've completed their developmental cycle and after artificial intelligence starts to permeate their economies. Every economy experiences an initial burst of wealth during its developmental phase, but ignoring the question of how income and wealth are distributed is like building a skyscraper on a swamp. *Their economies and societies will inevitably collapse* for the same reasons that Western economies and societies are collapsing today. The MHI and MST upgrade buggy Globalism 1.0 to Globalism 2.0, which protects the Capital-Labor Duality and ensures the broadest possible creation and distribution of wealth *in every country* for generations to come.

How Many Companies is Enough?

Can We Determine the *Optimal* Number of Firms in Each Industry?
Given the widespread suffering and grotesque wealth disparities caused by *model-driven* Globalism 1.0 today, I'm usually suspicious of anybody who uses economic models and formulas to answer complex socioeconomic questions. However, this is an important question because the purpose of the MST is to achieve a broader distribution of wealth and market power, which can only be achieved by increasing the total number of viable, independent firms throughout the global economy. But let's be clear: Unlike the vaguely defined "benefits to society" and absurd assumptions of Globalism 1.0 economic models, here we have a precisely defined goal—increase the number of viable, independent firms worldwide—which we can precisely measure at any time.[149] That means we can compare our expected results to real-world realities at any moment to determine how we are progressing toward our goals.

---

[149] The precise number is unique to each industry. Government analysts and practitioners within each industry can use the analytical tools I've provided to determine the optimal number of firms for any industry they want to analyze.

More Companies = Broader Distribution of Wealth and Power. We can *reasonably* expect that increasing the number of small- to medium-sized companies in each industry and within each country will result in a broader creation and broader distribution of wealth and power than we see from Broken Capitalism today. It's also possible to *reasonably* estimate the optimal number of firms in each industry based on the analytical tools I've provided in this book. My mathematically inclined readers can perform these calculations on their own if they want to confirm the concrete benefits to society provided by the MST. However, this is not necessary for anybody who intuitively understands the long-term implications of everything I've written up to this point.

Calculating the *Optimal* Number of Firms in an Industry. The number of firms in each industry is determined by three primary factors: the size of each market as measured by total industry revenue (R), the fixed cost required by each firm to enter the market (F), and the sensitivity of an industry's supply of a good to changes in the price of that good, i.e., the elasticity of supply (E). This can be visualized and calculated using the following formula, which I call the "Optimal Competition Formula" (OCF):

$$n = \sqrt{\frac{1}{E} * \frac{R}{F}}$$

... where n = the number of firms in an industry producing a given good; R is the total revenue of the industry; E = the elasticity of supply; and F is the fixed cost of producing the good at each firm.[150]

Translating the *Optimal Competition Formula* into Real-World Insights. Any economic policy that is intended to maximize the number of viable companies and jobs in an economy must influence one or more of the three variables (R, E, F *or* "REF"). In other words, to confirm that the MST will increase the number of companies and jobs in any industry, we need to answer the following questions.

Industry Revenue (*R*): How Will the MST Impact Total Industry Revenue? The MST increases total production, which increases total revenue, *within each country's industries* by providing structural support

---

[150] Other economists have probably independently developed similar formulas, but I haven't seen my OCF in any formal Economics literature to date.

for more economically sustainable domestic price levels. This enables more domestic firms to operate in each industry within each country because there are more profits to distribute across a larger number of small- to medium-sized domestic firms. This creates greater domestic competition, more jobs, higher *real* median incomes, higher *real* GDP, higher purchasing power, and higher quality of life throughout each country.

Supply Elasticity (E): How Will the MST Impact Elasticity within an Industry? Supply-and-demand elasticity impacts companies by punishing firms for not gobbling up a large market share. Even if their products are inferior, sweatshop country labor and perpetually increasing returns to scale enable the largest corporations to disproportionately exploit the powerful effects of market elasticity and use volume pricing as a weapon to destroy domestic competition and consolidate the market even further. This process inevitably causes price levels to collapse into an economic singularity, from which no value or wealth can escape the gravitational force of the largest Transnational Cannibals. The MST stabilizes price levels throughout an industry to gradually neutralize the ability of any firm to use market elasticity as an anti-competitive weapon.

Fixed Cost (F): How Will the MST Impact the Fixed Cost of Each Firm in an Industry? The MST gradually affects a large corporation's shareholder dividends, not fixed costs.[151] In fact, the MST does not directly impact a firm's fixed or variable operating costs at all. By gradually increasing the resistance against a firm's returns to scale *and* return on investment, the MST gradually reduces shareholder dividends as a company starts to gobble up too much market share. This creates natural incentives for shareholders to invest in many more new companies that can offer higher investment returns at smaller scales of production. Thus, every corporation's market power throughout each country is structurally and automatically regulated by the MST without any active government intervention. The MST prevents firms from dominating domestic or global

---

[151] More precisely, it gradually affects net income after all wages, salaries, and other operating expenses are already paid. That's why the MST impacts shareholder dividends, not wages or salaries or other operating expenses. However, some executives and shareholders will likely use the MST as an excuse to squeeze their employees, which is a byproduct of their greed, not a defect in the MST. But over the long-run, executives and shareholders that do that will cause their companies to collapse because smaller, more profitable companies will poach their employees.

markets and becoming *too-big-to-fail* Transnational Cannibals.

Measuring & Modeling Human Welfare

The Real Societal Welfare Model. Recall the question at the beginning of this chapter: Should we maximize *output* or human life? Globalism 1.0 cheerleaders cling to the delusion that "national welfare" and "benefits to society" increase when GDP increases, while ignoring the impact of monetary inflation and the most important question of all: Where is all the money going? If GDP rises, but the MHI in a country also rises, that means more companies and jobs are being destroyed than created and the labor force participation rate is falling, which means real unemployment is rising, which reduces real median income, all of which reduces the standard of living and total welfare for a population. For the math geeks, these conditions can be modeled using formal propositional calculus in what I call the Real Societal Welfare Model:

$$(((GDP \uparrow \lor GDP \downarrow) \land MHI > 2{,}500) \rightarrow (LFP \downarrow \land RU \uparrow \land RMI \downarrow)) \vdash RSW \downarrow$$

Where GDP = Gross Domestic Product, MHI = Market Health Index, LFP = Labor Force Participation Rate, RU = Real Unemployment, RMI = Real Median Income, RSW = Real Societal Welfare.

GDP is Irrelevant to Human Welfare if the MHI is Rising. You don't need to be a math geek to understand the underlying principle in the logic above: If the MHI is rising, it doesn't matter which direction GDP is moving because an increasing MHI *guarantees* that any increases in GDP will simply result in a net destruction of jobs and a higher concentration of income, wealth, and market power into the claws of a smaller number of corporations. If Globalism 1.0 cheerleaders want to pretend to know what they're talking about by using fancy math and models to guide their economic policies, then the core logic of their models should at least measure what really matters to actual humans. Globalism 1.0 cheerleaders cannot credibly claim to care about any "benefits to society" if they insist on using nonsensical models that ignore the most important factors that determine human economic and physical welfare.

GDP Grossly Inflates National Economic Health. The government's official GDP formula grossly inflates the true health of any economy that is dominated by Transnational Cannibals.[152] This is because GDP is heavily weighted toward consumption. This is a flawed methodology because, if most of the consumption is fueled by unproductive debt, and if all the products consumed are provided by an economy dominated by Transnational Cannibals that destroy a population's purchasing power by destroying the population's jobs, the GDP formula tells us virtually nothing about the true economic health of the population. Using *real GDP* helps to reduce the impact of monetary inflation within the calculation, but real GDP still tells us nothing about the true economic health of a population because it ignores the question of how income is distributed. That's why the most meaningful broad measure of a population's economic health is *real median income*.

Policymakers Use GDP to Deliberately Deceive Citizens. Anybody who has studied economics formally knows that GDP and per-capita GDP are woefully inadequate measures of a population's welfare; so there's no question that economic policymakers in every advanced economy today are aware that GDP is terribly misleading. If you confront them on this point, they will give you lame excuses like, "We know it's not perfect, but it's the best tool we have." Of course, this is nonsense because the U.S. Government and the governments of most G20 countries already measure real median income. So why do they focus everybody's attention on GDP as a measure of the performance of their economic policies? Because they know that replacing the misleading GDP metric with real median income in their official reports would shine a bright light on how broken their economic policies are and how their policies deliberately skew the flow of income and wealth toward Transnational Cannibals and the Predatory Cannibals that control them.

Dead Weight Loss

Dead Weight Loss Caused by Monopolies. When abusive monopolies artificially restrict supply and demand in an industry, economists apply the label "dead weight" to the small portion of economic activity that does not

---

[152] The official GDP formula: GDP = C + I + G + (X - M) or GDP = private consumption + gross investment + government investment + government spending + (exports - imports).

occur because of the monopoly. They call it "dead weight" because *they assume* there would be an even greater *theoretical gain to society* if the economy was perfectly optimized according to their models. In the case of monopolies, dead weight losses do indeed occur because monopolists restrict supply to inflate prices and they keep the monopoly profits, which reduces the income and wealth available to the rest of society. This lost income and wealth caused by monopolies can be legitimately perceived as a "dead weight loss" to society.

Dead Weight Loss Caused by Trade Barriers. Economists also believe that dead weight losses occur when most types of trade tariffs and quotas are implemented because these trade barriers increase economic friction between nations, reduce international trade, slow down the flow of income and capital between countries, and reduce overall societal welfare. In the context of the incoherent patchwork of special interest-driven tariffs and quotas that dominate the global economy today, yes, dead weight losses often do occur when tariffs and quotas are used as economic weapons to prejudicially punish countries and industries; or to prejudicially protect a small number of politically well-connected corporations.

Dead Weight Loss *Does Not* Apply to the MST. It's reasonable to expect dead weight losses in the context of prejudicial trade barriers that trigger tariff wars and all manner of international trade and diplomatic maladies, but applying the concept of "dead weight loss" to the country- and industry-neutral MST is nonsensical. The entire purpose of the MST is to structurally guarantee maximum competition, stabilize price levels and the Middle Class within every country, and prevent the ultimate loss to every *society*: the degradation and collapse of every economy and society in every country on Earth.

Escaping Dead Weight Loss Prison. There are many economists who still believe that a global economy can be precisely engineered with Globalism 1.0 economic models to optimize every penny of productivity on the entire planet without regard for all the cultural, sociological, and geopolitical factors that drive economic activity in the real world. These people will have the hardest time understanding why the concept of dead weight doesn't apply to the MST. For these people: Remember that a theoretical "loss to society" is not "dead weight" if the theoretical "gains to society" never existed in the first place. And what relevance does the theoretical notion of "dead weight" have to the billions of people worldwide who are suffering because of absurd assumptions and flawed economic models that have unleashed the twin scourges of Globalism 1.0 and Broken Capitalism into our world?

The Stability Premium Prevents the Collapse of Capitalism. For those who are still not convinced that dead weight doesn't apply to the MST, look at it from this perspective: Within the context of the MST, any theoretical dead weight is more accurately classified as a small "stability premium," which serves as a socioeconomic vaccine that inoculates the world against the disease of Globalism 1.0 and prevents the catastrophic collapse of Capitalism. This stability premium benefits all members of every society in every country by ensuring that consumers *and* producers can sustainably coexist. Without price level stability, and without the sustainable coexistence of consumers *and* producers *in every country*, a capitalistic global economy cannot survive.

Resistance Is Futile

MHI + MST Ensures Simple, Transparent Accountability. The Market Health Index (MHI) covered previously gives any citizen the ability to monitor the concentration of market power (including the *VIC*) in any industry at any time. The Market Stability Fund (MSF) account balance can be publicly published to show citizens how much MST is collected each year. And the SBA's expense budget can also be published publicly. These published account balances and budgets would enable citizens to hold the SBA accountable whenever it uses the MSF to rebalance any lingering market deficiencies that may be choking small- to medium-sized companies.

The MST Naturally Resists AI Domination. From the perspective of a corporation, artificial intelligence is simply another way to dominate a market. The largest Transnational Cannibals today are already dominating the world of AI and using it to increase their market power. AI can amplify returns to scale and economies of scale more than any technology in human history, but the MST creates natural structural resistance to all forms of market domination, including AI-based domination. This means that no single company will be able to runaway with a market just because they have the biggest AI budget. Even as AI proliferates throughout the global economy, the MST will ensure that innovative entrepreneurs will still be able to create new companies, attract investors, and earn an income. With the MST, no firm or cartel of firms would be able to dominate all the opportunities available in any particular industry. This is the best way to preserve the maximum amount of human jobs possible, regardless of how sophisticated AI becomes in the future.

The Market Stability Act. If each government around the world managed their MST policy like I've described in this chapter, unemployment rates worldwide would decrease dramatically, median incomes would rise significantly, the poverty rate in most countries would fall substantially, and overall quality of life would stabilize *and be sustainable* for centuries to come. All these benefits would come from a simple act of Congress, which I call the "Market Stability Act." Given the overwhelming benefits to the Middle Class and small- to medium-sized companies, widespread political support would be strong, which means the Market Stability Act could be passed relatively quickly.[153]

The Difference Between Pro-Big Business and Pro-Business Community. Many people claim to be "pro-business," which makes it seem like they support the entire business community, but they're usually not *pro-business community*. Specifically, they support *particular business interests* that *benefit them*, but they don't really want *competitive markets* in any meaningful sense. To demonstrate this, simply ask them what they think about the MST. If they give you incoherent excuses about how they think it would not work, they're likely pro-big business, but not pro-business community. If they really supported competitive markets, they would not be opposed to policies that make it hard for Transnational Cannibals to dominate the world and easy for small- to medium-sized companies to proliferate and make their entrepreneurial founders rich.

Resistance is Futile. The MST stabilizes and preserves the price levels within each domestic economy, which is necessary to preserve the quality of life and the business communities within each country. After one large, democratic country adopts the MST, every democratic government around the world would be forced by their own citizens to adopt it, too. This would be an example of a positive "Prisoner's Dilemma": Not implementing the MST while *the other guy* implements it would put all countries that don't implement the MST at a strategic disadvantage. Politicians who resist the MST to preserve the status quo will feel like

---

[153] Of course, that assumes Congress can act in the best interest of the American people and resist the self-interested howls of their corporate donors, which is a big assumption. That's why these policies need to be supported from the grassroots by nonpartisan organizations like The AngelPay Foundation and others.

they're punching at a tsunami.

The TPP Proves People Power Works. The Trans-Pacific Partnership (TPP) international trade agreement was the Transnational Cannibals' ultimate fantasy, which almost came true, but so far it has been defeated by a fierce public outcry of citizens worldwide. Once the secret text of the TPP was leaked to the public and the masses of humanity in each country learned the truth, they realized that their economies and their national sovereignty were in serious jeopardy. People rose up and the TPP came crashing down. The TPP illustrates how no democratic government would be able to resist the political pressure as citizens worldwide rise up and demand structural economic parity with the MST.

The MST is Essential to Fixing Broken Capitalism. With the Survival Motive automatically enforced by the MST, the profits, market power, resources, and political influence within any industry would never disproportionately concentrate into the hands of a single board of directors or a single bloc of shareholders. The MST automatically distributes resources, power, and wealth across many more companies worldwide, which is essential to restoring trust, integrity, and competition in economies worldwide. In other words, it's essential to fixing Broken Capitalism.

Unlearning Globalism 1.0 Propaganda. The principles that I've summarized in this chapter might seem counter-intuitive for some people who have been brainwashed by the neurotoxin of Globalism 1.0. It can be a jarring experience to unlearn corporate and government propaganda that has been deeply embedded into our brains from years of multi-billion-dollar social engineering campaigns. Nevertheless, these principles should make perfect sense to anybody who understands that the global concentration of wealth and power into the claws of a tiny number of Transnational Cannibals inevitably destroys companies, jobs, industries, economies, political systems, and societies.

Key Points

- **We Have the Economic Policy Tools.** The Market Health Index (MHI) *measures the existing concentration* of a market. The Optimal Competition Formula (OCF) *calculates the optimal concentration* of a market. The Market Stability Tax (MST) *automatically enforces* market stability, which ensures the broadest possible distribution of companies, value, wealth, and market power throughout every country. The Market Stability Fund (MSF) is the national treasury account *within each country* that holds all the proceeds from the MST until the Small Business Administration (SBA) in each country distributes the funds throughout the small- to medium-sized business community in the form of training, low-cost loans, and startup incubation facilities. All these tools can be implemented *without any direct government intervention in any market.* These and the tools in the next chapter are the economic policy tools that can fix Broken Capitalism at the structural level.

- **We Have the Incentive.** Broken Capitalism is destroying the Capital-Labor Duality, which means it's destroying the very essence of what it means to be human in a capitalistic society. These problems will be dramatically amplified if we don't fix Broken Capitalism before artificial intelligence (AI) causes billions of humans to be *economically useless and politically restless* in our lifetime. The MST ensures that AI will never lead to an even more grotesque concentration of wealth and market power than we see today. We don't need any more incentives to *take action now.*

- **The Longer We Wait, the Longer We Suffer.** There are many things that we can do at the grassroots level in every country. The nonprofit, nonpartisan AngelPay Foundation is my team's contribution to the solution, but we need many more people and organizations to join us to achieve a sufficient scale to make the kind of impact that is necessary to compel policymakers in every country to implement the nonpartisan policies described in this book. As a society, the longer we wait, the more entrenched the Transnational Cannibals become in every political system, which makes it ever-more difficult to inspire politicians to defy their corporate paymasters. The longer we wait, the longer we all suffer from Broken Capitalism.

- Chapter 11 -
Trust-Based Capitalism

"The welfare of the people is the ultimate law." – Cicero

Are Corporations People?

The Non-Birth of Corporate Personhood. After a series of state court verdicts in the early 19th Century which incrementally increased the power and privileges of corporations, the doctrine of "corporate personhood" became U.S. federal law several years after the controversial 1886 U.S. Supreme Court ruling in *Santa Clara County v. Southern Pacific Railroad Company.*[154] Ironically, the court's ruling was about a mundane tax issue, which had nothing to do with corporate personhood. In fact, an official verdict on corporate personhood was never delivered by the court, which was confirmed by Chief Justice Morrison Waite in 1886 when he said, ". . . we avoided meeting the constitutional question in the decision," in response to the court reporter's question about rendering a verdict on corporate personhood.[155]

    A Magical Non-Verdict Becomes the Law of the Land. Ignoring the Chief Justice, the court reporter, J.C. Bancroft Davis, who was a former President of Newburgh and New York Railway, inserted his own commentary into the text of the Supreme Court's decision, indicating the court had ruled in favor of corporate personhood.[156] Despite Chief Justice

---

[154] "Santa Clara County v. Southern Pacific R. Co. 118 U.S. 394 (1886)." Justia Law. Accessed April 4, 2017.
https://supreme.justia.com/cases/federal/us/118/394/case.html.

[155] Magrath, C. Peter (1963), Morrison R. Waite: The Triumph of Character, New York: Macmillan, p. 117,

[156] Ibid. See also: "Alaska Bar Association: Counsel, Beware of Those Headnotes,

Morrison's explicit admission that the Supreme Court never ruled on the issue of corporate personhood, that *non-verdict* magically mutated into a court precedent based merely on a court reporter's unofficial notes, upon which judges in later court cases based their *official* verdicts.[157] This accumulation of self-referential court cases ultimately resulted in a change to U.S. federal law, which now states:

> *In determining the meaning of any Act of Congress, unless the context indicates otherwise . . . the words "person" and "whoever" include corporations, companies, associations, firms, partnerships, societies, and joint stock companies, as well as individuals;*[158]

The Paradox of Corporate Rights. The logical basis for the doctrine of corporate personhood is difficult to overcome for its opponents. I'm obviously opposed to abuses of corporate power, but I don't think there is any intellectually or philosophically consistent way to claim that individuals have constitutional rights while a group of individuals within an organization does not have constitutional rights. This is the crux of the *Citizens United* debate and all other debates associated to campaign finance reform. However, these debates miss a deeper point: The problem is not corporate money itself; the problem is the size of corporations, which gives them too much financial and political power in the first place.

The MST Reduces Corporate Abuse of Political Systems. By structurally preventing corporations from becoming Transnational Cannibals and amassing the financial power of small- to medium-sized countries, the Market Stability Tax (MST) covered in the previous chapter substantially reduces the ability of corporations to manipulate political systems. That means the MST automatically helps to resolve the paradox of campaign finance reform. I've already written extensively about this topic in my article, "The Paradox of Campaign Finance Reform" at Eanfar.org; so for our purposes in this book, let's focus on taking the concept of *corporate*

Advises The Editor." Accessed April 4, 2017.
https://www.alaskabar.org/servlet/content/counsel__beware_of_those_headnotes__advises_the_editor.html.

[157] Gans, David H., and Douglas T. Kendall. "A Capitalist Joker: The Strange Origins, Disturbing Past, and Uncertain Future of Corporate Personhood in American Law." J. Marshall L. Rev. 44 (2010): 643.

[158] 1 U.S. Code § 1

personhood to its logical conclusion, as it relates to Broken Capitalism.[159]

If Corporations Are People, Then . . .

Corporate Governance is Structurally Corrupt. Corporate governance is not necessarily always corrupt by the moral failings or conscious intent of corporate executives and shareholders; it is *structurally corrupt* by design, which is what gives absolute power to a board of directors that are totally controlled by the shareholders. This absolute power is great for the wealthiest shareholders because they're not suffering from the civilizational decay caused directly by the Transnational Cannibals they control; so of course they would prefer not to change the rules of the game. But when the rules of any game are destroying your economy and your society, either the game or the rules must change.

If Corporations Are People, Then. . . Many corporate executives and shareholders hide behind the legal fiction that *corporations are legal persons*. Regardless of whether we agree with the legal justification for this principle, let's take the logic of "corporations are people" to its logical conclusion. Imagine that every corporation is an autonomous *conscious* entity, separate and apart from the workers *and* the shareholders. How would a conscious corporation behave? How would it perceive the role of Labor versus the role of shareholders in the value creation process? Would a conscious corporation allow shareholders to dominate the governance process or would it demand a more equitable allocation of power between capital, Labor, *and itself?*

How Would a Conscious Corporation Distribute Profits? If shareholders were not able to force a conscious corporation to distribute profits the way they do today, would a conscious corporation divide *its* profits the same way that self-interested shareholders divide a corporation's profits today? It's important to remember that the profits of a corporation today don't automatically flow to the shareholders. The shareholders must compel a board of directors to force the executive management of the corporation to distribute those profits to the shareholders at periodic intervals. Until the profits are actually distributed from the corporation, the

---

[159] "The Paradox of Campaign Finance Reform." Eanfar.org, July 8, 2016. https://eanfar.org/paradox-campaign-finance-reform.

shareholders do not receive those profits. So a conscious corporation could block all profits from flowing to anybody, including Labor and shareholders, until *it* determined how those profits should be distributed.

Shareholders Could Not Bully a Conscious Corporation. Now let's imagine that shareholders are perceived by the conscious corporation in exactly the same way that Labor is currently perceived by shareholders today: *as an expense.* From the perspective of a truly impartial, conscious corporation, the profits are generated *within its own corporate body.* "How dare those shareholders tell me how the profits within my own body should be distributed!" a conscious corporation might say. Neither Labor nor Capital (shareholders) would have any special claim on a conscious corporation's profits.

Dividends and Wages Are the Same to a Conscious Corporation. Strip away all the "shareholder value is king" brainwashing that became institutionalized in the 1980s and we come to an inescapable conclusion: Workers and shareholders both represent *an expense* to the corporation because they both take money out of the corporation. Of course, shareholders conveniently perceive the value *they extract* from corporations as "dividends" while claiming the value that *workers extract* is a "wage expense." But there is no fundamental difference—both wages and dividends extract value from the corporation in the form of a transfer of financial value from one account to another. The payments merely have different labels.

A Conscious Corporation Would Protect the Capital-Labor Duality. Now let's say the conscious corporation is thoughtful, has no conflicts of interest to make it biased in favor of workers or shareholders, cares about the health and integrity of its home society and economy, and genuinely seeks to achieve fairness, justice and equity in all its decisions. In this case, the conscious corporation would perceive the workers and shareholders as "beneficiaries" rather than as "expenses." Thus, a conscious corporation would feel a fiduciary duty and have the structural incentives to distribute *its* profits to the two groups of beneficiaries according to what is best for the Capital-Labor Duality, not according to the principle of domination that dictates how corporate income is distributed today.

A Conscious Corporation Would Distribute Income More Equitably. If *corporations are people* and if they had a mind of their own, they would treat Labor and Capital as two co-equal partners because neither one of them can produce a penny of value without the other. The capitalists' machines sit dormant and collect dust without the labor power to animate them into productive value creation engines. The worker's labor power is inert if it has no capital equipment and facilities to convert labor power into finished goods and services that can be sold in a market economy. A conscious, impartial corporation would respect this Capital-Labor Duality and allocate *its* income between Capital and Labor much more equitably than self-interested shareholders do today. (We'll discuss how the concept of a "conscious corporation" applies to the real world later in this chapter.)

Why Are Shareholders Allowed to Dominate Corporations? What is the fundamental principle that makes this overwhelming imbalance of power so deeply embedded in the mind of a shareholder? Is it merely an expression of abject self-interest? Is there an intrinsic force in physics or nature that requires a capitalistic society to be dominated by Transnational Cannibals and the shareholders that control them? Is there any principle in law or nature that requires the interests of shareholders to be elevated above all other concerns in a capitalistic society? Of course, the answer to all these questions is certainly "no." Shareholders dominate capitalistic societies today solely because they have collectively engineered the rules of the game to favor their interests over the past few decades. Now the game inequitably serves their interests at the expense of the health and stability of their home societies.

Adam Smith on Labor. Many people have never read the foundational documents of Capitalism written by Adam Smith, David Ricardo, John Stuart Mill and the other Godfathers of Capitalism. So when they encounter anything that seems to contradict what they are spoon-fed on Wall Street or the mainstream financial news media, their first instinct is to label it as Socialism, Marxism, or Communism. So what exactly did Adam Smith, the father of modern economics and Capitalism, have to say about Labor?

> *The annual produce of the land and labour of any nation can be increased in its value by no other means, but by increasing either the number of its productive labourers, or the productive powers of those labourers who had before been employed. . . . Labour, therefore, is the real measure of the exchangeable value of all commodities. . . . Labour was the first price, the original purchase-money that was paid for all things. It was not by gold or by silver, but by labour, that all the wealth of the world was originally purchased . . . In the long-run the workman may be as necessary to his master as his master is to him, but the*

necessity is not so immediate.[160]

And about the unhealthy greed of capitalists, Smith said:

> *Our merchants and master-manufacturers complain much of the bad effects of high wages in raising the price, and thereby lessening the sale of their good both at home and abroad. They say nothing concerning the bad effects of high profits. They are silent with regard to the pernicious effects of their own gains. They complain only of those of other people.[161]*

Regarding Labor wages, Smith said:

> *A man must always live by his work, and his wages must at least be sufficient to maintain him. They must even upon most occasions be somewhat more, otherwise it would be impossible for him to bring up a family, and the race of such workmen could not last beyond the first generation. . . . Political economy, considered as a branch of the science of a statesman or legislator, proposes two distinct objects: first, to provide a plentiful revenue or subsistence for the people, or more properly to enable them to provide such a revenue or subsistence for themselves; and secondly, to supply the state or commonwealth with a revenue sufficient for the public services. It proposes to enrich both the people and the sovereign.[162]*

Was Adam Smith a Communist? If you presented Adam Smith's quotes above to any self-described capitalist today, most of them would probably assume they were written by Karl Marx. Many people don't realize that Marx derived most of his core ideas from Adam Smith; yet, for the past 150 years, Marx has been inaccurately lambasted as a communist and Smith has been praised as the champion of free-market Capitalism. There is much to appreciate about Adam Smith, but he is known by most people primarily because he gave us a memorable soundbite (his "Invisible Hand"), which is frequently taken out of context to justify all manner of corporate abuses of power and inequitable distributions of wealth. In reality, both

---

[160] Smith, Adam, and Alan B. Krueger. The Wealth of Nations. Annotated edition edition. New York, N.Y: Bantam Classics, 2003.

[161] Ibid.

[162] Ibid.

Smith and Marx contributed tremendously to humanity's understanding of socioeconomics; and you can clearly see in their writings that they both had a deep respect for what I call the Capital-Labor Duality.

The Ritual of Shareholder Domination Will Not Last. There is no fundamental principle in nature or law that requires shareholders to have god-like authority over everybody in a corporation. Again, this is not about *fighting for Labor rights*; it's about recognizing the fundamental hypocrisy and unsustainable flaw in the corporate governance culture of most corporations. This is not a flaw in Capitalism; it's a flaw in human nature that allows certain humans to hide behind a veil of mindless institutional rituals to justify their greed and their impulse to dominate others. The ritual of shareholder domination will crumble—either by revolutionary force or by socioeconomic entropy—as Broken Capitalism continues to inflict increasingly painful suffering upon billions of socially connected people worldwide.

The Law of Constant Wages is Broken

The Law of Constant Wages. Labor's average portion of Gross Domestic Income (GDI) historically hovered around 50% for over 100 years until the late 1970s.[163] The famous economist, John Maynard Keynes, said the constancy of wages was "one of the most surprising, yet best-established facts in the whole range of economic statistics."[164] In fact, aggregate wages were so constant throughout the 19th and 20th Centuries that economists gave this phenomenon a name: "Bowley's Law," which was named after Arthur Bowley who identified this phenomenon in his 1937 book, *Wages*

---

[163] Some economists may be familiar with the Cobb-Douglas 1929 (March) research paper, "A Theory of Production," in which they said Labor's aggregate share of GDP was approximately 75%. Remember, they are using Gross Domestic Product (GDP); whereas I'm using Gross Domestic Income (GDI). In an earlier footnote I explained the problems with using GDP and why GDI provides a more appropriate and reliable long-term benchmark. Most importantly, the differences between these two benchmarks are merely statistical measuring discrepancies; these discrepancies cannot lead to any actual differences in the final outcome of a 50/50 distribution of income between Capital and Labor at the individual company level nor at the aggregate economy level.

[164] Keynes, John Maynard (1939). "Relative Movements of Real Wages and Output". The Economic Journal. 49 (193): 48. JSTOR 2225182.

and Income in the United Kingdom since 1860.

The Law of Constant Wages is Broken. The economic turmoil of the 1970s caused by the Vietnam War, President Nixon's idiotic fiscal and monetary policies, and the massive increase in federal spending for President Johnson's Great Society social programs gave corporate raiders an excuse to lobby Congress for labor, tax, and trade policies that served their interests under the guise of *fixing the economy*. Those policies— implemented between the 1970s and 1990s under Republican *and* Democratic administrations—have decimated the Capital-Labor Duality. Breaking Bowley's Law has predictably devastated the Middle Class. Now Labor's share of GDI is hovering around 40%, and is guaranteed to continue falling over the long-run if Broken Capitalism is not fixed.

Data Source: U.S. Bureau of Economic Analysis, Shares of gross domestic income: Compensation of employees, paid: Wage and salary accruals: Disbursements: To persons [W270RE1A156NBEA]; Federal Reserve Bank of St. Louis.

The trend in the chart above has led to the mountainous wealth gap between Capital and Labor illustrated in the following chart.

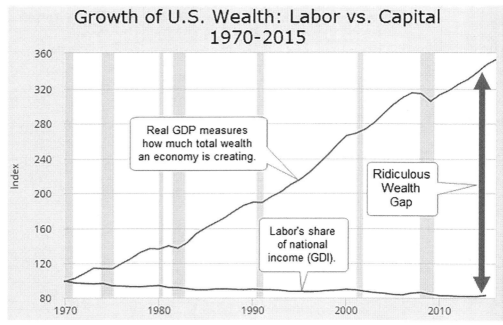

Data Source: U.S. Bureau of Economic Analysis, Shares of gross domestic income: Compensation of employees, paid: Wage and salary accruals: Disbursements: To persons [W270RE1A156NBEA]; Federal Reserve Bank of St. Louis.[165]

Re-empowering Labor Unions is Not a Sustainable Solution.[166] Many Labor rights activists believe the problem is merely an imbalance of power. They're often too young to remember how powerful labor unions actually were prior to the 1980s. The socioeconomic reforms implemented after World War II and during the 1960s gave labor unions unprecedented political influence over American economic policy. This is

[165] This data set includes all forms of worker compensation, including employer-funded 401Ks, pensions, healthcare benefits, etc. So anybody who says "The wealth gap doesn't take benefits into account. . . ." doesn't know what they're talking about or they're a partisan political operative.

[166] Labor unions may not appreciate all these comments, but the facts of history speak for themselves. I appreciate that labor unions fight for labor rights, but I seek to fix Broken Capitalism by restoring the Capital-Labor Duality so that both Labor *and* Capital are treated fairly and compensated equitably. Fixing Broken Capitalism encompasses much more than the relatively narrow agenda pursued by most labor unions, but they are not mutually exclusive. I hope labor unions recognize that this book is aligned with their long-term interests, too.

why the "Labor's Share of Gross Domestic Income" chart above shows Labor's share of national income *above* 50% prior to the 1970s. In fact, labor unions successfully pushed corporate shareholders below the equitable 50/50 share of Gross Domestic Income almost every year after World War II. Labor unions became so powerful that former Federal Reserve Chairman, Arthur Burns, said in 1972:

> *The hard fact is that market forces no longer can be counted on to check the upward course of wages and prices even when the aggregate demand for goods and services declines in the course of a business recession. During the recession of 1970 and the weak recovery of early 1971, the pace of wage increases did not at all abate as unemployment rose. . . . The rate of inflation was almost as high in the first half of 1971, when unemployment averaged 6 percent of the labor force, as it was in 1969, when the unemployment rate averaged 3 1/2 percent. . . . Cost-push inflation, while a comparatively new phenomenon on the American scene, has been altering the economic environment in fundamental ways. . . . If some form of effective control over wages and prices were not retained in 1973, major collective bargaining settlements and business efforts to increase profits could reinforce the pressures on costs and prices that normally come into play when the economy is advancing briskly, and thus generate a new wave of inflation. If monetary and fiscal policy became sufficiently restrictive to deal with the situation by choking off growth in aggregate demand, the cost in terms of rising unemployment, lost output, and shattered confidence would be enormous.*[167]

The Real Reason Reagan Crushed the Unions. At the height of their power, labor unions were just as greedy as the Predatory Cannibals that control the largest corporations today. Republicans and many Democrats in the 1970s were genuinely afraid of the negative inflationary impact that the unions were having on the economy. Even before Nixon killed the Gold Standard in 1971, inflation had been rising for years and was already at six percent. When the OPEC oil embargo hit the U.S. economy in late 1973, inflation was already at 10%. The embargo only lasted five months, but inflation continued to rise throughout the 1970s. Virtually all

---

[167] Burns, Arthur F. Reflections of an Economic Policy Maker: Speeches and Congressional Statements, 1969-1978. AEI Studies; 217. Washington: American Enterprise Institute for Public Policy Research, 1978.

mainstream economists of that era believed the labor unions were a major factor in the rising inflation because they were pushing up aggregate wages beyond the historical 50/50 ratio, which was not in the best interest of the broader economy.[168] This led to President Reagan's extreme response in the 1980s to do everything possible to crush the unions. That caused the pendulum to swing too far in the opposite direction, giving Transnational Cannibals far too much power today.

Shareholders *and* Labor Unions Become Predators When They Have Too Much Power. Like all special interest groups, both corporations *and* labor unions will seek to exploit the power of government to serve their narrow interests at the expense of the broader public interest. We often hear corporate executives and shareholders complaining about labor unions, but the history of labor unions *and shareholder unions* reveals that both groups act like thuggish gangs, seeking to smash the other group whenever they feel empowered by sympathetic politicians and distorted government policies. In fact, Adam Smith believed "the masters" (shareholding capitalists) were just as organized as organized labor; and he believed that anybody who doubts this is deeply ignorant. In Smith's own words:

> *We rarely hear, it has been said, of the combinations of masters, though frequently of those of the workman. But whoever imagines, upon this account, that masters rarely combine, is as ignorant of the world as of the subject.*[169]

Labor Unions and Shareholder Unions Are Equally Selfish. Today, the gang in power is the Predatory Cannibals, but Big Labor would not hesitate to resume its historically dominant position again if it had the chance. So let's not pretend that shareholder unions are more civil or justified in defending their rights than labor unions. Both groups selfishly defend their own interests at the expense of the public interest, which is

---

[168] To learn more about this phenomenon, see: Hetzel, Robert L. "Arthur Burns and Inflation." Richmond Federal Reserve Bank, 1998.
https://papers.ssrn.com/sol3/papers.cfm?abstract_id=2126277. Also see: Ferrell, Robert H., ed. *Inside the Nixon Administration: The Secret Diary of Arthur Burns, 1969-1974.* 1st edition, Edition. Lawrence, Kan: University Press of Kansas, 2010.
[169] Smith, Adam, and Alan B. Krueger. The Wealth of Nations. Annotated edition. New York, N.Y: Bantam Classics, 2003.

why structural corporate governance mechanisms need to be in place to prevent both groups from harming society.

America's Golden Age Was Built Upon the Foundation of a Strong Capital-Labor Duality. The golden age of the U.S. economy emerged after 1945 and lasted until about 1970. During that time, the Capital-Labor Duality was strong, the U.S. was the most prosperous country in the world, Labor and Capital both received approximately 50% of national income, and the overall quality of American life was the highest in U.S. history. That unprecedented period of prosperity was no accident; it was the inevitable outcome of a strong Capital-Labor Duality, among other post-war advantages that were all derived from a strong Capital-Labor Duality.

Stop the Vicious Cycle of Thuggery by Legislating Capital-Labor Equity. The Capital-Labor Duality in the post-war era was held together by the relative balance of political power that existed between Capital and Labor during that era, which no longer exists today. That balance has collapsed because there is no institutional structures in place that are strong enough to enforce the broad creation and broad distribution of national income. And given all the overwhelming structural forces in favor of Transnational Cannibals and the Predatory Cannibals that control them today, there is no realistic way to restore the integrity of the Capital-Labor Duality without *legally enforcing* the same 50/50 distribution of income that fueled the post-WWII economic boom.

There is Nothing Sacrosanct About the Phrase "Laissez-Faire." Every major U.S. market—including labor, banking, healthcare, housing, insurance, all manufacturing industries, education, defense, telecom, energy, stocks, bonds, commodities, infrastructure building, legal services, and many more—is suffering from significant-to-severe market failures today because of the grotesque distortions caused by Predatory Cannibals and their patrons in Washington. These market failures exist because the federal government has been *intervening to help Big Business* since the 1980s while small- and medium-sized businesses and the Middle Class are being choked into extinction. As much as I hate government intervention, I hate seeing my country collapse even more; and the inertia supporting Predatory Cannibals today is too powerful to take a Laissez-Faire approach. No matter how much our Libertarian friends chant "government is evil," there's no realistic way for the U.S. economy to magically heal itself without direct and decisive government action to restore the Capital-Labor Duality.

The Virtues of the 50/50 Ratio

Collective Labor Bargaining is a Primitive, Destructive Relic. With the benefit of several centuries of hindsight, it should be clear to any nonpartisan human today that it's beyond stupid for millions of workers and shareholders to collectively waste billions of dollars and man-hours every year *fighting* over an aggregate wage level that was collectively constant for over 100 years prior to the 1980s. All the fighting and mutual waste and abuse between Capital and Labor occurred simply to preserve the natural 50/50 ratio. The knee-jerk reaction of Neoliberal ideologues will likely be, "Exactly! The 50/50 ratio is the rational outcome of the free market," but this is ideologically-driven nonsense. All that waste and abuse *is not* an expression of the *virtues* of a free labor market; it is a primitive ritual and relic of the Industrial Revolution when humans did not have statistical tools and computers to see that the optimal, ethical, politically and economically sustainable income distribution between Capital and Labor has been—and will always be—50/50.

50/50 is Not Merely a Simplistic, Sentimental Ratio. It would be a mistake to perceive the 50/50 ratio as merely a simplistic, sentimental appeal to morality or arbitrary fairness. The 50/50 ratio is a verifiable statistical equilibrium that was inherent within the DNA of Capitalism for over 100 years; *and* the 50/50 ratio represents a deep truth about human civilization and human nature: Human civilization is only possible when humans feel they are treated equitably. Without a feeling of equity, humans have no dignity, which means they have no happiness. Without a reasonably accessible path to happiness, humans will engage in every conceivable form of warfare until they are mutually annihilated or mutually satisfied, which can only occur when they feel they are treated with mutual respect and compensated equitably.

The 50/50 Ratio is the Golden Rule of Value Creation. The 50/50 ratio is the only mathematical ratio that logically and philosophically communicates equity, respect, trust, and fairness, all of which are essential to the health of every economy and society. There is no other ratio that more efficiently achieves the optimal aggregate income allocation between Capital and Labor throughout an economy so that time and resources are not wasted on unnecessary labor wage fighting and class warfare. There is no other ratio that is simpler to implement and maintain as a matter of corporate governance and national labor policy. There is no other ratio that is more philosophically, technically, legally, and institutionally resilient to special interest manipulation once it becomes the law of the land. And there is no other ratio that more effectively preserves the Capital-Labor Duality while simultaneously and dramatically reducing the total amount of wasteful government bureaucracy in our lives.

50/50 Eliminates the Slippery Slope of Arbitrary Labor Rights. Politicians love to use labor policy as a bargaining chip in political elections, which creates incentives to classify certain fringe benefits like paid vacations, pension plans, health insurance, college tuition assistance, etc., as "worker rights." This is a slippery slope with endless opportunities for career-minded politicians to expropriate corporate profits to subsidize their pet labor policies. It also makes the entire labor policymaking process vulnerable to ideological extremism, which pushes labor policies to one side of the ideological spectrum or another, depending on the politically motivated whims of the government at any point in time. All the political distortions and economically wasteful lobbying associated to these arbitrary *rights* would not be necessary if Capital and Labor simply shared corporate income 50/50.

Arbitrary Rights Violate the Principle of Value Creation. Fringe benefits like paid vacations and employer-subsidized health insurance (in the U.S.) are politically popular around the world because they partially offset the grotesque plunder of the Middle Class by Transnational Cannibals. However, demanding payment for any activity that doesn't directly create value for an organization violates the fundamental principles of equitable value creation and value exchange at the heart of the Capital-Labor Duality. This kind of logical inconsistency undermines the sincerity and credibility of labor rights activists because it creates the appearance of hypocrisy when they don't argue from a structurally neutral philosophical position. Trading all the arbitrary fringe benefit *rights* for a true 50/50 split of corporate income between Capital and Labor resolves this problem because it's a more objective, fair and equitable exchange of value. And it would eliminate the opportunities for politicians to manipulate labor policies for political gain.

Fringe Benefit "Rights" Are Not the Same as Human Rights. Truly legitimate labor rights like child labor laws and the right to safe working conditions that prevent bodily harm are obviously important and should be protected. Other basic human rights that extend constitutional rights to labor policy are also generally reasonable in a civil society. For example, no organization should be allowed to deliberately discriminate against employees based *solely* on congenital characteristics like gender, race, ethnicity, species, etc. These basic human rights in the workplace will become even more important in the future as artificial intelligence and cybernetic organisms ("cyborgs") threaten the existence of all humans. Those are truly *human rights*; in contrast, fringe benefit *rights* are merely economic concessions that corporations often make to keep the masses relatively docile while they do everything possible to perpetuate all the benefits that they receive from Broken Capitalism today.

Trust-Based Capitalism

Trust Law. The behavior of the "conscious corporation" described previously reflects the basic real-world mechanics of Trust Law today, which has been well-established for nearly 800 years since 12th-Century England. A "corporate trust" is a legal entity similar to a corporation, but it is managed by an *impartial* trustee or Board of Trustees for the benefit of the trust's beneficiaries. A trust can generate income and hold any number of assets, businesses, and investments, and it needs to distribute income to groups of people just like a corporation. But unlike self-interested executives, shareholders, and board members in a corporation, the trustee has no inherent conflicts of interest that skew income distribution decisions toward any particular group of beneficiaries.

A Trustee's Incentives Are Aligned with All Beneficiaries. Unlike board members of corporations, Trust Law imposes the highest fiduciary duty on trustees to prevent unreasonable loss to the trust's beneficiaries. Trustees get paid a fixed administrative fee for managing all the income distribution processes associated with a trust. This means trustees have no vested interest in the performance of the trust; thus, they cannot be easily corrupted by any of the trust's beneficiaries like executives and board members are often corrupted by the overwhelming influence of shareholders today. The trustee's incentives are fully aligned with the best interests of *all* the beneficiaries of the trust, not only one special class of beneficiaries called "shareholders."

Trusts Can Restore the Balance of Power. There is no legitimate technical, legal, or philosophical reason why corporations should not be managed the same way corporate trusts are managed today. This would fix the gross structural imbalance of power inside corporations. This structural imbalance of power is what enabled corporate raiders in the 1980s to exert overwhelming influence over every corporation—directly or indirectly—which has corrupted the incentives and decision-making processes of public company executives. Once the raiders had control of corporate boardrooms, it was easy to compel senior executives to destroy and export American jobs and expropriate American technologies and intellectual property to foreign sweatshops. This is what enabled foreign companies to expand their operations at lightning speed so that they could compete directly with American productivity while the raiders vacuumed up all the skyrocketing profits that came from squeezing the American labor force out of the river of wealth.

Every Economy Requires Trust. It's fitting that a corporate fiduciary trust also happens to be the single-most important word in all relationships: "trust." In fact, "trust" must be the guiding principle at the heart of every capitalistic society. Without trust, voluntary economic transactions cannot take place because nobody wants to engage in commerce with people they can't trust. Updating corporate governance, tax laws, and creating strong financial incentives for capitalists to manage their corporations with a "Trust-Based Governance Model," rather than shareholder-dominated fiefdoms, would realign the incentives of all stakeholders so that a trusting and mutually beneficial relationship between Capital and Labor is restored.

Trust-Based Capitalism Reduces Corporate Governance Complexity. The administration of any trust is straight-forward for the trustee, there would never be any major labor disputes, and every society that adopted "Trust-Based Capitalism" would no longer be ripped apart by disloyal corporations and gluttonous corporate raiders. This would eliminate all the nonsense, drama, and corruption that dominates so much of corporate governance throughout the world today. Strategic and executive decisions would still be made by executive management with feedback from workers, but the 50/50 Ratio of income distribution between Capital and Labor would be firmly established and enforced by a Trust Agreement, which cannot be manipulated by self-interested executives and shareholders.

The Restore Trust Act. A fiduciary corporate trust structure would *simplify* and restore integrity to corporate governance, which means these changes could be phased in far quicker than any of the loophole-infested legislative monstrosities that we've seen in recent years. The Dodd-Frank Act, FATCA, and the Affordable Care Act have taken years to implement because they're far more complex than my proposed "Restore Trust Act" (RTA). The RTA could be gradually implemented over two to three years, which would enable industries to adopt the new Trust-Based Governance rules in an orderly fashion. This would be more than enough time to implement the far simpler systems and governance processes of Trust-Based Capitalism. So there's no *non-greedy* excuse that RTA opponents can make to reject the RTA, especially because virtually every wealthy person in the world today already uses trusts for their own personal estates, precisely because they're trusted, reliable, legal vehicles to efficiently manage income generating assets.

The Genesis of Anti-Trust Law. During the late 19th and early 20th Centuries, Broken Capitalism emerged in the form of the "Robber Barons." These were famous industrialists like John D. Rockefeller, J.P. Morgan, Andrew Carnegie, and others who accumulated vast fortunes and market power using anti-competitive tactics that would be punished under criminal laws today. The majority of Antitrust Law that exists today was created during this era because the Robber Barons used trusts to secretly consolidate many companies under common ownership, then use their market power to kill competition and control large swaths of the U.S. and global economies.

Robber Baron Trusts Are Not RTA Trusts. The Robber Barons used trusts like modern-day holding companies because corporations at that time were not yet allowed to acquire ownership in other companies. "Trust-Busters" like U.S. Presidents Teddy Roosevelt and William Taft became famous for breaking up the Robber Barons' trusts. However, corporate trusts today are much more strictly regulated than the trusts of the Robber Baron Era, which means it would not be possible to exploit RTA-based corporate trusts to dominate markets and industries.

Going Public Requires Trust-Based Governance. Any company that wants to *go public* to gain access to billions of dollars of *other people's money* in a public stock market should be required to act in the best interest of the general *public*, not only in the interest of a small group of self-serving shareholders. The best way to guarantee a fiduciary level of trust with public funds is to require corporations to convert to the Trust-Based Governance Model as part of the IPO process.

IPOs Are the Best Time to Become Trust-Based. The IPO process is already very tedious and time-consuming; so the Trust-Based conversion process would be a comparatively trivial administrative step. In fact, a Trust-Based conversion would *simplify* the IPO process in many ways because the Trust-Based Governance Model eliminates many of the conflicts of interest and risk factors that are investigated and nominally mitigated by mountains of legal and regulatory paperwork throughout the IPO process.

Trust-Based Governance: Private Companies. In theory, Trust-Based Governance is possible in any company of any size, but in practice, the benefits to society are less significant for private companies than they are for large, public companies. Additionally, private companies are typically managed by their founders, which has two important consequences:

(1) Founders have much more pride in their companies than non-founders and they have much more to lose in terms of wealth and reputation if they manage their companies recklessly. This is why founder-managed companies rarely suffer from major scandals. So the risk mitigation benefits of Trust-Based Governance are not usually necessary in founder-managed companies.

(2) Company founders usually feel they deserve a majority of the income generated from their entrepreneurial risk-taking, which causes them to feel morally justified in resisting the 50/50 Ratio at the heart of the Trust-Based Governance Model.

Trust-Based Governance: Public Companies. In contrast to private companies, nearly all large public companies are managed by non-founder executives and shareholders. Non-founders have no legitimate justification to claim a majority of a company's income. The founders took the greatest risks and suffered through the hardest years to take the company to an IPO, which is why *they should* be more generously rewarded than any other group. But after the IPO is complete, there is no legitimate justification for executives and shareholders of public companies to resist the 50/50 Ratio and Trust-Based Governance Model.

Size Matters. Companies and the behavior of their executives don't begin to substantially impact large populations—and thus, should not be burdened with unnecessary rules and regulations—until the companies grow to a significant size. Significant existing market share and/or rapidly increasing market share are usually prerequisites for a successful IPO. As a result, there is no significant societal benefit derived from compelling companies to adopt Trust-Based Governance until they are big enough to justify an IPO. But during the IPO process, they certainly should be compelled to perform the Trust-Based conversion just like they're compelled to do many other things if they want to successfully complete an IPO and take money from public investors.

Impact on Stakeholder Incentives: Founders. By the time a company is ready for an IPO, it already has enough employees to justify the 50/50 Ratio between Capital and Labor. And at that point, the founders are usually already wealthy, but if they're not for some reason, they certainly will be wealthy after they're able to sell their founder's stock into the public market after the IPO. So nothing about the Trust-Based conversion prevents entrepreneurs from building great companies and getting rich.

Impact on Stakeholder Incentives: All Others. Trust-Based Governance does not prevent companies from attracting and generously rewarding talented employees. It does not prevent strong shareholder ROI. It simply ensures that, after a company starts interacting with public shareholders and impacting larger populations and the environment, the company is going to start operating with a higher fiduciary and societal duty to its home country. Specifically, it's going to start supporting the Capital-Labor Duality, rather than only serving self-interested shareholders and Predatory Cannibals who usually don't give a damn about their home country.

Trust-Based Shareholders. Shareholders would still be shareholders, they would still vote on all corporate governance matters, but they would have no influence over the fundamental 50/50 compensation structure of the company *after an IPO*. In a Trust-Based public company, the 50/50 Ratio is sacrosanct and immutable to protect the inherent co-equal duality of Capital and Labor. All forms of compensation would be based on the 50/50 Ratio. All individual worker and shareholder compensation would be allocated according to the framework described below.

Trust-Based Compensation. After a company performs an IPO, becomes a public company, and completes the Trust-Based conversion, its bylaws or Trust Agreement (in the case of an actual corporate trust) would provide 50% of all corporate income to the "Shareholder Pool" and 50% of all corporate income to the "Worker Pool." The following table illustrates a simple scenario to make the math easy to understand, but this Trust-Based compensation framework can easily scale to any size of income, shareholders, and workers.

Total Company Income (BEFORE Wages/Salary Expense)	$1,000,000	

Dividends to Shareholder Pool (100 Total Outstanding Shares)		
Shareholder 1 (50 Shares)	$250,000	
Shareholder 2 (50 Shares)	$250,000	
Total Shareholder Pool	$500,000	

In a Trust-Based company, shareholders still have incentives to minimize the total number of shareholders.

Wages/Salaries/PS to Worker Pool		
	Annual Wages/Salary	Annual PS
Worker 1	$20,000	$14,247
Worker 2	$25,000	$17,808
Worker 3	$22,000	$15,671
Worker 4	$35,000	$24,932
Worker 5	$25,000	$17,808
Worker 6	$15,000	$10,685
Worker 7	$40,000	$28,493
Worker 8	$50,000	$35,616
Worker 9	$25,000	$17,808
Worker 10	$35,000	$24,932
Totals	$292,000	$208,000
Total Worker Pool	$500,000	

In a Trust-Based company, shareholders and management perceive the Worker Pool as a fixed cost. This creates a structural incentive for them to hire as many employees as possible to maximize total labor value received in exchange for the 50% Worker Pool cost. It also incentivizes workers to work as productively as possible to avoid hiring more employees so they can keep more of the Worker Pool profit share (PS).

Individual Shareholder Compensation. Within the Shareholder Pool, the scenario above includes two shareholders, each owning 50% of total outstanding shares. However, there could be any number of shareholders, with each shareholder owning any percentage of outstanding shares, which would determine how much income each shareholder receives from the Shareholder Pool. This is exactly the same way that shareholder dividends work today.

Individual Worker Compensation. Within the Worker Pool, the scenario above includes 10 workers, but it can easily scale to a labor force of any size. Each worker is given a minimum base wage/salary, which can be negotiated just like individual wages and salaries are negotiated today, but in a Trust-Based company, there is much less incentive to waste time fighting over the base wage/salary. This is because Trust-Based companies would be required to have a worker profit sharing program (indicated by "PS" in the table), which *must distribute the remaining 50% Worker Pool income to all the workers* on a pro rata basis (based on each worker's wage/salary) or based on any performance criteria that executive management deems appropriate.

The False Social Equality of Labor Wages vs. Capital Returns. Some people try to justify higher income to Capital with comments like, "Labor wages are guaranteed, but investment returns are not; therefore, Capital assumes more risk than Labor and should be compensated for this higher risk." Statements like this imply a false legal, philosophical, and societal benefit *equality* between Labor wages and Capital returns. When human labor is exchanged for a wage, that exchange represents *a sale* of a precise quantity of human labor in exchange for a precise wage. This is fundamentally *a sales transaction based on a contractually agreed upon exchange of specifically defined value.* Sales transactions are, by definition, qualitatively different from open-ended, speculative investment transactions for many legal, philosophical, and societal reasons beyond the scope of this book.

Should Labor Wages Have a Higher Priority than Capital Returns? The concept of "risk" due to *uncertain returns* is a relevant factor when prioritizing multiple speculative investment options, *but not* when prioritizing fundamentally different sales and investment transactions. This is why Labor wages are given higher payment priority than shareholder dividends in legal bankruptcy proceedings. Thus, in this context, applying the concept of "risk" to Labor wages is nonsensical, which means trying to justify higher compensation to Capital, merely because capital investments are speculative, is also nonsensical. However, although they are not *equal* in terms of their benefits to society, from a public policymaking perspective, the principle of *equity* is what logically and philosophical justifies the 50/50 Ratio in the distribution of income between Capital and Labor.

Trust-Based Communities

Trust-Based Governance Aligns All Stakeholder Interests. In a Trust-Based company, all workers would be automatically incentivized to work as productively as possible to help the company earn as much income as possible. They would feel respected and appreciated, which would dramatically increase the overall morale and happiness of the labor force and the broader communities in which they live, transforming them into

Trust-Based Communities. As a result, Trust-Based Governance aligns the interests of all employees, shareholders, executive management, and community stakeholders. This creates sustainable, long-term incentives for all stakeholders to sincerely work together to make their companies and communities as successful, peaceful, and prosperous as possible.

What Creates Welfare States? Nearly $1 trillion of American taxpayer funds are spent *every year* on federal and state welfare programs.[170] These programs provide cash assistance, healthcare and medical provisions, food assistance, housing subsidies, energy and utility subsidies, education and childcare assistance, subsidies and assistance for various basic services . . . but all the social and economic problems associated with Broken Capitalism keep getting worse. All these programs fundamentally exist because Broken Capitalism is destroying the Capital-Labor Duality.

Trust-Based Communities. In a capitalistic society, business enterprises are the core socioeconomic units that control the wealth creation and distribution process. If companies are not guided by Trust-Based principles that are structurally enforced by Trust-Based government regulations, the community and the broader economy will inevitably disintegrate. Requiring public companies to become Trust-Based would rehabilitate economically distressed communities, reduce racial tensions, improve communication between ethnic groups, increase civic engagement, reduce crime and violence, and increase the stability and prosperity of the Middle Class. Trust-Based Governance would have a greater positive impact than all government-based social welfare programs *combined.*

Trust-Based Governance Automatically Enforces Good Behavior. Trust-Based Governance automatically creates structural incentives that promote good corporate behavior with minimal government regulation. Fewer scandals, less fraud and abuse, and less severe economic crises means there would be fewer reasons for politicians to regulate every industry to death. Then regulators could focus their time and taxpayer resources on only the most severe cases of corporate malfeasance. Less regulation, less crime, and happier communities would result in more

---

[170] Rector, Robert. "Examining the Means-Tested Welfare State: 79 Programs and $927 Billion in Annual Spending." Washington, DC: The Heritage Foundation, 2012. http://www.budget.house.gov/uploadedfiles/rectortestimony04172012.pdf. Note: Regardless of the ideological bias of the Heritage Foundation, the data provided in this report should be disturbing to everybody.

liberty, more widespread prosperity, and a more robust and competitive economy.

Welfare States Are Not Necessary in Trust-Based Economies. A $1-trillion-per-year welfare state is not necessary when Capitalism is configured to broadly create and broadly distribute wealth. So the cure is *not more government welfare programs*; the cure is to create Trust-Based Communities by enforcing Trust-Based corporate governance. This is the only way to nurture the Capital-Labor Duality and re-ignite the value creation engine at the heart of every community and economy.

Suicidal Minimum Wage Laws

Fixed Minimum Wages Are a Regressive Tax on Small Companies. Any minimum wage that does not take into account a corporation's market share will inevitably be a regressive tax on smaller companies. This makes it even more difficult for them to compete against big companies that have the scale and resources to absorb the significant cost of a minimum wage. This is why minimum wages impact the small- to medium-sized business community far more than they impact big companies, but small- to medium-sized companies *create over 80% of all new jobs*. This is another example of how U.S. economic policies are structurally engineered to eliminate competition from smaller companies and destroy domestic jobs, which helps big companies get even bigger.

Destroying Millions of Companies and Jobs Before They're Born. Nobody with real-world experience building companies from the ground up could rationally embrace fixed minimum wage laws for small and early-stage companies. The atmosphere of a startup company is so stressful and there are scant resources available to pay anybody anything, much less government imposed-wages, fringe benefits, and all the other costs associated with hiring new employees in today's over-regulated and over-litigated business environment. But that doesn't mean there are not many millions of people willing and able to take those jobs and help those companies grow until they are able to pay higher wages over time.

Fixed Minimum Wage Laws Are a Gift to Big Business. Why should any society allow minimum wage laws to prevent small- to medium-sized companies from being born and creating jobs when there are millions of unemployed and under-employed people in every country who are willing and able to work for lower wages, who desperately need *any income* they can find, and who desperately need work experience for their résumés? Regardless of their intent, all-or-nothing fixed minimum wage laws are one of the biggest gifts to Big Business and they give Transnational Cannibals even more excuses to export jobs and abandon their home country.

Fixed Minimum Wage Laws Amplify the Negative Impact of Robots and AI. Anybody who understands the *Law of Supply and Demand* knows that when the price of something rises, there will be less demand for it. So when bureaucrats with no real-world business experience raise the price of labor by implementing *fixed* minimum wage laws, organizations of all sizes are obviously going to buy less labor and replace humans with cheaper robots and AI. How does this improve the labor force participation rate? How does this support the Capital-Labor Duality? How does this do anything positive for the majority of humans? Regardless of the intent, a *fixed* minimum wage law is the most idiotic economic policy that a government can implement at a time when robots and artificial intelligence are pounding on every human's office door. This begs the question: Why do politicians keep implementing idiotic fixed minimum wage laws? Because it benefits Big Business and Transnational Cannibals, of course.

The Graduated Minimum Wage

Introduction to the Graduated Minimum Wage. The only labor wage policy that would be financially sustainable for *all* companies, politically sustainable for politicians, and philosophically tolerable to conservatives and liberals alike, is what I call the "Graduated Minimum Wage" (GMW). The GMW neutralizes all the emotionally-charged controversy over minimum wage laws by automatically resolving the most significant problems that small- to medium-sized companies complain about, while simultaneously providing a philosophically consistent, fair, and equitable wage policy framework that all labor rights activists can embrace.

Like the MST, the GMW is Based on Market Share. In the previous chapter, we learned how the Market Stability Tax (MST) creates gradual structural resistance against the abuses of Transnational Cannibals, but the same concept can be used to achieve more equitable economic outcomes with virtually no active government intervention across many corporate governance policies. In this case, the GMW works by gradually and automatically increasing the minimum wage rate that companies must pay their employees as their market share increases each year. This ensures that new and relatively small companies have the opportunity to grow and become competitive with larger companies, but as they grow, they are gradually required to share more of their wealth with their workers.

The GMW vs. Today's Complex Patchwork of Minimum Wage Laws. As of 2017, the federal minimum wage is $7.25, but every state currently sets their own minimum wage. States like Georgia and Wyoming have a $5.15 minimum wage, while Washington, D.C.'s minimum wage is the highest in the nation at $11.50. The average between the lowest and highest minimum wages nationwide is $8.33. So let's round this up to $10.00 to make it easier to see how the GMW works, as illustrated in the following table:

Example Industry
Graduated Minimum Wage Scale

	Mkt Share	Effective Min Wage	% of Max FMW
Company 1	30%	$10.00	100%
Company 2	25%	$9.55	96%
Company 3	15%	$8.41	84%
Company 4	10%	$7.60	76%
Company 5	8%	$7.19	72%
Company 6	5%	$6.39	64%
Company 7	4%	$6.04	60%
Company 8	2%	$5.08	51%
Company 9	1%	$4.27	43%
Company 10	0.10%	$2.40	24%
Total	100%		
Max Federal Min Wage (Max FMW)	$10		
Biggest Company Mkt Share	30%		

The GMW Explained. In the Example Industry illustrated in the table above, the biggest company has 30% market share, which automatically defines the market share threshold that corresponds with the Maximum

Federal Minimum Wage (Max FMW) for that industry, which is $10.00 in this case. The *Effective Minimum Wage* is automatically calculated based on the market share of each company *relative to the "Biggest Company Mkt Share."* The "% of Max FMW" is the percentage of the Max FMW that each company must pay their employees. This dynamic formula automatically scales to any number of companies and any combination of market shares in any industry. For the math geeks, here's the GMW Formula:

$$\{M_n = M_B \rightarrow W_E = W_{Max}\} \vee \left\{M_n < M_B \rightarrow W_E = W_{Max} * \left(\frac{M_n}{M_B}\right)^{\frac{1}{4}}\right\}$$

. . . where M_B = the market share of the biggest company within each industry; M_n = the market share of the *nth* company in the industry; W_{Max} = the Max FMW; and W_E = the Effective Minimum Wage.

Graduating from Partial to Maximum Minimum Wage. Companies with no market share obviously have less resources to pay their employees. Instead of preventing these companies and jobs from existing at all, the GMW gives them an opportunity to grow until they have more resources to pay higher wages. As their market share increases, companies gradually pay a larger percentage of the Max FMW. The full Max FMW is paid only by the largest companies that have the largest market share, and hence, the most resources to afford the Max FMW. Until a company gets to that point, they are only required to pay a pro rata portion of the FMW, but of course they can pay their employees more than the Max FMW if they want to, just as companies can today.

The GMW Eliminates Labor Wage Policy Conflicts. The GMW eliminates the need for the existing complex and conflict-inducing patchwork of state and federal minimum wage laws because it's automatically and dynamically customized for every company's particular ability to afford a minimum wage based on each company's specific market share within its industry. This creates a consistent nationwide labor wage policy based on a dynamic wage rate formula that is easily applicable to all states. Additionally, the GMW eliminates all labor wage policy conflicts between state and federal governments because it eliminates their biggest source of tension: The federal government trying to impose a *fixed minimum wage* that doesn't account for each state's unique economic conditions.

The GMW Satisfies Labor Rights Activists Without Added Costs. Virtually all labor rights activism is targeted at big corporations because the activists know that the biggest corporations today are the most aggressive at pushing workers' wages down. The GMW ensures that the biggest companies always pay the maximum amount required by law while also maximizing the total number of jobs available throughout the economy, which is also important to labor rights activists. Every labor rights activist can appreciate how difficult Broken Capitalism makes it for small companies to compete with Transnational Cannibals and other large companies; so there's no rational reason for activists to oppose the GMW. And big companies already have to pay the Max FMW or the state's minimum wage (whichever is higher); so the GMW doesn't impose any additional costs on big companies.

The GMW is Logistically and Politically Easy to Implement and Enforce. The GMW Formula ensures that the biggest company(s) in each industry pays the full Max FMW while smaller companies in the same industry pay a pro rata percentage of the Max FMW based on their market share.[171] This entire process is easy to automate and easy for the IRS to calculate and enforce because the data for every company's revenue and corresponding market share is already collected. As a result of all these benefits, the GMW eliminates all the political pressures at the state *and* federal levels that create friction and ideological conflict over labor policies.

The GMW vs. Welfare Transfer Payments. Compared to nonproductive and wasteful corporate and social welfare programs that demoralize the human spirit and destroy the incentive for welfare recipients to find new jobs, the GMW is a much more sustainable and effective fiscal policy mechanism to achieve the federal government's alleged goals of full employment, widespread prosperity, and low inflation. As robots and artificial intelligence continue to master every human activity on Earth, there is no rational reason to cling to suicidal labor policies that are obviously hostile to the growth of companies and human jobs.

Enforcing Corporate Loyalty

Prepare for the Propaganda Campaigns. Of course, Big Business and Transnational Cannibals will not like the nonpartisan solutions recommended in this book and they will falsely claim it's hypocritical to

---

[171] If two or more companies are tied with the biggest market share, they would all pay the same Max FMW of $10.00 because they all control an equally dominant position in the industry.

have a bias for small- to medium-sized companies. Don't be deceived by their guilt trips, crocodile tears, and self-serving propaganda. They know the status quo serves their interests; so many of them will say and do anything to preserve the status quo. Regardless, there's no *non-greedy* way for them to objectively argue against the economic, social, and political stability benefits associated with the nonpartisan policies described in this book.

There is No Shame in Prioritizing Human Life Over Corporate Gluttony. The explicit purpose of the solutions in this book is to eliminate the existing systemically destructive bias for Big Business and replace it with an explicit systemic bias for small- to medium-sized companies *because this is the only way to fix Broken Capitalism.* There is no shame or hypocrisy in configuring Capitalism to have a strong systemic bias for small- to medium-sized companies when business and political leaders prioritize human life over corporate gluttony.

The Existential Importance of Loyalty. Trust and loyalty are crucial, symbiotic elements of every relationship. Without loyalty, there is no trust; and without trust, there is no reason to be loyal. If corporations want the benefits of being domiciled in their home countries, they need to respect the relationship that they have with their home countries by operating in the best interest of their home societies. Citizens should be able to trust that corporations in their country are not conspiring against them at every board meeting. The only way citizens will feel that level of trust is if Transnational Cannibals stop deliberately destroying the Capital-Labor Duality.

Should Governments Enforce Corporate Loyalty? Some liberty-minded people bristle at the idea that *corporate loyalty* to a country can be enforced by government. Given the abusive history of most governments, my instinct is to distrust all governments; so I used to feel uncomfortable with this idea, too, until I connected the following important dots.

- Corporations exist to serve *real humans*, not the "economic units" and "indifference curves" used in unrealistic economic models.

- Nearly all humans are each a citizen of only one country; this is their *home country*.[172]

- Democratic governments are legally obligated to serve *specific* citizens,

---

[172] Less than 0.1% of humans have citizenship in more than one country.

not a vague *global society*.

- Virtually all humans live in one country and one society for their entire lives; this is their *home society*.

- Each country can only be truly supported by its own *home economy* because no other country has any obligation or permanent incentive to support another country's existence.

- Humans cannot survive or thrive if the Capital-Labor Duality within their home society is constantly assaulted by saboteurs with the financial power of a foreign country operating *inside* their home country.

- The gluttony of Predatory Cannibals creates structural incentives for them to exploit and ultimately destroy the Capital-Labor Duality *in every country*.

- The mutated corporate DNA of all Transnational Cannibals today compels them to devour all resources in their path.

- Robots and artificial intelligence amplify the destructive economic and political power of Transnational Cannibals and national governments. This creates incentives for corporations and governments to combine their resources to collude against human populations, which further amplifies their collective and coercive power. The only way to prevent this creeping power from destroying the liberty and prosperity of the general public is to inject a deliberate bias into economic and political systems to diffuse power across the greatest number of humans and organizations.

- Unless corporate loyalty, broad wealth creation and distribution are built into the structure of each domestic economy based on the principles in this book, Transnational Cannibals will soon irreversibly control every government on Earth, which will destroy the economies and societies in every country on Earth.

The Carrot and Stick. A government should provide the carrot of attractive business conditions *and* the stick of vigorously enforced rules that discourage corporate disloyalty. In this context, "disloyalty" is any corporate action intended to replace domestic labor with foreign labor, prop up foreign supply chains to avoid domestic supply chains, engage in monopolistic behavior that reduces competition in domestic markets, and engage in political lobbying for economic policies that destroy the purchasing power of domestic workers, which destroys the Capital-Labor Duality upon which every capitalistic society depends.

Offshoring vs. Outsourcing. When a firm pays an independent supplier in a foreign country to produce intermediary components for the firm's own final products, that is "outsourcing." In contrast, when a firm transfers its own production processes to a foreign country, invests in its own facilities in the foreign country, retains control over those foreign facilities, and trains foreign residents to perform jobs that were previously performed by residents in the firm's home country, that is "offshoring." "Outsourcing" is legitimate international trade; in contrast, "offshoring" is performed purely to eliminate the home country's labor force and concentrate more wealth into the pockets of Predatory Cannibals.

Structural Incentives to Use Domestic Labor and Production. The MST would automatically and gradually increase the cost of outsourcing—and thereby make domestic labor and production gradually more attractive within each country—because all outsourced goods would be subject to the *VIC's* MST when they are imported into the home country. *This is not a penalty for outsourcing*; it's simply a structural incentive for companies to gradually turn to domestic labor and production as the scale of their business grows. In other words, it reverses the self-destructive incentives that Globalism 1.0 creates today.

Increasing the Cost of Corporate Disloyalty. In contrast to legitimate outsourcing, corporate disloyalty in the form of *offshoring* is purely intended to eliminate domestic labor. This form of corporate disloyalty should be perceived as treason and treated more harshly because it represents a deliberate assault on the Capital-Labor Duality of the firm's home country. Like outsourcing, offshoring would be subject to the MST when offshored products are imported; but companies that engage in offshoring should be regarded as pariah firms, pestered in every legal way possible by private citizens, and prosecuted to the fullest extent of the law by governments until they stop deliberately destroying their home country's Capital-Labor Duality.

Capital & Labor Co-Determination. Between the late 1970s and 2000, American corporations and politicians had a choice: (a) destroy the American labor force to squeeze more profits and political power into fewer hands; or (b) implement the policy of "co-determination" (as adopted in Germany), which would have given American corporations meaningful economic and political incentives to support American labor and the U.S.

economy. Co-determination is an inherent feature of Trust-Based Governance, which aligns the incentives of corporate shareholders, executives, and their labor forces. This ensures that all stakeholders are genuinely incentivized to work together in good faith to increase their productivity and share the rewards from their mutual success.

Self-Interest is Not a Trustworthy Principle in Economics. As an investor, entrepreneur, and board member in several companies over the years, I'm a capitalist, and it would be easy to continue benefiting from the existing rigged game. But after I realized how Broken Capitalism is destroying every economy and society on Earth, I could no longer look in the mirror and pretend that an imaginary *invisible hand* is going to magically transform my individual self-interest into a society worth leaving our children. No society can trust human self-interest as a governing principle in economics. This is why the practical, nonpartisan solutions in this book are essential to restoring trust and structural integrity in Capitalism and ensuring the highest possible quality of life for future generations.

Key Points

- **If Corporations Are People . . .** If capitalists want to pretend that corporations are *people*, then corporations need to behave like *responsible people*. Corporations also need to be held to the same criminal standard of treason *as people* when they deliberately destroy the Capital-Labor Duality at the heart of their home society.

- **The 50/50 Ratio is the Golden Rule of Value Creation.** No other ratio of income and wealth distribution in a capitalistic society will achieve sustainable peace, stability, and broad-based prosperity.

- **Trust-Based Capitalism Heals Nearly All Social and Economic Wounds.** Trust is the most significant factor in the success or failure of every form of human interaction. Without Trust-Based Governance guiding public companies, there is no reason for them to be loyal to their home societies, no reason for citizens to trust their intentions, and no effective or sustainable way to enforce good corporate behavior.

- Chapter 12 -
AngelPay:
Returning Wealth & Power
to the Creators of Value

"It is not what a man or groups of men say about value that counts, but how they act." — Ludwig von Mises

Thank You. Writing this book has been a gratifying journey. I hope it has added some meaningful value to your life. Thank you for exploring all these interesting topics with me. The more human communities understand the problems and solutions described in this book, the more they will come together to fix Broken Capitalism.

    The Purpose of this Final Chapter. I placed this final chapter at the end of the book for three reasons: (1) It describes what other like-minded humans and I are doing every day to fix Broken Capitalism; (2) it explains why I believe it's important to promote and support the nonprofit, nonpartisan AngelPay Foundation in every way possible; and (3) I'm not comfortable with self-promotion and I didn't want this book to be perceived merely as a brochure for AngelPay. I'm one of AngelPay's co-founders and I'm happy to share our message and mission with my readers, but obviously the principles in this book go way beyond AngelPay. Nevertheless, AngelPay is a meaningful part of the solution.

Organizational Purpose

Prioritizing Human Life and Happiness Over Profit. Many financial services companies seem to be guided by nothing more than the obligatory *customer-is-king* lip-service. Even when they start out on a good path, they often abandon their original core values because their profit-obsessed corporate structure and culture are fundamentally engineered to squeeze every penny from their customers, which creates endless conflicts of interest. This is what causes them to behave in ways that destroy the Capital-Labor Duality. As a nonprofit organization, The AngelPay Foundation is structurally and culturally engineered to maximize human life and happiness—not profit—but we ensure that the value we deliver to the communities we serve is financially sustainable.

The AngelPay Manifesto. I originally started writing this book to be the philosophical heart and soul of The AngelPay Foundation. My original title for the book was *AngelPay's Fair Capitalism Manifesto* and it was intended to help all our staff and associates efficiently learn what causes Broken Capitalism and what AngelPay is doing to fix it. Over time, people have encouraged me to share the book with a broader audience. It's still AngelPay's Manifesto, but it's not really about AngelPay—it's about the entire global economy and all of humanity. So I gave the book a new title that is more appropriate to the scope of its message. I hope others get as much value from it as we do at AngelPay.

The Genesis of AngelPay

The AngelPay Mission: Return wealth and power to the creators of value.

History of Innovation & Positive Impact. For decades, the AngelPay Team has directly contributed to the evolution of the global financial services sector. When we invented and founded Authorize.Net in 1996, there was no secure and scalable way to process payments and credit cards over the Internet. The technologies we invented gave birth to the global e-commerce sector and continue to empower billions of people worldwide, reduce poverty in virtually every country, and generate trillions of dollars of new wealth throughout the global economy. Today, Authorize.Net is the largest payment gateway provider in the world and has processed over $1 trillion to date.

Our Evolution. After we sold Authorize.Net, we had some time to think deeply about the many problems that have plagued the financial services sector for decades. Our solution to many of these problems is the nonprofit AngelPay Foundation. AngelPay is a 501(c)(3) nonprofit organization founded by the most experienced team in the global payments industry. AngelPay is our way of giving back to the communities that have been so good to us over the years.

A Growing Community. AngelPay delivers reliable financial services to a global community (the "AngelPay Community") of individuals and organizations with the lowest possible cost structure. AngelPay is best known for our nonprofit payment processing platform, but we also seek to use our skills, technology, and resources to provide other free and low-cost services, tools and leadership to serve the public interest in other areas of the financial services sector. Our organization's legal structure and strong focus on the AngelPay Mission ensure that our incentives are always fundamentally aligned with the interests of the communities we serve. This enables us to authentically promote the common good and improve the quality of life in the communities and organizations that depend on us.

A Quiet Revolution. We are the first and only *nonprofit* financial services company with a mission to *return wealth and power to the creators of value.* Additionally, we have many unique technological and competitive advantages that we've developed over decades of experience, which reinforce our ability to deliver secure, scalable, world-class services with the lowest possible cost structure in the industry. Most importantly, AngelPay embodies and exemplifies the positive spirit, nurturing community, and action-oriented philosophy that all humans should embrace if they want to fix Broken Capitalism.

World-Class Team. The services that the AngelPay Foundation provides to the AngelPay Community are delivered by the same team that invented secure and scalable e-commerce when we invented and founded Authorize.Net in 1996. Additionally, our team includes former ("rehabilitated," we humorously say) senior executives from some of the largest financial companies on Earth, in addition to former senior executives with experience in many other industries, professors from academia, and other like-minded business and community leaders. Without any exaggeration, I can say that our team has more experience in this industry than any other team in the world, which has given us deep technical insight into how to fix Broken Capitalism.

Our Greatest Contribution. Everybody on our team has observed first-hand throughout our careers how toxic and self-destructive the financial services sector has become. This is why everybody at AngelPay has enthusiastically supported the writing of this book. We are all proud of our previous accomplishments, but the AngelPay Foundation is by far the most meaningful and exciting organization that any of us have ever been involved with; and we invite you to join us online at AngelPayHQ.org and participate in any way you can.

AngelPay Community Values

- **Support Value Creators.** Provide our financial services at low or no cost to people and organizations that create meaningful value for humanity.
- **Promote Fair Capitalism.** Promote the principles of *Fair Capitalism* (as opposed to Broken Capitalism).
- **Share Knowledge & Protect Wealth.** Provide nonpartisan education, training, tools, and networking opportunities to help sincere humans and organizations understand and navigate global economic and geopolitical trends so they can create, contribute, and protect their wealth and power from Broken Capitalism.
- **"Pay What You Can" Membership Dues Philosophy.** We understand that every individual and organization is different and everybody has different financial pressures and resources. That's why we give our AngelPay Members the power to choose their preferred membership dues levels based on whatever they can pay. Individuals and organizations can choose how much or how little they want to contribute to support the mission of the AngelPay Foundation. In exchange, they can use any, all, or none of AngelPay's services—it's up to them. The membership dues proceeds enable us to grow the AngelPay Community and share the critically important, *nonpartisan* message in this book with as many humans as possible.

Authentic Alignment

AngelPay's Interests Are Aligned with the Communities We Serve. The AngelPay Foundation is the first and only nonprofit financial services company with a mission to *return wealth and power to the creators of value*. That means our interests and incentives are fundamentally aligned with the communities we serve. I'm not aware of any other company in this industry that can make that claim; and it's unlikely that any other company will ever be able to *credibly* make that claim because very few companies have the experience, credibility, technological infrastructure, philosophical awareness, and financial independence to operate as a true nonprofit organization. Their self-interested shareholders and inefficient business models make it structurally and fundamentally impossible for them to genuinely serve their communities without succumbing to many inherent conflicts of interest.

Deep Understanding of the Small- to Medium-Sized Business Community. When we founded Authorize.Net in 1996, we literally started the company from a garage, scraping and clawing every penny to pay our bills. That experience was incredibly difficult in the beginning because very few people (including all the major banks) believed it was possible to build a secure and scalable system to accept payments and credit cards over the Internet. Fortunately, we persevered and eventually we built Authorize.Net into the most recognizable brand in the global online payment processing industry. Our experience building a truly global company from the ground up and serving tens of thousands of merchant customers worldwide has given us deep insight into how Broken Capitalism is impacting the small- to medium-sized business community every day.

Do Big Companies Get It? The small- to medium-sized business community is the core of every capitalistic society. Without them, the Capital-Labor Duality dies and Capitalism collapses. This is why AngelPay focuses more attention on them. But to be clear: The AngelPay Team has over two decades of experience serving companies of all sizes. From Fortune 500 companies to startups, eCommerce shopping portals, to traditional Retail establishments—we have seen it all. In fact, larger organizations have much more to lose from Broken Capitalism; so they should be interested in understanding how to fix it, too. AngelPay is a meaningful part of the solution, which means there is no rational reason why large companies should not join and support the AngelPay Community, too.

Participating in Fair Capitalism

Creating a Foundation for Fair Capitalism. Capitalism works only when the creators and merchants of value within an economy are treated fairly. Regardless of their intentions, reckless vampire-squid banks and other Transnational Cannibals have become too big, too powerful, too greedy, and too destructive to the global economy. In contrast, AngelPay authentically exemplifies the positive core values and principles described throughout this book. In particular, AngelPay represents a clear alternative to the abusive, toxic status quo of the financial services sector today.

A Liberating Alternative to the Toxic Status Quo. With AngelPay as an alternative nonprofit financial services provider, no individual or company should ever knowingly choose to shackle themselves to service providers whose intentions and incentives are structurally hostile to the interests of their customers and communities. AngelPay is the only nonprofit financial services company that truly understands, respects, and nurtures the Capital-Labor Duality in every community that we have the privilege to serve. For this reason, I hope you will share AngelPay with all the business owners, artists, aspiring entrepreneurs, friends and family in your personal and professional networks.

"What's in it for Me?" This book is about the many dimensions of Capitalism on Earth today, including what it means to live in a capitalistic society. We are all forced to be capitalists or workers. Sometimes we are both, but unless you already have all the money you need for the rest of your life and you don't work or invest, you're not able to escape the reality of being a capitalist, worker, or both. In a capitalistic society, value must be created and exchanged, meaningful income must be earned, purchasing power and money must be available to pay the bills. With that in mind, every person reading this book should ask two rational questions: "What's in it for me?" and "What's in it for you?"

Business Leaders: Liberate Yourself. If you own or manage a company that needs financial services, AngelPay empowers you to escape the chains that shackle your organization to service providers whose interests are not fundamentally aligned with your interests. I invite you to join the AngelPay Community and experience the difference that the nonprofit AngelPay Foundation makes for your organization and for your life as a business leader.[173]

---

[173] Note: At the time of this writing, The AngelPay Foundation provides nonprofit payment and credit card processing services. However, we are growing and expanding our services as quickly as possible, including valuable nonprofit conferences and networking events that help business and community leaders understand and navigate the many risks and challenges associated with Broken Capitalism today. By the time you read this book, we should be able to offer a

Everybody Else: A Rare Discovery. It's difficult to find an organization that is truly able to help millions of people worldwide, reduce billions of dollars of waste and abuse throughout the global economy, while also providing a valuable service to help millions of companies and individuals make their entrepreneurial dreams come true. Our team at The AngelPay Foundation has been building exactly this kind of organization. We keep our marketing and advertising costs as low as possible so we can deliver our services with the lowest possible cost structure, which means we depend on the enthusiastic support of people like you to share AngelPay with your friends and family. If you (or somebody you know) are unemployed, under-employed, or just want to earn some extra income, please consider participating in the AngelPay Rewards Program (AngelPayHQ.org/rewards), which generously compensates hard-working Affiliates for helping us grow the AngelPay Community and sharing the solutions in this book.

The AngelPay Team: Our Incentives. Everybody on our team has already proven themselves professionally in many ways. We don't have anything more to prove to the business world and we don't have any shareholders pushing us to compromise our principles. At this point in our lives, we only care about fixing Broken Capitalism because that's the only thing that matters to the quality of life for our children and future generations. Like all nonprofit organizations, AngelPay has operating expenses. For example, we must attract and retain talented people, which means we must generate enough income to pay them competitive salaries and we must maintain a secure and reliable infrastructure. However, AngelPay is a 501(c)(3) nonprofit and "non-stock company," which legally means we have no shareholders and no structural conflicts of interest. That's why our incentives are truly aligned with the interests of the communities we serve, the AngelPay Mission is truly about "returning wealth and power to the creators of value," and everybody on our team is truly committed to fixing Broken Capitalism.

Income vs. Profit. It's important to remember that "income" is not the same as "profit." All nonprofit organizations must generate income from services and/or donations, but they make sure their income is allocated to accomplishing their nonprofit purpose. That means there is no profit to distribute to shareholders after they pay for all their nonprofit

broader spectrum of nonprofit services.

operations, which is OK because a true nonprofit organization does not have any shareholders. In this regard, AngelPay is no different than any other nonprofit organization.

Inspiring Mission. We hope you are as inspired by the AngelPay Mission as we are. Many of our team members volunteer their time for free or at deep discounts to support the nonprofit AngelPay Foundation. We also believe giving generously to our Members and Affiliates is a better use of our financial resources than sending all that money to expensive PR and marketing firms. So please support the AngelPay Mission by visiting AngelPayHQ.org today, share this book with everybody you know, and share the positive spirit of the AngelPay Foundation with as many of your friends and family as possible.[174]

Conclusion: It's Always Darkest Before the Dawn

Business Leaders, Policymakers, and Citizens. As the world nervously watches the Toxic Cloud of Broken Capitalism cast an ever-darkening shadow across the global economic landscape, we can derive some solace from the old proverb, "it's always darkest before the dawn." However, most governments around the world are woefully unprepared to deal with the economic and social problems that exist today, much less the problems that are rapidly approaching. I hope citizens, sincere business leaders, and good-faith policymakers in the U.S. and around the world will come together and sincerely consider the solutions described in this book.

I wish you luck and success in all your endeavors.

My best,

Ferris Eanfar

Key Points

- **Focusing on What Matters.** The nonprofit, nonpartisan AngelPay

---

[174] All book sales proceeds support the nonprofit AngelPay Foundation.

Foundation prioritizes human life and happiness over profit, but we create opportunities for individuals and organizations to participate in Fair Capitalism more profitably.

- **Structurally Aligned Incentives.** AngelPay's legal structure and the AngelPay Mission ("Returning wealth and power to the creators of value.") ensure that our incentives are always fundamentally aligned with the best interests of the communities we serve.

- **Unparalleled Experience and Commitment to Fixing Broken Capitalism.** The AngelPay Team has the skills, experience, credibility, technological infrastructure, financial independence, and deep philosophical awareness to truly understand Broken Capitalism in every earthly dimension. That's why we are obliged to do something about it, but we can't do it alone. Please join the AngelPay Community today.

Before You Go: Why Are Book Ratings Important?

In today's hyper-connected world, books live and die by online ratings. The algorithms at the most popular online bookstores push books up or down their book lists based on how many positive ratings they receive. Thus, without positive ratings from thoughtful readers like you, this book may not be seen by enough people to make the positive impact that it can make. If you appreciate this book, please consider posting a positive rating online wherever you obtained it. Every rating counts because they add up over time and help draw attention to the important principles and solutions in this book. If you have negative feedback, please consider sending it privately to BCfeedback@Eanfar.org. All feedback is appreciated, but negative public feedback is not necessary when an author or publisher provides a feedback mechanism directly to readers. Thank you!

Your Country Needs You Now.

If you understand why it's important to fix Broken Capitalism, please give this book a positive rating online and tell at least 10 people about it today.

Home: Eanfar.org | **Facebook:** Facebook.com/Eanfar
Twitter: @FerrisEanfar | **AngelPay:** AngelPayHQ.org

About the Author

You can visit Ferris' LinkedIn page (https://LinkedIn.com/in/ferriseanfar) for the most up-to-date summary, but in brief: Ferris Eanfar has over 20 years of experience in technical, financial, media, and government intelligence environments. He is a Senior Partner at Vision Bankcard and the CEO and co-founder of The AngelPay Foundation, the first and only nonprofit financial services company dedicated to returning wealth and power to the creators of value. Ferris' professional background includes payment and credit card processing, asset management, commodities trading, Artificial Intelligence engineering, book publishing, military and government affairs. He is a U.S. Air Force veteran and he worked in the U.S. Intelligence Community as a Cryptological Linguist with a Top Secret (TS/SCI) security clearance. He has written dozens of articles and a few books in the field of International Political Economy (see Eanfar.org), including *Broken Capitalism: This Is How We Fix It*, which provides unique insight into what is wrong with the global economy and how to fix it.

Ferris enjoys spending time with family and friends, traveling to interesting places, playing and composing piano music, and writing nonpartisan books and articles about the geopolitical, economic, social, technological, and philosophical phenomena that govern planet Earth. Ferris has numerous technical and financial certifications and his formal education was in Cryptological Linguistics at the Defense Language Institute and International Political Economy at Penn State University.

Index